AMERICA'S TEAM

THE OFFICIAL HISTORY OF THE DALLAS COWBOYS

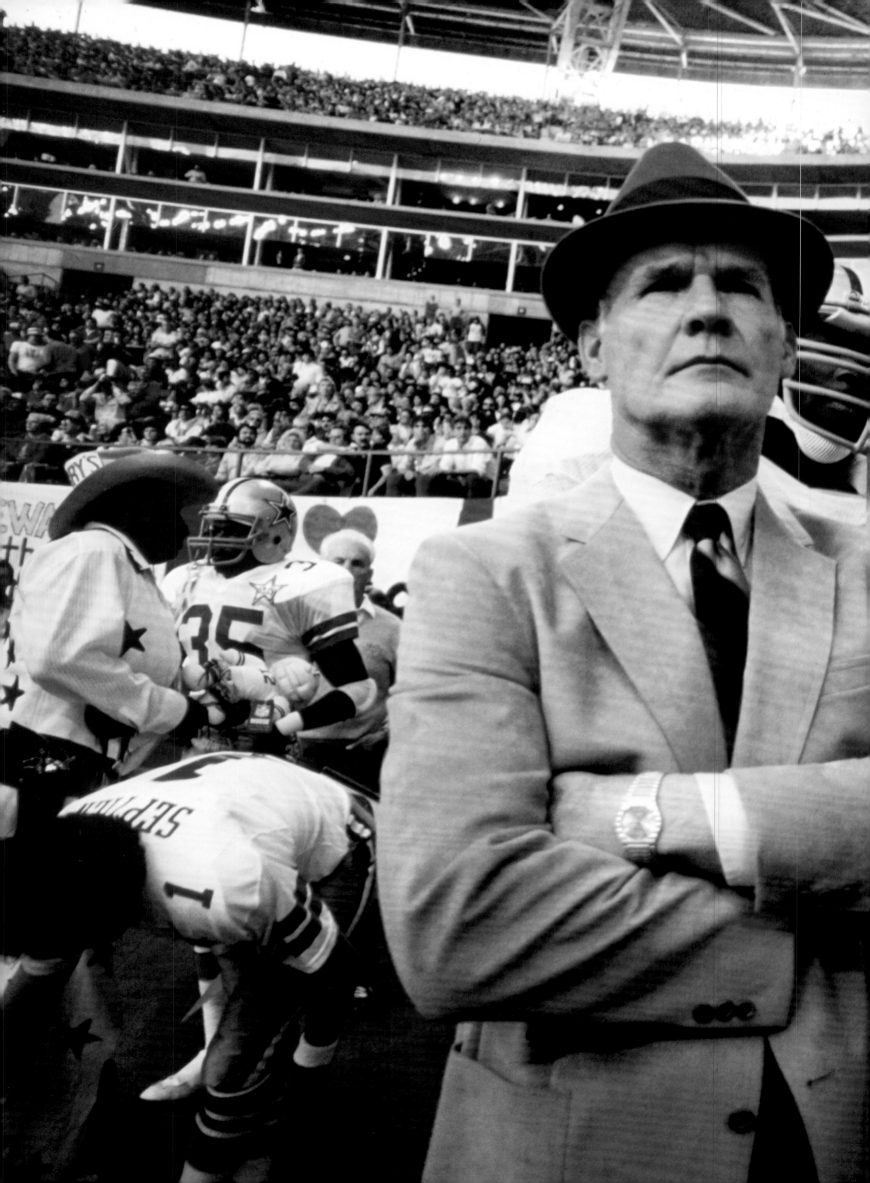

WRITTEN BY **JEFF SULLIVAN**   FOREWORD BY **JERRY JONES**

AMERICA'S TEAM

THE OFFICIAL HISTORY OF THE DALLAS COWBOYS

1960 **50** 2010

INSIGHT EDITIONS

San Rafael, California

Photo credits

Dallas Cowboys Archives (unless otherwise noted)

Russ Russell/Dallas Cowboys (pgs. 52, 67, 77, 94, 99, 101, 103, 106, 159, SBXXX-1, SBXXX-3, SBXXX-4, SBXXX-8, CS-2)

Ron Scribner/Dallas Cowboys (pgs. 92, 96-97, 101, 146-147, 162, 164-165, 179, 182, 199, 212, 217, 218, 228, 241, SBXXX-1, SBXXX-8)

James Smith/Dallas Cowboys (pgs. 2-3, 12, 13, 15, 18-19, 155, 156, 174, 182, 183, 199, 201, 205, 207, 217, 231, 239, 256, 258, 261, 265, CS-1, CS-3, CS-4, CS-7)

Barbara Alper (pg. 17); Bobby Badger (pg. 260); Bruce Bennett/Getty Images (pg. 94); Vernon Biever (pgs. 54, 58, 60-61); David Boss/US Presswire (pg. SBVI-7); Ralph Cole/ Ralph Cole Photography (pgs. CS-1, CS-8); Collections of the Texas/Dallas History and Archives Division, Dallas Public Library (pgs. 20, 29, 50); Shealah Craighead, courtesy of the George W. Bush Presidential Library (pg. 265); Dallas Morning News (pg. 80); Mark Davis/Davis Studios (pg. 272); Malcom Emmons/US Presswire (pg 85); Bukki Erwin (pgs. 108-109); Tom Fox/Dallas Cowboys (pgs. CS-5-6); Richie Humphreys/Dallas Cowboys (pgs. 245, 261, 265, back endpaper); Timothy Hursley (CS-7); Bob Laughead/ Laughead Photographers (pgs. 6, 21, 24, 29, 33, 40, 49); John Mazziotta (pgs. 51, 210, 216, SBVI-1, SBVI-5-6); New Orleans Times-Picayune (pg. SBVI-7); NFL Films (pg. 242); Herb Noseworthy (pgs. 30, 50, 75, 224); Todd Photography/toddphoto. com (pgs. SBXXX-2, SBXXX-5-6); University of Arkansas (pg. 14); Copyright 2004 USA Sports, Inc. (172-173); David Woo/Dallas Morning News (pg. 112)

AP Photo (pgs. 42-43, 82, 83, 218, 226, 229, SBXII-8); AP Photo/NFL Photos (pgs. 64, 130, 137, 150, 216, 218, 221, 225, 226, 232, 233, 243, SBVI-3, SBVI-4, SBXXVII-5-6, SBXXVII-7, SBXXVIII-1, SBXXVIII-3, SBXXVIII-4); AP Photo/Rick Bowmer (pg. SBXXVIII-4); AP Photo/Mark Duncan (pg. 125); AP Photo/Ron T. Ennis (pg. 168); AP Photo/Mike Fuentes (pgs. 270-271); AP Photo/John Gaps III (pg. SBXXX-4); AP Photo/Eric Gay (pg. 153); AP Photo/Tony Gutierrez (pg. 202); AP Photo/Jerry Hoefer (pg. 91); AP Photo/Linda Kaye (pg. 148); AP Photo/David Longstreath (pg. SBXXVIII-4); AP Photo/Donna McWilliam (pg. 175); AP Photo/Doug Mills (pgs. 120, 160, 211, SBXXX-7); AP Photo/Chris O'Meara (pg. SBXXVII-1); AP Photo/Susan Ragan (pg. SBXXX-7); AP Photo/Ed Reinke (pg. SBXXVII-7); AP Photo/Jeff Robbins (pg. SBXXX-7); AP Photo/ Phil Sandlin (pg. 76); AP Photo/Tim Sharp (pgs. 148, 155); AP Photo/Matt Slocum (pg. 184); AP Photo/David Stluka (pgs. 181, 187); AP Photo/Elaine Thompson (pg. 193); AP Photo/Greg Trott (pg. 243)

Library of Congress Cataloging-in-Publication Data available.

ISBN: 978-1-60887-009-7

ROOTS of PEACE ⊕ REPLANTED PAPER

Insight Editions, in association with Roots of Peace, will plant two trees for each tree used in the manufacturing of this book. Roots of Peace is an internationally renowned humanitarian organization dedicated to eradicating land mines worldwide and converting war-torn lands into productive farms and wildlife habitats. Together, we will plant two million fruit and nut trees in Afghanistan and provide farmers there with the skills and support necessary for sustainable land use.

Manufactured in China by Insight Editions

10 9 8 7 6 5 4 3 2 1

INSIGHT ⊛ EDITIONS

3160 Kerner Blvd., Suite 108
San Rafael, CA 94901
www.insighteditions.com

Pages 2–3: Waving the Cowboy flag.
Pages 4–5: Tom Landry.
Page 6: Sonny Gibbs arrives after being drafted.

IN HONOR OF THE DEVOTION TO THE MOST BRUTAL OF ATHLETIC COMPETITIONS, WHERE THE AVERAGE CAREER EXTENDS FEWER THAN FOUR YEARS AND THE PAIN ENDURES A LIFETIME.

WITH THE HEARTFELT GRATITUDE AND APPRECIATION OF MILLIONS, THIS BOOK IS FOR THOSE WHO SACRIFICED A PART OF THEMSELVES IN TRANSFORMING AN EXPANSION FRANCHISE INTO AMERICA'S TEAM.

TABLE OF CONTENTS

JERRY JONES
FOREWORD

Growing up, football could not be described as fun for me. Never was, from the very beginning, that first season of flag football in sixth grade. Baseball was fun.

Football was a whole bunch of getting knocked down, or setbacks, and then achieving success moments after the feeling of having been down. The very nature of football is not a natural thing. You're supposed to stand up in front of 300-pounders and not be crumpled despite your instincts telling you that you will be.

Initially, football was about will as I forced myself to extend, prepare, and listen to the coaches and those who had played the game before me. I wanted to get better, not only for my own personal goals, but also for the feel of a victory after having invested that much work and focus. That has always been a high for me, whether 12 years old in North Little Rock or 67 years young in Arlington.

Other sports offer more multiples of success, more feel-good moments. In football, though, there are significantly fewer feel-goods, but there are higher highs. And the highs have always been the reason why I've been excited by the game. One high, one afternoon of glory, has always been worth many days or even weeks of lows for me.

My dream growing up was to be involved with professional football, ultimately to own an NFL franchise. My college thesis was titled "The Role of Oral Communication in Modern Day Collegiate Football." After we won the 1964 national championship at the University of Arkansas, a reporter asked me what my aspirations were, and as a 184-pound guard, obviously I knew I wouldn't be playing ever again. I told him, "I just want to be involved with football."

My father, Pat, was talking to a newspaperman at the inauguration of Missouri governor Warren E. Hearnes in January of 1965. It wasn't for a story, just small talk, and the guy asked my father about his children. My dad said he wasn't worried about his daughter, but that every time he talked to his son, "All he wants to speak of as far as his future goes is being a part of professional football." Dad told the man, who later wrote about the encounter, "Football is all he wants to talk about. I don't know if he's going to amount to anything."

I KNEW HOW FORTUNATE I HAD BEEN TO HAVE THAT MUCH SUCCESS, AND I NEVER, EVER, EVER, WANTED TO RISK IT AGAIN, EVER . . . AND THEN ALONG CAME THE DEVIL CALLED THE DALLAS COWBOYS.

After graduating, already married to Gene with my oldest son, Stephen, in the crib, I went to work for my father's insurance company. But football was never far from my thoughts.

When Joe Robbie bought the Miami Dolphins in the summer of 1965, I went down there and tried to acquire a minority ownership, and while he was extremely helpful and informative, there wasn't an opportunity for me. A year later, there was a legitimate chance to purchase the San Diego Chargers—then of the AFL—for $5.8 million, but the financial commitment was too much.

At that point, I figured professional football ownership had passed me by, the dollars and cents beyond my means, so thereafter it was more of an ordinary interest. However, as my business became oil, I would always keep up with the structuring of the league and expansion franchises. I would see that information and force myself to memorize it, although again, the reality of it was the NFL had become so capital-demanding that I wasn't financially qualified. For more than 20 years, I never made an official inquiry toward buying a team.

In 1987, though, a good friend of mine brought me to the San Francisco 49ers headquarters shortly before training camp started, and Bill Walsh, bless him, generously took the time and offered his perspective. He really spent a lot of time with me and shared his views on the ownership there and the NFL. It was the most tremendous of educations. And by that time, I had become financially qualified to be an owner.

I will say that when prosperity came in oil, I hid those assets from myself, figuratively speaking. I knew how fortunate I had been to have that much success, and I never, ever, ever, wanted to risk it again, ever . . . and then along came the devil called the Dallas Cowboys.

From the instant I read in the newspaper they were for sale, I made my mind up. I never would've risked what I had gained at that juncture to make more money or to have more business. I just didn't want that. But for the Cowboys, I did risk the bulk of what I was about, in the form of liquidity.

Those were tough economic years in Texas. I had to borrow the cash I didn't have to consummate the $160 million commitment, and I had to use my other assets to make up the difference. It was known as a total equity purchase as far as the collateral was concerned. In other words, I could've taken everything I used to buy the Cowboys and done a $2 billion takeover.

So as far as risk, I probably did not make the smartest business decision. If you saw the financials of what I purchased, you would not respect me as a businessperson. That's how much I wanted it. I knew it was a bad business decision before I signed the papers.

The day before we announced the deal, after Bum Bright and I shook hands and agreed to the terms, three or four of us drove out to Texas Stadium. I was so proud of that stadium and its reputation as "the home of America's Team." That was probably the most surreal moment of my life. I asked someone there to turn on the lights, and I walked out to the star at midfield. I laid down, spread my arms toward the edges of the star, and just stayed like that for a minute or so.

◄ Members of the Arkansas Razorbacks 1964 national championship team, including Jerry Jones (No. 61) and Jimmy Johnson (behind No. 81).

▲ Jerry Jones celebrates on the sidelines.

Looking back, I wish the situation with Tom Landry had been handled differently. Yet, I'm not exactly sure how. Bum implored me to let him inform Coach Landry of the situation, that I was bringing in Jimmy Johnson, but I felt it was my responsibility. I wanted to fly down to Austin and tell him in person out of respect. My admiration of Coach Landry and what he was about as a man was a huge part of my inspiration to buy the Dallas Cowboys.

But I never considered anyone else besides Jimmy to be the head coach. Of course, we were roommates at Arkansas and had remained friendly. In fact, several months went by after we started, before we ever sat down and signed a contract. We just started working. I have every bit of respect for his intellect and, oh boy, is he smart. Jimmy is one of those guys who would've been a success in anything he ever tried.

That first year, I spent so little time sleeping that I would stay many nights at my office. I didn't even sleep sometimes, and when I did, the slightest disturbance would wake me up. Consequently, after living a pretty healthy life those first 46 years, I developed an arrhythmia, which is an irregular heartbeat. It has been happening ever since, and there is no question that it's caused by stress and lack of sleep.

I was aware what people and the media were saying about me, and while the words hurt, I think they served as an inspiration because I really wanted to show them they were wrong. I have always operated better in adversity and am, admittedly, motivated by fear. There was definitely no honeymoon period for me, but I understood why.

There was a sense of vindication, though, when we won that first Super Bowl at the Rose Bowl. When we first arrived at the stadium, three hours or so before kickoff, I grabbed a football and when no one was looking, I walked down to the end zone and yelled, "Touchdown!" and spiked the ball. After having been knocked down so many times, we had reached the top, the highest of highs.

As for "the divorce" after winning the second Super Bowl, if we had not enjoyed that level of success, I know I would've been easier to deal with. But I also think Jimmy could've had more tolerance in the relationship as well. Our success had bought us all kinds of time to have an awkward situation relative to our relationship. We had earned that time, but I didn't use that time. In other words, I could have said, "Let's just not talk for awhile." That could've been instrumental toward buying us one more year together so we could try to win that third straight Super Bowl. And you know, I might have been more tolerant also if I had not known Barry Switzer—who had coached Jimmy and me at Arkansas—was available.

After the press conference when Jimmy resigned, I'm sitting in my office when Barry arrives. He says, "Where's Jimmy at?" I told him, "He's gone, Barry." And he says, "Look, I came down to take the job, but I was hoping Jimmy wasn't gone yet because I wanted to get you two in the room—me and the two of you—and ask you both, 'How could you [mess] this up?'"

Jimmy and I are like brothers, though, that's probably the best analogy. I love him.

Of course, Barry stepped into a tough spot. He came in by himself, inherited Jimmy's staff and our players. I really thought he did a heck of a job here, though, and he's the best pure evaluator of football talent I've ever been around.

I've cried twice after losses, the first being the San Francisco playoff game that would've sent us to a third straight Super Bowl. I could not stop crying after that one; that certainly was the most disappointing loss of my life. I honestly thought we had the best team. At the same time, I was so proud of my guys and the coaches in almost coming back from being down 21–0 in the first quarter.

The second time was the opening night defeat in Houston in 2002. Losing to an expansion team in Texas was pretty tough. That one really hurt, right here in our state.

Winning that third Super Bowl, beating Pittsburgh in Tempe, I know a lot of people say nothing tops the first one, but for me, that one was right there after what had happened with Jimmy and the reaction to me bringing in Barry. That was pretty special.

Maybe I was naïve, but I really thought we had a chance to win another Super Bowl after that. I knew we were losing a lot of talent to free agency, but if you look at most championship teams, their core players were in their thirties. I was thinking Troy [Aikman] had a long run in him, I really did. And to me, he was the best quarterback in the league. Emmitt [Smith] had done such a great job of maintaining himself physically and avoiding injury, and Michael [Irvin] was in the prime of his career.

I thought Chan Gailey did a nice job; in fact, I think one of my biggest regrets looking back is letting him go after just two seasons. But shortly thereafter, it's like a credit card, we reached the max right around the time Dave Campo took over in 2000. I don't blame him at all; that's important to stress. Dave Campo never had a chance as head coach. For two years there, a third of our dollars counting against the cap were for players no longer with us. Dave never had a chance.

Success in the NFL always goes back to the quarterback; it falls on him. And that's why we struggled in the post-Aikman years. Bill Parcells came in and really did an incredible job making the playoffs that first year in 2003. And we were fortunate to develop a quarterback of top-tier talent in Tony Romo. I think if we had won that playoff game at Seattle, Bill's fourth season, he would've come back for another year. Fortunately, we were able to bring in Wade Phillips, who I feel has done a superb job, winning two division titles in three seasons.

For me, the five crowning achievements of my ownership have been the three Super Bowls, the new stadium, and our involvement with the Salvation Army. Also, being able to work alongside my family these last 21 years has been the most rewarding experience of my life.

I loved working with my father, and there's also a different trust level when family is involved. I always thought that if we had stayed in business together, we would've had that much more success. When I bought the Cowboys, I did not want to make that mistake with Stephen, Charlotte, and Jerry Jr. I was determined not to wake up 30 years later and say, "I love my kids so much, but I wish we could have done this thing together because it would've meant so much more to me."

▲ (left to right) Salvation Army Major George Hood, Charlotte Anderson, Gene Jones, and Jerry Jones meet with Sheryl Crow, who performed during the Cowboys' 2005 Thanksgiving halftime show.

> **FOR ME, THE FIVE CROWNING ACHIEVEMENTS OF MY OWNERSHIP HAVE BEEN THE THREE SUPER BOWLS, THE NEW STADIUM, AND OUR INVOLVEMENT WITH THE SALVATION ARMY.**

And no one—I mean absolutely no one—could fully appreciate the efforts of my wife, Gene, during our time with the Cowboys. After raising our three exceptional children, often by herself, she was instrumental in our transition to the North Texas community. She just has this genuine kindness and affection that brings out the very best in people. So much of what has been accomplished the last 21 years with this team wouldn't have been possible without Gene. Coincidentally, she and I first met at the freshman orientation at Arkansas in September 1960, which, of course, is the same month the Cowboys played their first game.

Still, despite this being very much a family business, we have never felt like the owners of the Dallas Cowboys. When I hear these numbers on how much the franchise is worth, they mean absolutely nothing to me. I have no comprehension of this team ever being sold out of this family, but it's not our team. We maybe manage the day-to-day operations, but the Dallas Cowboys are, well, America's Team. They belong to the most passionate and loyal fans in the world.

Firmly believing this, there aren't enough words to express my heartfelt gratitude for having been a part of the first 50 years of this franchise. As a dear friend once said, "How 'bout them Cowboys!"

INTRODUCTION

First, the Yanks were an utter and complete failure in every sense of the word in 1952. Then there was this undersized running back with the genius IQ, his old man among the richest men on the planet. And the song, the song was big.

Likely no Dallas Rangers without the song. But then this other gazillionaire's son decided to start his own league and, well, that was just a mess, although not quite on the scale of the Yanks.

And that's how the Dallas Cowb . . . er, Rangers were born into this world the afternoon of October 19, 1959, in Chicago.

A trio of men was entrusted to nurture this expansion franchise, three men and a baby—one of whom was actually a baby photographer. There was also a television executive and an engineer. Not exactly what one would expect.

The three faced the most daunting of tasks in assembling a football team from scratch without the assistance of the college draft, and they even traded their first pick in the following year's draft for a lawyer who stood five inches shy of six feet. He would be their starting quarterback.

Oh, and the dungeon, almost forgot the dungeon. Well, maybe it was a medieval castle, no one was certain. Jungle Jamey might have known, but more times than not, he was occupied with his rabbit or his longtime friend John F. Kennedy.

High school and college football were considered so entrenched among their respective fan bases that while football was always king in Texas, many felt the professional variety would never succeed. This was back in the 1950s, and the belief was certainly proven when a nomadic franchise—formerly of the All-America Football Conference, absorbed by the NFL—landed in Dallas via Baltimore and New York in January of 1952. At the time, NFL commissioner Bert Bell said, "The enthusiasm of Texans for football is the greatest in the country."

Sure enough, the team formerly known as the Yanks was quickly renamed the Texans, the Dallas Texans, an ownership group of 16 strong anchored by 32-year-old textile manufacturer Giles Miller. The team would play home games at the Cotton Bowl where more than 75,000 fans routinely jammed for collegiate contests featuring SMU, Texas, Oklahoma, and TCU.

▲ (left to right) Tex Schramm, Bedford Wynne, Clint Murchison, and Tom Landry.

The National Football League was coming to Dallas!

Some 44 days after their season-opening 24–6 loss to the New York Giants at the Cotton Bowl on September 28, the franchise folded, the Texans playing their final five contests on the road, funded by the league. They finished 1–11 and were outscored by 245 points.

However, the franchise and its players survived, landing once again in Baltimore as the Colts. Five years later, Johnny Unitas and the team formerly known as the Dallas Texans won the 1958 NFL Championship, defeating the New York Giants, 23–17, in "The Greatest Game Ever Played." Still, the interest in a professional football franchise in Dallas was not dead.

Clint Murchison Sr. was among the richest of Texas oilmen, appearing on the cover of *Time* magazine in 1954 with an estimated net worth of more than $300 million. He was also friends with longtime FBI director J. Edgar Hoover and heavily involved in national politics. His philosophy was simplistic enough, once telling his sons, "Money is like manure. If you spread it around, it can do a lot of good. But if you let it pile up in one place, it just stinks."

The second of three sons, Clint Jr. was brilliant with a devilish sense of sarcasm and a lifelong love affair with football. Honestly, who knew that the Massachusetts Institute of Technology—among the vaunted of academia—even fielded a football team? Quantum physics was nothing compared to dodging tackles on the MIT team as a 130-pound halfback with poor eyesight.

THEY WERE BOTH WILLING TO SPEND MILLIONS. MONEY WAS NO OBJECT REALLY. LOSE $5 MILLION THE FIRST THREE YEARS? NO PROBLEM; WHERE DO WE SIGN? THE ISSUE, THOUGH, WAS LACK OF OPPORTUNITY.

Later in life, Clint Jr.'s three sons would barely see him during the workweek; dad was always busy. But come YMCA and Pop Warner football practices and games, their coach, their father, was always present and accounted for.

H. L. Hunt had absolutely zero interest in football. Another Texas oil mogul, Hunt was wealthy beyond the definition, often referenced in print as the richest man in the world. Conversely, his son Lamar loved the game and was a backup end at SMU.

Around the time the Baltimore Colts were winning the NFL Championship, Lamar Hunt, 26, and Clint Murchison Jr., 35, each desperately desired inclusion in the world of professional football, their respective adoration for the game outweighing any and all financial risks. They were both willing to spend millions. Money was no object really. Lose $5 million the first three years? No problem; where do we sign?

The issue, though, was lack of opportunity.

George Halas, coach and owner of the Chicago Bears and without question the most powerful man in football, was also the chairman of the NFL Expansion Committee and had no plans whatsoever of adding a 13th or 14th franchise.

That is until Hunt decided he was no longer waiting. The NFL wouldn't award him a team? He'd simply start his own league. And on July 29, 1959, the American Football League was opened for business with franchises in Dallas, Houston, New York, Denver, Los Angeles, and Minneapolis. Boston and Buffalo quickly joined, giving the league eight teams for its inaugural season of 1960.

Less than a month thereafter, Halas and friends decided that expanding the NFL was, in fact, the most brilliant of ideas, an obvious counter to Hunt's start-up. Halas introduced Murchison and his partner, Bedford Wynne, as the new owners of a Dallas team at a press conference in Chicago on that fateful October day in 1959. The price tag was $600,000 and included an expansion draft where Dallas would select 36 players from the other 12 teams.

Unfortunately, they still needed unanimous approval from the dozen NFL owners, and that vote wasn't slated for more than three months at the annual league meeting in Miami. And while 11 votes were considered a virtual lock, there was a minor problem brewing in the nation's capital.

Washington Redskins owner George Preston Marshall believed his team held territorial rights to the South and would one day serve as the cornerstone of a Southern television network. He feared placing a team in Dallas would significantly hinder his plan; never mind there are roughly 1,350 miles between the cities. Regardless, Marshall, among the more stubborn of men, wasn't casting a favorable vote to expansion anywhere south of the Mason-Dixon Line.

But this was before Marshall learned that Murchison, that whippersnapper down in Dallas, was responsible for "stealing" his pride and joy, the team's song, "Hail to the Redskins." The lyrics to the tune were written

▲ Players huddle up during a 1961 game at the Cotton Bowl.

by his wife, Corinne Griffith, no less, the former silent-screen starlet who, incidentally, was born in Texas.

Marshall was furious that Murchison had somehow a year earlier acquired the music to the song for $2,000 via an associate, Tom Webb, who was friends with the composer, Barnee Breeskin. Marshall told one and all that Murchison was "obnoxious," to which the latter replied, "If he thinks I'm obnoxious now, how will he feel when he meets me?"

Long story short, the pair met just two hours before the league gathering in Miami on January 28, 1960, and actually got along splendidly, with Murchison giving Marshall the copyright to the music in return for his vote. The new team was approved, and the Dallas Rangers became a reality.

Murchison didn't wait until the owners' decision, though, to surround himself with the best and brightest men available, a trio that would remain in place for an incredible 29 years.

First he hired 39-year-old Texas Earnest Schramm Jr., "Tex" to one and all, as his general manager/vice president at $36,500 per year with stock options. Since resigning as the general manager of the Los Angeles Rams in the spring of 1957—where he hired future NFL commissioner Pete Rozelle as publicity director in 1952—Schramm had been working in the sports department of CBS Television in New York.

Prior to entering the world of professional football, Schramm was a sportswriter for the *Austin American-Statesman*, having graduated from the University of Texas with a journalism degree in 1947. Before a job interview over lunch in late 1959, Murchison and Schramm had never met, a recommendation from Halas leading to the meeting.

The two men then focused their attention toward landing New York Giants defensive coordinator Tom Landry as their head coach, a former All-Pro defensive back and punter who was also a product of the University of Texas. During the 1959 season, Giants head coach Jim Lee Howell cited his assistant as "the greatest football coach in the game today."

On December 28, 1959, Landry signed a five-year contract with an annual salary of $34,500 and was introduced as the first head coach of the Dallas Rangers. Before inking the deal, Landry and Schramm spoke of an agreement that would serve as the backbone of the franchise for nearly three decades.

"Tom knew he had authority over the players and everything that had to do with the playing of the game. I had the remainder," Schramm later recalled. "There's one thing you must have in football: one continuous line of authority. The players had to understand that, as far as they're concerned, Landry is the boss. They had to understand that the only person I will listen to is Landry. Secondly, they had to understand that I had that kind of backing from Murchison. If everyone doesn't know that there's a definite line of authority, you have chaos."

Shortly thereafter, Schramm hired Gil Brandt, who was running a baby photography business in Milwaukee, as his director of player personnel and scouting director. Brandt never played or coached football previously and wasn't even 30 years old, but he had done some scouting work for Schramm back with the Rams.

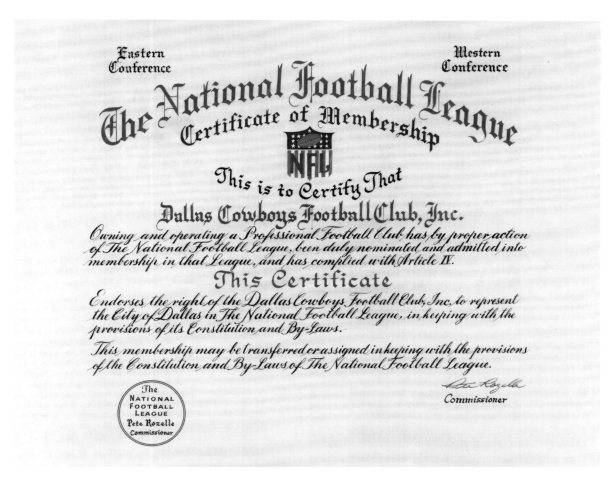

Eastern Conference

Western Conference

The National Football League

Certificate of Membership

NFL

This is to Certify That

Dallas Cowboys Football Club, Inc.

Owning and operating a Professional Football Club, has by proper action of The National Football League, been duly nominated and admitted into membership in that League, and has complied with Article IV.

This Certificate

Endorses the right of the Dallas Cowboys Football Club, Inc. to represent the City of Dallas in The National Football League, in keeping with the provisions of its Constitution and By-Laws.

This membership may be transferred or assigned in keeping with the provisions of the Constitution and By-Laws of The National Football League.

The NATIONAL FOOTBALL LEAGUE Pete Rozelle Commissioner

Commissioner

▲ The Dallas Cowboys' Certificate of Membership into the NFL.

En route to piecing together a makeshift roster for that 1960 inaugural season without the benefit of the NFL Draft, which took place before the league meetings, the Dallas Rangers were no more. In the March 18 editions of multiple local newspapers, there were numerous headlines and references to the Rangers. Two days later, with no explanation to speak of, the Dallas Cowboys were signing rookie free agents and promoting season tickets.

Luckily, in 1970 Murchison explained what took place amidst a series of articles he wrote for the team's *Insider Newsletter*: "It came to me right away, like a bolt from the blue: *The Dallas Rangers*. Now there, I declared, was a name for a football team if ever there was one. Its connotations were historical, proud, tough. My grandfather, who was one, would have loved it."

At least he would have loved it more than Tex Schramm, who started hollering that there already was a team in Dallas called the Rangers. Even worse, allowed Tex, it was a (minor league) baseball team. The media would confuse the two.

Almost immediately, Murchison and Schramm agreed to change the team name but struggled with the solution. Through this stretch, the media and team press releases referred to the club as the Dallas Rangers. Finally, in mid-March of 1960, a decision was made. Schramm called Murchison at the airport and demanded a resolution. He read each of the three finalists aloud, and before hanging up the phone, Murchison said, "Okay, let's go with Cowboys."

The choice of wearing blue was a relatively easy one, Murchison concluded, since Hunt's Texans had already revealed their red uniforms.

Five years later, during the offseason, Schramm told a reporter than Murchison was floating the idea of changing the moniker back to Rangers. The morning the information appeared in the newspaper, Murchison's office was flooded with calls. He later wrote to the newspaper that his office received 1,148 calls, with the response breakdown as follows:

Keep the name Cowboys: 1,138

Change the name to Rangers: 2

Murchison is stupid: 8

Following pages: Quarterback Don Meredith avoids a tackler in the Cowboys' first win in franchise history, a 27–24 victory over the Steelers on September 17, 1961.

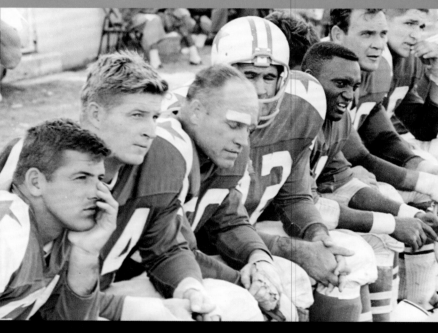

(left to right) Cowboys fan Bubbles Cash; Bill Howton; 1961 bench; Ralph Neely; Eddie LeBaron; Frank Clarke.

GROWING
PAINS

1

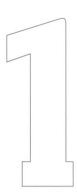

Tom Landry never planned on becoming a head coach, having earned an industrial engineering degree from the University of Houston during the offseasons early in his NFL playing career.

Always the overachiever, he already owned a business administration diploma from Texas. In fact, the 1959 campaign, as defensive coordinator of the New York Giants, was supposed to be his last in the coaching ranks.

"I had decided that I didn't really want to coach at about the time I was approached by Clint Murchison," Landry said in 1984. "(Giants) head coach Jim Lee Howell was stepping down. If I had seriously thought I wanted to pursue a coaching career, I'd have stayed in New York. But I had decided to work my way out of football.

"If anyone but Dallas had tried to hire me, I probably wouldn't have seriously considered the offer. But since my family was already living in Dallas, I decided to give it a shot for a while and just see how things worked out."

Suffice it to say, few things worked out that inaugural season of 1960, although the Cowboys were able to sign quarterback Don Meredith and University of New Mexico fullback Don Perkins to personal services contracts and eventually acquired each rookie's NFL draft rights from the Bears and Colts, respectively, for future selections. A sympathetic George Halas, Chicago's owner and head coach, picked Meredith with the sole purpose of dealing him to the Cowboys, in part to keep him from the rival AFL. For obvious reasons,

Meredith, a two-time All-American at SMU, would've been a coup for Lamar Hunt and the Dallas Texans who had also drafted him. However, the $150,000 offered by the Cowboys over five years was simply too much money.

Still, two players do not make a football team. Player personnel director Gil Brandt furiously signed any and all rookie and veteran free agents he could find for the Cowboys, also flying to California for an expansion draft on March 13. Each of the 12 NFL teams could protect 25 of its 36 players, with Dallas selecting 3 from every club.

"We were given each team's list of protected players 24 hours before the draft," Brandt said.

The draft brought an array of veteran players—or, as legendary Dallas sportswriter

◄ The Cotton Bowl.

QUARTERBACK
EDDIE LeBARON

On winning the Bronze Star and Purple Heart in the Korean War:
"When you first get there, you never think you'll be hit. I got used to it all after awhile, but it's easy to see why some of these guys come back with psychological trauma. People used to always ask me what it was like to have a 300-pound defensive lineman like Big Daddy Lipscomb coming after me, and I'd just smile and say, 'Big Daddy isn't anywhere as bad as a 150-pound Korean solider with a machine gun. Give me Big Daddy anytime.'"

On playing quarterback at five feet seven inches:
"Throwing over people was never an issue for me. That was really the least of my concerns; I could throw nearly 80 yards, but I didn't have much arm strength for the 40-yard out to the sideline, where it needed to be zipped in there. My game was a lot of rollouts, fakes with the football to keep the defense guessing, fake runs, fake passes, keep moving. I remember at a Pro Bowl one time, Y. A. Tittle and I were practicing. He threw side-armed and we looked at it. Turns out, I released the football from a higher point than he did."

Blackie Sherrod wrote, "semi-old timers"—14 of whom would never play for the Cowboys. No matter, in late June the Cowboys dealt their 1961 No. 1 pick to the Washington Redskins for the rights to quarterback Eddie LeBaron, a three-time Pro Bowler dubbed the Little General for his heroics in the Korean War and his size (five feet seven inches, 168 pounds). The thinking was twofold: he would make the team more competitive in the short-term while also serving as a mentor to Meredith.

"I was done playing when Tex [Schramm] called me," LeBaron said. "I had retired from the Redskins, and my family and I had moved in January 1960. A friend of mine was an oilman in Midland [Texas], and I was going to practice law and get involved with the oil business. I was enjoying it, too.

"Tex called in May, the same time I was about to take the Texas bar exam. He called three or four days before I was going to take the test. I was a great fan of Landry, and while I knew of Tex, I really knew nothing of him.

"The Giants had called a few months earlier and wanted me to come up and start for them. They even had a job at a law firm for me and I thought about it, but said, 'No, I don't think so.' But the fact that Landry was the coach definitely had me intrigued. We played against each other when I was with the Redskins, when he was a player-coach, and I had tremendous respect for him as a defensive back, a coach, and a person. He was a smart player and a smarter coach."

"So I took the bar exam, and then flew out of Austin to Dallas where Gil Brandt picked me up at the airport. Landry and I really made an immediate connection, and I decided to give football another shot. Another factor may have been we weren't as highly organized as I would've liked that final year in Washington and no one was more organized than Landry."

For the record, LeBaron passed the bar.

With the roster continuing to evolve and the first training camp coming soon upon them, the Cowboys mailed out 200,000 letters in hopes of securing a solid base of loyalists at the Cotton Bowl. There would eventually be exactly 2,165 charter-season ticket holders.

The collection of football talent that assembled for the first day of that 1960 camp at Pacific University in Forest Grove, Oregon, was lacking, well, football talent. Sure there were a few solid veterans (wide receiver Billy Howton, linebacker Jerry Tubbs, LeBaron), but the overwhelming majority were either well past their gridiron prime or would never experience one.

Landry later admitted that he revised his initial five-year plan of competing for a championship that very morning, some 39 rookies in tow. Still, the much-anticipated—at least by the press corps—"Landry Mile" debuted nonetheless, with not a single player reaching the coach's goal: six minutes for backs, an extra 30 seconds for linemen.

Rookie end Greg Altenhofen, who failed to survive final cuts, was first across the finish line in six minutes, 19 seconds. The players would run the mile throughout camp, several times per week, until they reached their allotted time. This ritual would not change in the ensuing 28 training camps.

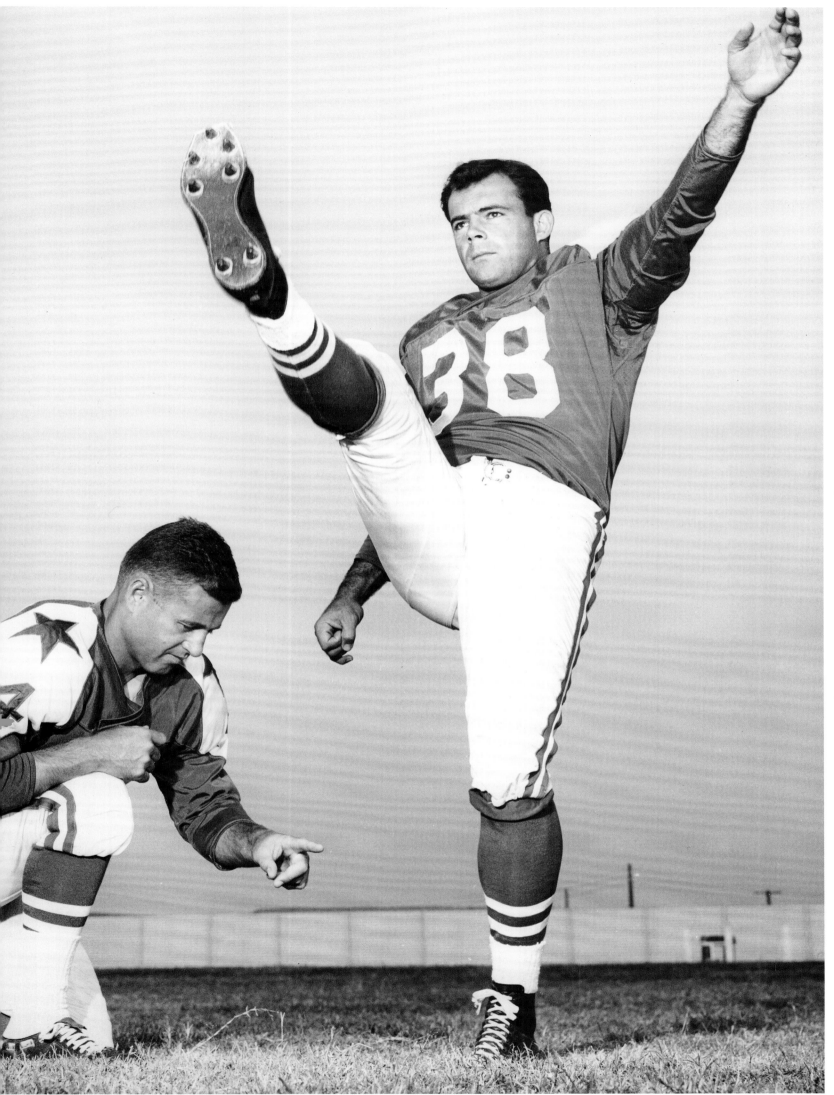

Not all was dire and dour, though, for Jungle Jamey was on hand to provide a degree of entertainment. The King of Gate Crashers, James Bacilerri, a fan and acquaintance of Landry's from back in New York, walked around barefoot, slept on the practice field, and bragged to players about his friendships with Charles de Gaulle, Bob Hope, and JFK. Joining Jungle for this particular visit was a leashed white rabbit he named Texas Freeloader.

In reality, training camp was small time for J. J., who went on to crash numerous Super Bowls, Heisman Trophy presentations—once dressing up as Santa Claus—and even John Kennedy's 1961 presidential inauguration. But when he wasn't traveling the country in his broken-down 1949 Ford, bear meat dangling from the antenna, his hometown was nearby Portland. Also, he idolized Landry, who found him mildly amusing and completely harmless.

As for his feelings about Schramm, well, that was another story entirely. Jungle Jamey simply had no use for Tex, once telling him during a team dinner, "You're no athlete. What are you doing here if you're no athlete? I'll tell you what, you're a freeloader, that's what."

Apparently, the irony was lost.

Landry eventually convinced Schramm to allow J. J. to accompany the team to Seattle for its first preseason game. However, even Jungle Jamey was smart enough to avoid joining the Cowboys on their trek to Delafield, Wisconsin, for their last two weeks of the preseason.

Their home base was the St. John's Northwestern Military Academy, which featured bats flying around the hallways, minimal light in the rooms, and an ever-present odor of . . . let's just leave that to the imagination. The players called it the dungeon and twice hung Brandt in effigy, as he was responsible for the site, having been promised months earlier that the dorms would be remodeled well before their arrival.

"If it wasn't the worst place I've ever been in my life, it's pretty darn close," Tubbs said five decades removed from the visit. "The building we slept in was out of the Middle Ages; really should've had a moat around it. Dark and dreary, depressing, the dungeon wasn't a nice place."

The Cowboys' regular-season debut, in the rain no less, took place at the Cotton Bowl on September 24, 1960. LeBaron delivered the ball in stride to tight end Jim Doran in the first quarter, the 75-yard scoring strike accounting for the first points of the infant franchise. Alas, his 345 passing yards weren't enough, as future Hall of Fame quarterback Bobby Layne—who played his prep ball mere miles away at Highland Park High School—tossed four touchdowns in Pittsburgh's 35–28 decision. The halftime performance of Roy Rogers and his horse, Trigger,

---

**LINEBACKER AND
LONGTIME ASSISTANT COACH
JERRY TUBBS**

On the Flex defense:
"It wasn't the sexy, razzle-dazzle defensive scheme many people made it out to be. But you had to know what you were doing, had to be well coordinated with your teammates because everyone was responsible for a specific job rather than sitting back and reacting to the offensive play. As the middle linebacker, my job was based on how the linemen attacked their gaps. Often, I would be in position to make the tackle."

On how his relationship with Tom Landry evolved from a player to an assistant coach:
"I'm not sure there was a terrible amount of change except that maybe as a player you did exactly what he asked of you, and as a coach [you'd be] asked for input. We weren't bosom buddies, but he treated his coaches with class and respect. There was a coaches' meeting once a week at his house, and he hosted parties now and then where the assistant coaches were always invited. He was also a man of his word. If he said something, you could believe it. He was tough, too. World War II tough. Tom Landry was the real-life John Wayne."

didn't fare much better, with kids pelting the duo with ice as they emerged from the end zone.

The incident cemented a philosophy from which Schramm would rarely stray in the years to come, no matter how much the attendance dwindled those first few seasons.

"Tex decided that rather than spend a lot of money on promotions, we'd spend what money we had available on scouting and personnel," Brandt said. "He felt that winning would promote itself."

The following week, in front of a sparse home crowd of family and friends estimated at 18,500, the Cowboys nearly upset that season's eventual NFL champion, the Philadelphia Eagles, losing 27–25. Thereafter, the defeats were mostly one-sided, Landry's units lacking depth, especially in the secondary. The offensive line was also a work in progress, the running attack barely mustering 1,000 yards in 12 contests.

Yet, under no circumstances would Landry veer from his long-time vision.

"I remember one game in St. Louis that first season," LeBaron recalled 49 years later. "Before the game, I pulled him aside and said, 'Tom, you're making this too complicated. We can beat these guys if you simplify the offense.' And he said, 'We're not trying to beat St. Louis this week, we're trying to build a team that can beat the Cleveland Browns and win championships, and we don't have the players for that yet, but we're not going to alter the system because of that. When we have the players, this system will work.'

"I'll never forget that, even then, Landry wanted to build long-term; he wasn't worried about wins and losses those first few seasons if it impeded the long-term growth. And Tex and Clint stood by him."

While the inaugural campaign was without victory, the Cowboys—as 14-point underdogs—salvaged a 31–31 tie against Landry's former team, the Giants, at Yankee Stadium on December 4. The following morning, at Dallas Love Field airport, two fans greeted the team, one holding a sign that read, WELL DONE COWBOYS.

"May sound funny, but tying the Giants was like winning the world championship for us," Tubbs said. "I never lost a game in high school or college; we were 31–0 my three years at Oklahoma. But that tie meant so much to me and all of us."

The 1960 Dallas Cowboys finished 0-11-1 and were outscored by nearly 200 points. While the official attendance was announced at 10,000, fewer than 3,500 fans showed up for the final home game against San Francisco on November 20, leading a visiting scribe to joke, "There aren't enough Texans here to defend the Alamo."

PUNTER
DAVID SHERER

On Don Meredith:

"I played with Don at SMU; he was the best man at my wedding. He was always the life of the party because he possessed such a great mind. People may not realize how smart Don was. He never forgot someone's name. I mean he could meet them once for two seconds and would remember the guy's name five years later. That's why he did so well with *Monday Night Football*. He was such a natural fit with not only his personality but [also because] he never forgot anything. Don never had to work at it; he was just being himself."

On Tom Landry:

"The most fun I ever had playing was staying out after practice and punting with Tom Landry. He loved punting. He was an advocate of the two-step punt and was always trying to get me to switch from my three-step technique. At least once a week during the season we'd have contests, sometimes we'd be out there 45 minutes. Looking back, I think it relaxed him. Even that first year, he was so intense in practice, he wasn't close to any of the players. But I loved the time he spent with me. I'd say the punting contests were pretty even; he could kick it pretty good."

Following pages: Lee Roy Jordan's cleats.

30,000	Attendance at the first home game in franchise history, a 35–28 loss to the Pittsburgh Steelers at the Cotton Bowl on September 24, 1960.
554	Receiving yards for tight end Jim Doran in 1960, the team's lone Pro Bowler that inaugural season.
460	Passing yards Don Meredith earned in a 31–24 loss at San Francisco on November 10, 1963, a franchise record.

55

RING OF HONOR FULLBACK
DON PERKINS

On running the "Landry Mile" as a rookie in 1960:

"He wanted all of us to run a mile the first day of training camp. Tom's criteria was six minutes for the backs and receivers; I think the linemen were given an extra 30 seconds. I wasn't in the best shape of my life, had gained 30 pounds or so since my last college game [at New Mexico], as the Cowboys said they wanted me to play fullback. Then again, I had never run a mile in my entire life. I failed miserably. It's been 50 years now, but I still remember walking and crawling most of the final two laps.

"Afterward, Coach Landry called me in for a private meeting. He told me he was disappointed and that he thought I was more determined and took better care of myself. That really hurt my feelings. I never wanted to disappoint Tom Landry. You know, though, in nine years, I never came close to running that mile in six minutes. Bob Hayes and Bob Lilly never did either, so at least I was in good company. The three of us were always running extra laps during training camp."

Robert Lewis Lilly grew up in Throckmorton, Texas, his family's hometown since before the Civil War. His earliest memories were on the farm, 14-hour days the routine when he wasn't attending school. When Lilly was a boy, his father, whom he idolized, took him to watch his first football game.

"My father's hero was Sammy Baugh, who played at TCU from 1934 to 1936," Lilly said. "When I was eight years old, in 1947, my father started taking me to TCU football games. There was this guy my father knew from Fort Worth who worked one of the gates and let us in for free. That was the only place I watched a football game growing up, even through college."

Lilly started out playing quarterback—the next Slingin' Sammy perhaps? Just one minor problem: while Baugh played in the NFL at six feet two inches and barely 180 pounds, Lilly was six feet three inches and more than 200 pounds before his first day of high school. By the time he was earning All-American honors at TCU as a defensive tackle in 1960, Lilly was six feet five inches, 250 pounds with extraordinary, almost superhuman natural strength. Former Horned Frogs teammate Harry Moreland once said, "If I was as big and strong as Lilly, I would charge folks just to live."

Fittingly, Lilly became the first draft selection of the Dallas Cowboys, 13th overall in 1961. The pick was acquired from Paul Brown and Cleveland literally at the draft itself, with Schramm making a mad dash to Cleveland's table as Brown was pondering his options. The deal included the Cowboys' No. 1 pick in 1962 and starting offensive tackle Paul Dickson. And while some may have dreaded the thought of joining a winless team, Lilly was not among them.

"I couldn't have been happier; I wanted the Cowboys to take me," he said. "My father was able to see every one of my home games until he passed away in 1970. If not the Cowboys, the AFL Dallas Texans were my second choice. I just wanted to be close to home."

There was definite improvement in 1961, with the Men of Landry defeating the Pittsburgh Steelers, 27–24, in the season opener at the Cotton Bowl for the first victory in franchise history. Both LeBaron and Meredith threw for 160-plus yards in the win, while Howton, the first player in NFL history with 500 career receptions, finished with 138 yards and a score.

"That first win against Pittsburgh, I remember that the players, myself included, thought we were going to win before the game started," LeBaron said. "We believed in Tom very deeply. I remember we took the lead in the third quarter on a [45-yard] touchdown pass in which Billy Howton broke off a post pattern, and I saw what he was thinking beforehand, and we hooked up."

The influx of talent—including Don Perkins, who missed the 1960 season with a broken foot; fullback Amos Marsh; linebacker Chuck Howley; and Bob Lilly—led the Cowboys to a stunning

4-3 start before a disappointing 0-6-1 finish. Perhaps more important, Landry's platoon quarterback system first emerged, with both LeBaron and Meredith sharing snaps in 8 of the 14 games in 1961.

"I kind of liked the shuffling quarterback system, but I know Don hated it," LeBaron said. "For me, as long as I had first and third downs, it was great. I could go over and talk with Landry, and we could go back and forth on the play call for third or first down while the second-down play was taking place."

Of course, LeBaron was the first and last Cowboys signal caller over the next dozen or so years who wouldn't have a complaint with the theory of alternating snaps and/or possessions.

The 'Pokes—the moniker often referenced by media and fandom alike—continued to show progress in 1962, finishing 5-8-1 and scoring 398 points, second most in the NFL. Five players were tabbed as Pro Bowlers: cornerback Don Bishop, Perkins (945 rushing yards), LeBaron (95.4 quarterback rating), Lilly, and Tubbs. Dandy Don Meredith also made the leap, with 15 touchdown passes and just eight interceptions.

The Cowboys appeared on the brink of success, having outscored opponents, 280–245, through the first three quarters on the year. Their fourth-quarter collapses could be attributed to both a young defense and a lack of depth.

"The NFL roster limit then was 33 players, and if you started the game on defense, you were expected to play every down, all four quarters. Special teams, too, usually," Lilly said. "That's not an excuse, but it was a different game. We knew, Coach Landry knew, it was going to take some time, and in 1962 the offense was there, but the defense wasn't."

The defense wasn't alone, however. The fan base also wasn't there. Attendance was abysmal, dropping eleven percent from the previous season to 21,778 per game, a number that was incredibly generous in comparison to warm bodies at the Cotton Bowl. For the November 11 game with the Giants, Murchison sent iconic New York City restaurant owner Toots Shor a rather large carton along with a letter:

Dear Toots:

Enclosed are the box seats for the New York–Dallas game Sunday about which I spoke to you Friday night. And in case you want to bring any of your friends, I am also sending you Sections 1, 2, 3, and 4.

Sincerely,

Clint

DEFENSIVE BACK
CORNELL GREEN

On not having played college football:
"I played basketball at Utah State, so yeah, I was shocked when Gil Brandt showed up and wanted to sign me. I played one year in high school, that's it. I never expected to even make it through that first training camp in 1962, but three years later, there I was in the Pro Bowl. I was pretty proud of that. I give all the credit to our defensive backfield coach, Dick Nolan, who later became the head coach of the 49ers. He taught me football."

On the transition from basketball to football:
"The physical aspect of the game wasn't too tough for me, but the actual rules—I literally didn't know the rules at first. I just thought you could kick anyone's butt. If a receiver ran by me, I just tackled them. Coach Nolan explained I couldn't do that, but I still must've averaged a pass interference call a game those first few years. My hands weren't that good either. I wasn't used to concentrating on catching the ball. In basketball, you could catch it with one hand, that was pretty easy. And if you dropped the ball, you could still dribble."

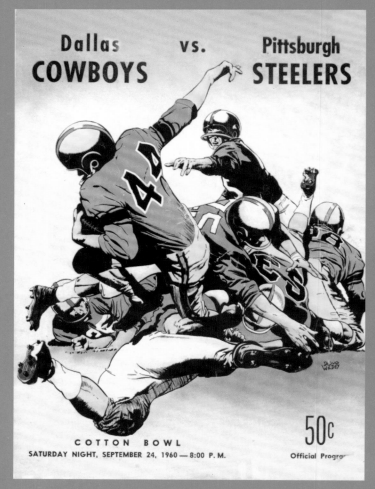

Dallas vs. Pittsburgh
COWBOYS STEELERS

COTTON BOWL
SATURDAY NIGHT, SEPTEMBER 24, 1960 — 8:00 P.M.

50c
Official Program

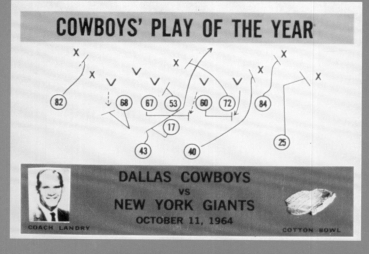

COWBOYS' PLAY OF THE YEAR

DALLAS COWBOYS
vs
NEW YORK GIANTS
OCTOBER 11, 1964

COACH LANDRY

COTTON BOWL

There were 10,000 unsold tickets included with the carton.

As for their crosstown rivals, despite having won the AFL Championship, the Dallas Texans weren't having much success at the box office either. Thus on May 22, 1963, Hunt, in a sacrifice that put his league before his team, accepted a generous offer from Kansas City and relocated the soon-to-be-named Chiefs.

"There was no conceivable way for both the Texans and Cowboys to continue to operate in Dallas and be successful," said Hunt, who remained a Dallas resident until his death in 2006. "The Cowboys had a certain built-in advantage in that if they ever were successful on the field they were playing in the NFL. There's a question as to how long you can lose money in a business and still make economic sense."

Both the Texans and the Cowboys were no doubt still losing significant dollars at the time, with Murchison later joking of Hunt's decision, "We flipped a coin, and I lost."

But the owner's fortunes were ever so slowly beginning to change. *Sports Illustrated* predicted that the Cowboys, with three NFL Drafts, a plethora of trades, and several undrafted free-agent signings behind them,

OWNER CLINT MURCHISON'S THREE SONS
CLINT III, BURK & ROB

On their father:

Clint III: "My father was much more involved with Tex Schramm than people realize. Tex would call him on almost every decision. But dad never involved himself with Tom Landry in terms of offering coaching ideas or such. There's that one story about dad recommending a reverse with Bob Hayes, and Landry ran it the first play of the game for like minus-nine yards, and he never said another word."

Burk: "Dad felt the streets outside the Cotton Bowl were dangerous and felt like the Cowboys needed a better place. [Dallas mayor] Erik Jonsson was an egghead; he had no clue the impact a stadium downtown would've had. There were ninety acres where Reunion Arena was that were available in west downtown. That's where dad wanted to build. He wanted to create the most fan-friendly stadium the world had ever seen."

Rob: "Dad possessed a real passion for football. He was a visionary; he saw the future of the NFL before almost anyone else did. I remember sitting with him at games. He was stoic. I never recall him cheering. He wasn't friendly with more than a handful of players. Ralph Neely was probably his favorite."

would win the conference championship in 1963. In addition, a radio contract was signed with four states (Texas, Louisiana, Arkansas, and Oklahoma) carrying the 'Pokes. Somewhat lofty expectations, sure, but not deemed unrealistic by the team, fans, and media alike.

Looking back, this was the most instrumental of seasons in the defense's maturation process, with cornerback Cornell Green and end George Andrie, both in their second campaigns, joining rookie linebacker Lee Roy Jordan and Chuck Howley as worthy representatives of Landry's Flex. More crucial, though, was a midseason position change for Lilly, from end to tackle, his natural position.

In the end, though, the Cowboys finished a bitterly disappointing 4–10.

For the first time, patience was no longer stressed; penance, in the form of a sacrificial lamb, was deemed necessary. Many felt Landry, having compiled a record of 13-38-3 through four seasons, must be fired.

Speculation rampant, Murchison called for a press conference on February 5, 1964, where he stunned one and all by announcing he had just inked Landry to an unprecedented ten-year contract extension.

Following pages: Jerry Tubbs and Eddie LeBaron become actual cowboys for a promotional stunt.

100	Yards of cornerback Mike Gaechter's team record interception return for a touchdown against the Philadelphia Eagles on October 14, 1962.
25	Interceptions thrown by Eddie LeBaron in 1960, which remains tied for a franchise record. Danny White also tossed 25 in 1980.
16	Degrees at kickoff of Dallas' road game at St. Louis on December 15, 1963, the coldest regular-season game in franchise history. The Cowboys won 28–24.
13	Wins compiled by Tom Landry during his first four seasons (1960–1963) as head coach. He was given a 10-year contract extension following the 1963 campaign.

DIRECTOR OF PLAYER PERSONNEL
GIL BRANDT

On how the Cowboys changed the NFL Draft:

"Some teams would literally show up at the draft with a *Street & Smith* college football magazine, having never seen or spoken with a single prospect. No one wanted to change. Tex knew someone at Delta Air Lines, and they were using computers, so we bought our own in 1960 and started inputting any and all data we could find on potential draft picks. We also had scouts working for us from almost every college in the country, usually assistant coaches. We'd pay them $50 in the spring and $50 in the fall to scout a game or spring practice of another team. They'd also tell us who the best players at their schools were.

"We started the Wonderlic Test in 1961, the 40-yard dash, having players measured and weighed, having them jump, whatever we could think of. Ten percent of potential draft picks are great, 10 percent are lousy, and 80 percent look alike. A housewife can tell you the 20 percent at the top and bottom, the trick is evaluating everyone else in the middle."

"That should quiet people down," Murchison said at the time. "That is in line with my philosophy that once you get a good man, you keep him."

For Landry, the vote of confidence, which included an offer to purchase 20 percent of the team, served as a defining moment in his coaching career.

"That was the most significant thing that ever happened to me," Landry said in 1984. "I'm sure when that happened there were a lot of shocked reporters in that room. It came as a surprise. Everybody thought Clint was going to make a coaching change. From then on, I really dedicated myself to be a football coach.

"Clint Murchison was so important to the long streak we had. He never put pressure on me, never asked me a question in all those years. Anytime we got in a slump, he was the first to write a note with something clever on it. Today, everybody panics after two or three years."

Murchison's oldest son, Clint III, who was finishing up high school around the time of the contract extension, said, "I remember being old enough to think (the extension) wasn't a smart move. I wasn't alone in that thinking."

The 1964 NFL Draft was noteworthy for both the immediate dividends paid, thanks to first-round selection Mel Renfro, one of the finest athletes to ever wear the Cowboys uniform, and the long-term investments eventually gained. Bob Hayes, the future Olympic gold medalist with a limited football pedigree from Florida A&M, was taken in the seventh round and was followed by Heisman Trophy–winning quarterback Roger Staubach of the Naval Academy, who faced a four-year military commitment, being selected in the tenth.

Still, results were lackluster, with Dallas finishing 5-8-1 in 1964 despite a huge spike in fan support. More than 38,000 strong came out per game at the Cotton Bowl, almost double that of two seasons previous. Only Lilly and Renfro were named to the Pro Bowl, while Meredith, finally entrenched as the undisputed starter following LeBaron's retirement, struggled, throwing just nine touchdowns against 16 interceptions and taking 58 sacks. And while some on the outside questioned his commitment to the sport, his teammates were in awe of his toughness.

RING OF HONOR DEFENSIVE TACKLE
BOB LILLY

On his legendary strength:

"Some was probably just family genes. My father could pick up a car engine with his bare hands, and my uncle was a champion boxer in World War II. My father was a custom farmer. When I was 11 years old, I was put in charge of the hay. I drove the tractor, baled, raked, and hauled the hay. To dump the hay from the tractor, we would put rocks under it and back it up, so two or three times a day, I was lifting the front of the tractor, about 800, 900 pounds. I didn't lift an actual weight until 1967, my seventh season with the Cowboys."

On his nickname, "Mr. Cowboy":

"I really didn't like that tag for the longest time. I think Roger [Staubach] was first responsible for it. I thought there were a lot of guys who deserved it more than me. Anyway, now, I guess, I've just grown used to it. That's what everyone calls me. I still think there are a lot of guys you could be calling that. I certainly don't have any plaques at my house with 'Mr. Cowboy' on it."

"Don Meredith broke his nose 26 times and never took himself out of the game; there was no tougher football player," Lilly said. "He was a superb athlete and a lot better quarterback than he was given credit for."

Nonetheless, the Cowboys chose quarterback Craig Morton out of the University of California with the sixth overall pick of the 1965 draft, just a year removed from selecting both Staubach and fellow signal caller Jerry Rhome in 1964. Still, Landry stuck with Meredith.

Ask those in the visiting locker room on Halloween 1965, buried within the bowels of Pitt Stadium following an embarrassing 22–13 loss to the Steelers, a team headed for a 2-12 finish. For that's where the path of the franchise was forever altered. At that moment, the Dallas Cowboys were 20-51-4. Over the next 20 years and two months, their regular-season record would be 213-81-2.

"Tom Landry cried," Lilly recalled of that day. "He said we did everything he asked and maybe he wasn't the right coach. We realized that he wasn't the problem, we were."

Others players in attendance said Landry mentioned resigning.

"He was crying not so much about the game as about me," Meredith said. "He had wanted me to do well, and I was awful. I stood up and swore I was going to work harder and we would win, but people kept sitting there with their heads down."

Two days later, back in Dallas, Landry called Meredith into his office, saying, "Don, you're my quarterback. I believe in you." Both men broke down.

The Cowboys won five of their last seven, and posted their first non-losing campaign at 7–7. Meredith finished with superb numbers (2,415 yards, 22 touchdown passes) while Hayes literally reinvented the wide receiver position, averaging 21.8 yards per catch with speed never before witnessed in the NFL . . . or anywhere else for that matter. The defense boasted five Pro Bowlers, having allowed the third-fewest points in the league.

"We knew we were ready following 1965," Brandt said. "The goal was no longer incremental improvement; we wanted to win the NFL Championship."

DAN JENKINS
FUNNY OLD COWBOYS

Reminiscing about the early days of the Dallas Cowboys has to begin with poor Eddie LeBaron trying to see over the line of scrimmage without a stepladder, and tireless Frank Clarke continually racing down the sideline in search of any forward pass that might not land at the feet of a soft drink vendor working the aisle in a yawningly empty Cotton Bowl.

But the team was socially acceptable right away, thanks to the fondness that many folks had for Clint Murchison Jr., Bedford Wynne, and Tex Schramm and the efforts they made to paint the territory Cowboy blue.

Incidentally, that color seems to have changed into a darker shade through the years. In the beginning it stirred around in there somewhere between the baby blue of the University of North Carolina, Dodger blue, royal blue, and what can only be described as Chevrolet blue.

In any case, it was a brave man who chose to appear in public—particularly anywhere near a truck stop—in a cashmere blazer of this curious color, a coat that had been given to him by the Cowboy organization in appreciation of his support.

> **MEREDITH LIKED TO JOKE THAT LANDRY WOULD STAND AT THE BLACKBOARD AND SAY, "IF WE DO THIS, THEY'LL DO THAT," AND WHEN DANDY WOULD INTERRUPT AND SAY, "WHAT IF THEY *DON'T* DO THAT?" LANDRY WOULD REPLY, "THEY WILL."**

Yes, I confess I was presented with one of those blazers, like a few other members of the press, but I promptly hid it in a closet at home while remarking to my wife, "I'm giving the band a night off."

Those first three seasons from 1960 through 1962 were fun days for the press when the Cowboys competed with Lamar Hunt's Dallas Texans for the favor of the fans and affection of the media. This struggle may have reached its peak one Sunday in the Cotton Bowl when the Texans—the future Kansas City Chiefs—promoted a game as "Barbers' Day." All those wearing white smocks would be admitted free. Whereupon the scant thousands who showed up were draped in everything from bed sheets to tablecloths and looked less like barbers than Klan members mingling with dental assistants.

But I digress. Don Meredith took over as quarterback of the Cowboys in 1963, and thus began a six-year saga of Whose Team Is This, Anyway?

Did it belong to the witty and charming Dandy Don, whose gifted leadership and passing arm often relied on instinct, or was it run by the stone-faced man in the hat, coach Tom Landry, who believed strongly in his own wisdom and demanded obedience to his *X*'s and *O*'s?

The situation may have occasionally caused Landry to reach for the Anacin bottle, but it merely gave Dandy Don ammunition for humor. Meredith liked to joke that Landry would stand at the blackboard and say, "If we do this, they'll do that," and when Dandy would interrupt and say, "What if they *don't* do that?" Landry would reply, "They will."

But sometimes they didn't. And a large share of the blame for the loss would be heaped on Dandy Don. Which once resulted in Gary Cartwright's immortal resurrection of the Four Horsemen in the *Dallas Morning News*, only this time his names for them were "Pestilence, Famine, Death, and Meredith."

▲ (clockwise from top left) The 1960 quarterbacks: Eddie LeBaron, Don Meredith, and Don Heinrich; actor Ken Curtis, *Gunsmoke*'s Festus, has some fun with Dave Edwards; Players posing for a 1962 promotion; Chuck Howley recovers a fumble.

Of course, as we know, a bunch of Cowboys would eventually start a trend of winning more games than they lost, having been hammered into shape by Tom Landry's calculus and the offensive fireworks of Dandy Don and such cohorts as Bob Hayes, Danny Reeves, Don Perkins, and Ralph Neely, not to overlook the defensive heroics of Bob Lilly, Chuck Howley, Mel Renfro, Cornell Green, and Lee Roy Jordan.

Those were the most prominent pioneers of a future dynasty.

It should also be remembered that by 1965 the Cowboy uniforms had happily changed from goofy blue and white to sensible blue and silver.

Naturally, it was left to Dandy Don Meredith to have the last word on that entertaining era.

"Tom Landry was a perfectionist," he said. "If he was married to Raquel Welch, he'd expect her to cook."

Dan Jenkins has been a renowned sportswriter for the past five decades, having authored over 500 articles for Sports Illustrated *as well as books* Semi-Tough *and* Jenkins at the Majors. *He remains a senior columnist for* Golf Digest.

(left to right) 1968 training camp; Lance Alworth; Pettis Norman in the 1967 Championship Game; the Cowboys offices; an impassioned fan; playing the College All-Stars in 1972; Cornell Green.

2

DANDY, DOOMSDAY, AND CAPTAIN
AMERICA

1966–1973

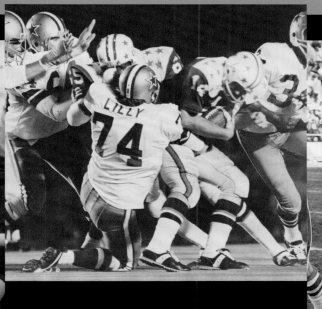

More than four decades removed, the memories are stunningly vivid. The victories and defeats, the iconic plays of a generation, are certainly satisfying to reminisce about, yet the personal relationships endure well beyond the snaps of the pigskin.

★ ★

The examples are in abundance, the admiration and respect the highest accord of sincerity.

Coming off arguably his best season in 1968, one that included a third straight Pro Bowl nod, Don Perkins, at 31 years of age, decided to hang up the cleats. At the time, Tom Landry said, "His best years I've ever seen are the last two. I think he has ended his playing days at least three years too soon."

Asked of his decision nearly 42 years later, Perkins said, "I might've had some good years left, but I wasn't going to hold off my backup much longer. He could catch better than me and was ready for the job. It was his time, and I thought retiring was the best thing for me. I had a good run and didn't want to become one of those disgruntled backups finishing their careers. The closest friendships I've ever had were those I developed with the Cowboys; there was a special bond between the players back then."

Walt Garrison, a fifth-round selection in 1966, spent three seasons behind Perkins at fullback. Born and raised just north of Dallas, Garrison was riding bulls and steers at his uncle's farm when most kids were still watching *Howdy Doody*. Though his first, second, and third loves were the rodeo, a friend of his father's landed him a football scholarship at Oklahoma State courtesy of the governor of New Mexico—long story—where his freshman coach was Sammy Baugh.

His initial three campaigns with Dallas were a learning process with just 479 rushing yards and 11 receptions, his duties primarily coming on special teams.

Still, at almost every practice and game, there was Perkins showing Garrison new techniques, teaching him how to read the linebackers, explaining the intricacies of playing fullback in the NFL. Finally, at one point Garrison said to him, "Don't you realize I'm trying to beat you out for playing time?"

Perkins didn't hesitate in his response: "I want to win a championship, and the better you are, the stronger we are as a team. If you're better than me, you should be playing."

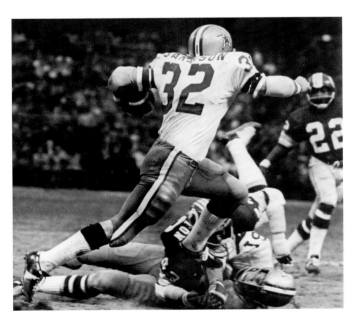

▲ Walt Garrison.

▲ Boyd Dowler scores for Green Bay in the 1966 Championship Game.

▲ Gil Brandt.

THE OFFICIAL BREAKTHROUGH, THE LEAP, CAME IN 1966 AS THE COWBOYS LOOKED UNBEATABLE IN THE EARLY STAGES, OUTSCORING THEIR FIRST FOUR OPPONENTS 183–45.

As Garrison finishes the story, he's told of what Perkins said of his retirement, that he wouldn't have been able to hold him off another year. The most affable and versed of storytellers, Garrison is now silent. He starts a sentence, or at least a syllable, before again pausing.

"Don Perkins is my hero. He's also the best fullback in the history of the Dallas Cowboys."

This mutual respect shared as teammates and men was by no means an isolated occurrence as the Cowboys embarked upon their unprecedented run of sustained success, a magnificent tally of 20 consecutive winning seasons from 1966 to 1985. The bond between Perkins and Garrison represents that of many, those who came together under a common leader, a shared character, and a singular goal.

"We were just a bunch of guys who loved each other," Bob Lilly said.

Indeed, it would be naïve to think this collection of individuals was connected by mere coincidence.

"Character was a huge factor, absolutely huge," Gil Brandt said. "We would ask everyone we could about a player we were looking at bringing in. Not what he could do on the field, but what type of person he was. We tried to stay away from players with character issues or off-the-field problems. Tom [Landry] felt very strongly about this.

"Now, you call a collegiate head coach and ask about his player, and you're going to get 'Great kid, great student, highest character,' because it makes their program look better the higher he's drafted, especially by the Cowboys after we started having some success.

"So what we did, we entered into the computer all the birthdays of the assistant coaches, the trainers, equipment managers of every college team, as well as the birthdays of their wives and kids. And we sent them all birthday cards, maybe a nice Dallas Cowboys pen, a poster of their favorite player, whatever. So when we needed to know about a player, we called the trainer, the equipment manager, asked about their families, and then got the inside scoop on the kid."

The official breakthrough, the leap, came in 1966 as the Cowboys looked unbeatable in the early stages, outscoring their first four opponents 183–45. Yes, 183 points, as in nearly 46 per game, or 6 more than the 1960 Cowboys tallied all season. The 56–7 dismantling of Philadelphia on October 9 in front of nearly 70,000 fans at the Cotton Bowl remains the largest margin of victory in team history, with the 652 yards from scrimmage also a still-standing franchise mark.

The 'Pokes finished 10-3-1 and easily led the NFL with 445 points and 5,145 yards on offense. Halfback Dan Reeves, an undrafted free agent a season earlier who played quarterback collegiately at South Carolina, tied for the league lead with 16 total touchdowns, 8 rushing and 8 receiving, while Bob Hayes was simply altering how defenses played the game. His speed was above and beyond any mere defensive back or really any other human on earth. He led the league with 13 touchdown catches.

The defense, anchored by Pro Bowlers George Andrie, Chuck Howley, Cornell Green, Mel Renfro, and Bob Lilly, wasn't shabby either, allowing the second-fewest yards in the league (3,558) behind a potent pass rush that registered 60 sacks—then an unofficial statistic—including 12 at Pittsburgh in a 20–7 win on November 20.

The Cowboys secured the Eastern Conference title with a 17–7 defeat of the Giants in the regular-season finale, their plane greeted by more than 10,000 fans upon the team's arrival from New York. The process took all of seven years, but Dallas was now a professional football town with home attendance averaging more than 67,000 fans each game.

Next was Vince Lombardi and the Green Bay Packers for the NFL Championship at the Cotton Bowl on New Year's Day, the winner advancing to the inaugural AFL-NFL World Championship Game, later recognized as Super Bowl I. Alas, the dream died on the 2-yard line with the Cowboys unable to force overtime despite first-and-goal with 2 minutes, 19 seconds remaining following a pass interference call. The Packers prevailed, 34–27, and secured their fourth league crown in six years in the process.

RING OF HONOR DEFENSIVE BACK
MEL RENFRO

On Bob Hayes:

"He was amazing. I couldn't cover him in practice; no one could cover him. I was a world-class sprinter in college, ran a 9.5-second 100-yard dash and was part of a 440-yard relay team that broke a world record. Bob and I were the same age. I would line up 15 yards deep in practice on Bob. He'd come off the snap, I'd turn and run, the quarterback would throw the ball 40 yards downfield, and there was Bob slowing down to catch it with me still running behind him. I always laugh when people say Bob was the World's Fastest Human at the 1964 Summer Olympics. Trust me, Bob was the World's Fastest Human before that and for some time thereafter. You know what's scary? I always felt Bob never ran as fast as he could. He just ran as fast as he needed to."

On the Flex defense:

"The only thing I understood about the Flex was that the front seven would line up in funny positions. I have absolutely no clue to this day what the defensive line and linebackers were doing with the Flex. Luckily, it didn't really apply to the defensive backs."

THE OFFICIAL KICKOFF TEMPERATURE AT NOON WAS MINUS 13 DEGREES, THE WIND CHILL AROUND 30 BELOW. IN THE BROADCAST BOOTH, FRANK GIFFORD TOLD A NATIONAL AUDIENCE, "I JUST TOOK A BITE OF MY COFFEE."

The national and local media spun the outcome as the last stand of a worthy champion, one fortunate enough to have delayed the dawn of a new NFL power, the Dallas Cowboys.

One of the key components to the Cowboys' success in the mid-1960s and beyond was a revamped offensive line. In 1964, with six different guards making starts, the 'Pokes took nearly five sacks per game. Don Meredith was often the recipient of brutal physical beatings long before the league showed any interest in protecting its quarterbacks. Defensive players were allowed two and sometimes three steps after the quarterback released the ball to unleash their fury, with helmet-to-helmet hits the norm long before they were outlawed.

When Ralph Neely arrived at training camp as a rookie in 1965, he was unlike any offensive lineman on the roster. The All-American tackle from Oklahoma was huge, six feet six inches, 265 pounds, and—at least on the football field—mean and nasty. He was quickly nicknamed "Rotten" by his teammates.

"Don said I was the first offensive lineman bigger than he was. He didn't care how I tackled or hit defensive linemen. He was just happy they weren't kicking the crap out of him," Neely said.

Lilly, who faced him daily in practice, later said of Neely, "He's so good, he's the only player I ever knew who was never a rookie."

The following year the Cowboys selected guard John Niland with the No. 5 overall pick, which provided the offensive front a stabilizing foundation for the next decade. Neely and Niland combined for eight Pro Bowl nods and five All-Pro honors. Heck, Niland was so quick that he chased down a jewelry store robber in January 1969, running six blocks and through two stores in downtown Dallas before apprehending the culprit with $945 worth of diamond rings.

"It reminded me of the movies," Niland said.

Unfortunately, there would be no Hollywood ending in 1967. Entering the season as overwhelming favorites to win their first league crown, Dallas was inconsistent, losing three of its last five to finish 9-5. However, following a stunning 52–14 blowout of the Cleveland Browns in the Eastern Championship Game, there was much optimism and promise heading to Green Bay for a rematch in the NFL title tilt.

Several Cowboys players remember the weather being quite pleasant during their walk through at Lambeau Field on December 30. There was a little fog, but the wind was minimal, temperatures around 25 degrees. They slept that night with visions of redemption for the year previous, confident that now was their time to become the class of the NFL.

RING OF HONOR QUARTERBACK
DON MEREDITH

On his relationship with Tom Landry:
"I truly admired Tom in so many ways. When I first joined the Cowboys, I think I expected a different type of personal relationship with him. As a player, it was difficult to get to know Tom other than as a head coach. But as time went on, we came to appreciate each other's dynamics and could joke with one another."

On whether he retired from the game early:
"I could have definitely played a few more years with the Cowboys. I was only 30 at the time and was coming off a good season. But I made a personal decision that it was time to leave the game, and I really had no regrets."

On his most memorable game:
"Well, I had a few back at Mount Vernon High School! But with the Cowboys, it has to be the 1966 season against Green Bay, our first time in the Championship Game. Even though we lost, I felt like I was playing at my best, and I just loved the feel of that whole game. I was always disappointed that others didn't see it the same way."

"Mel Renfro was my roommate, and the wake-up call comes from the operator, and back then they would give the time and the temperature," Perkins said. "So Mel hangs up the phone, looks at me and says, 'The woman said 18 below 0. She must've meant above, right?' We went to look out the window, but it was all frost, a block of ice really.

"I don't remember individual plays from the game itself, just that it was constant pain. The biggest battles that day weren't on the field. They were on the sidelines for the heaters. The game was played at half speed; we all kept slipping around like the Ice Capades."

The official kickoff temperature at noon was minus 13 degrees, the wind chill around 30 below. In the broadcast booth, Frank Gifford told a national audience, "I just took a bite of my coffee."

There was no ground to be seen; the field was literally a block of ice, the vicious gusts of wind perhaps the most severe of deterrents.

"During pregame, I slipped and fell. The ice just ripped my skin off, like three inches of skin on my arm," Lilly said. "When we went into the locker room, we wrapped ourselves in Saran Wrap, put on two pairs of long underwear, wrapped our arms in rubberized tape, whatever we could think of.

RUNNING BACK
CALVIN HILL

On Tom Landry's offense:

"Coach Landry was an engineer. His offense was built from engineering concepts. If you, as a player, understood the basic concepts, the offense was very logical. Everything Tom Landry did was logical based on a statistical edge. The offense may have looked complex, but it was simple logic: A is greater than B. There was a lot of movement—different formations, double shifting, quick snaps—but it was based on angles, and with running plays, giving the ball carrier the best angle to gain positive yardage. You see so many backs nowadays running side to side or even backward looking for gaps. We were running forward looking for holes."

On Roger Staubach:

"We were rookies together. Roger was the hardest worker I ever saw on the football field. He possessed this extra level of competitiveness. He was a terrible loser. If the team lost, he always took that defeat upon himself. If we lost, Roger lost. His wife, Marianne, even called me once and asked if I could come over and talk with him. I tried, but I wasn't much help. When we lost a football game, it was like a funeral."

"There were these three guys drinking whiskey behind our bench when the game started, and before we took the field, they took their shirts off. They were yelling at us, but we weren't listening. We were more amazed they didn't have shirts on. We came back from that first series and they weren't there. I have always wondered what happened to those guys. No one knew. To this day, what, 43 years later, any time I see anyone from that game, I ask if they ever heard about those three guys.

"That was the only game I ever played in my life, at any level, where winning wasn't the main objective. Survival was."

After Green Bay took a 14–0 lead, the Cowboys scored 17 unanswered points, culminated by a stunning 50-yard halfback option pass from Reeves to wide receiver Lance Rentzel.

"Coach Landry had three or four exotic plays, that's what he called trick plays, in the game plan every game, and we had been working on that one for three or four weeks," Reeves said. "That was Meredith's play call, though. It was the first play of the fourth quarter, and we had called a ton of running plays, which Don thought set up the option toss, as the linebackers were coming up awful quick on the snap. He was right; it worked perfectly."

Green Bay's offense hadn't mustered more than 14 yards in any of its previous 10 possessions, at least before taking control at its own 32-yard line with 4:50 on the clock. Having advanced to the

1-yard line with less than a minute remaining, the Packers ran two unsuccessful running plays with Donny Anderson. Rather than kicking a tying field goal with 16 seconds remaining and no timeouts at their disposal, quarterback Bart Starr took a quick snap and plunged into the end zone.

As for the game-winning sneak, Landry said, "It was a dumb call. But now it's a great play."

Midway through the return flight to Dallas, a reporter—the media traveled with the team then—asked Meredith for his thoughts on the game. He said, "I'm sorry, but I just can't say anything about the game. I hope you understand. All I have to say is, there was trouble on every corner and it just didn't seem like Christmas."

Perhaps no defeat ever frustrated Landry more, especially with his former coordinator peer from the Giants on the opposing sidelines. The game would prove historic for another reason, marking the final game for Lombardi to lead Green Bay. He died less than three years thereafter.

In 1986 Landry wrote with admiration of his old rival in a special tribute for *SPORT* magazine, although he couldn't help himself in the second-to-last paragraph, illustrating the philosophical differences between the two:

> The thing you had to do against Lombardi was be tough and execute well, and you had to believe you could beat him. Even when we had a better team in the Ice Game on New Year's Eve 1967, the Packers still beat us on the last play with a quarterback sneak.
>
> His system was not very innovative. It was a tough, hard-nosed, fundamental type of football. But his strength didn't lie there. It lay in his ability to get people to perform. Better than they thought they could. No one was better than Vince in that area that I've ever seen.

The 1968 campaign was more of the same for Dallas, a somewhat disturbing trend taking shape, which led to the moniker "Next Year's Champions." The Cowboys breezed through the regular season at 12-2, winning 11 games by at least 13 points. For the year, they outscored opponents by 245 points, easily the most in franchise history.

Meredith, now 30 years old, was sensational, posting a career-best 88.3 quarterback rating as the offense easily paced the NFL with 431 points. Bullet Bob Hayes hauled in 10 touchdown receptions and returned two more via punt returns, including a 90-yarder against Pittsburgh. Then there was his 44-yard scoring grab at Philadelphia.

RING OF HONOR LINEBACKER
CHUCK HOWLEY

On being the only Super Bowl MVP from a losing team:

"Definitely a tough feeling, playing in the ultimate game, which the Super Bowl is, and being named the Most Valuable Player after losing [16–13 to the Baltimore Colts]. Even all these years later, I can't really explain it. I certainly wasn't jumping for joy in the locker room like every other Super Bowl MVP has, but I was proud of the accomplishment."

On the Ice Bowl:

"It was cold. As one of the guys on the field, I wasn't freezing; we warmed up a little just from the exercise of running around on defense. I felt worse for the guys on the sidelines not playing. That's when it was most brutal, when we were standing there not moving."

On the Pro Football Hall of Fame:

"I know a lot of people think I belong in there. I hear it all the time. I believe, sure, it's an accomplishment every athlete wants and strives for, but at the same time, it will be what it will be. I have the satisfaction of my teammates, the victories we shared together, and our Super Bowl VI victory."

Following pages (left to right): Jethro Pugh, Cornell Green, and Mike Gaechter try to stay warm during the Ice Bowl.

1,036	Rushing yards for Calvin Hill in 1972, the first 1,000-yard season in franchise history.
84	The distance in yards of Ron Widby's franchise-record punt at New Orleans on November 3, 1968.
63	Yards of the lone punt return touchdown in Cowboys postseason history, courtesy of Golden Richards, in a 27–10 loss to Minnesota in the 1973 NFC Championship Game.

"Bobby didn't like running slant patterns all that much, but he took this one and just . . . disappeared," Rentzel said. "I have never heard a visiting stadium that quiet. Franklin Field was silent. Players on both teams were all just looking at each other in utter disbelief. We didn't even run down to congratulate him. Everyone was ranting about Usain Bolt at the 2008 Olympics and I was thinking, 'I saw speed like that once.'"

But once again, the season of much hope and promise ended in crushing fashion with a 31–20 loss at Cleveland in the Eastern Championship Game, leading to a second trip in four years to the Playoff Bowl Game, or as middle linebacker Lee Roy Jordan called it, "The Toilet Bowl."

That would prove the final NFL contest for both Meredith and Perkins as the original Cowboys announced their retirements in July of 1969. Landry, among others, was absolutely shocked by Meredith's decision, saying, "I tried to talk him out of it. But if you lose your desire to play, then you shouldn't play."

Dandy Don was 34-13-1 his final 48 regular-season starts, although his detractors often cited his career 1-3 mark in the playoffs. He was the first face of the franchise, the local kid from Mount Vernon, Texas, and SMU who would become a national sensation in the *Monday Night Football* broadcast booth. As for his often-analyzed relationship with Landry, Meredith spoke fondly of his coach at his farewell press conference.

"I have come to love the guy," Meredith said. "I can tell you about his professional ability in just about any area you want to talk about. But also, he's the finest man I have ever known. I will miss him a great deal."

So within the span of a few weeks, 27-year-old rookie quarterback Roger Staubach went from fourth on the depth chart to Craig Morton's backup, the Cowboys having dealt Jerry Rhome to San Francisco shortly before Meredith's departure.

Since last taking a snap for the Naval Academy on November 28, 1964, Staubach's exposure to the gridiron consisted of playing catch in Vietnam, two seasons with the base team at the Pensacola Naval Air Station and two weeks at the 1968 Cowboys training camp, which prompted Meredith to say, "Anybody who takes a vacation and comes to two-a-days has got to be a little weird."

Not helping matters was the complexity of Landry's playbook, Staubach saying, "It's tougher than calculus." He showed enough initially that Landry decided against acquiring a veteran backup. Staubach's impact in his first two years, though, proved minimal: four starts, three touchdown passes, and 10 interceptions.

WIDE RECEIVER
LANCE RENTZEL

On Tom Landry:

"It's rare to be on a team that changed the way the league played the sport—that's catching lightning in a bottle. My first two years with Minnesota, I remember watching film on the Cowboys even when we weren't going to be playing them, the coaching staff trying to get in stride with Tom Landry's offense. You know, that was the true genius of Coach Landry. He invents the 4-3 defense, which made the 5-3-3 obsolete. Then when every other coach in the league starts using his defense, he comes up with an offense to beat his own defense. That's true genius."

On putting wide receivers in motion:

"No one had ever seen that before Landry sent me in motion the first time. It created immediate chaos for the defense. It forced them to make all kinds of choices instantly, and that gave us the advantage before the ball was snapped. Motion created mismatches, forcing a linebacker or safety to pick up a much faster wideout, and the defense didn't realize there was a mismatch until we were running for a 60-yard touchdown. Even then, I'm not sure they knew what happened."

The story of 1969 was a repeat of 1968, with the Cowboys rolling through the regular season at 11-2-1—rookie Calvin Hill and Walt Garrison combining for 1,760 rushing yards—before losing to the Browns in the Eastern Conference Championship, 38–14. The whispers were now shouting rants among the media and fans. Tom Landry and the Dallas Cowboys, 45-12-2 in their last 59 regular-season contests, simply could not win the big game.

There was an influx of talent thanks to the 1970 NFL Draft, including running back Duane Thomas, defensive back Charlie Waters, offensive lineman John Fitzgerald, and defensive end Pat Toomay. But surprisingly, long-term, the jewel of the class was an undrafted free agent from parts unknown.

"On the plane from Dallas to Los Angeles for training camp, a number of rookies were on the flight," Toomay said. "Margene Adkins, Denton Fox, and this other guy. He looked kind of lost. He was wide-eyed, his jaw sort of hanging open, as he wandered around. So there I was, headed for baggage claim, when this guy grabs me. 'Are you with the Cowboys?' he asks. I nod. 'Me, too,' he says. And then, sort of whispering: 'But I'm from Arkansas, and I haven't traveled that much. Do you know where we go?'

"A few yards away an airport employee stood talking on an intercom. I asked her where Cowboy players were to meet their buses. Smiling, she clicked a button on her intercom so that as she told us where to go, her directions were broadcast throughout the entire airport. 'Oh, my gosh!' yelped my new compadre. 'Can you believe what just happened?' My new friend introduced himself then. He was a free agent safety from tiny Ouachita Baptist University in Arkadelphia, Arkansas, his home. He, of course, was future Ring of Honor inductee Cliff Harris."

But 1970 didn't appear to be the season for the Cowboys either, especially following a stunning 38–0 defeat to the St. Louis Cardinals in the Cotton Bowl on *Monday Night Football* that dropped them to 5-4. It also marked the first regular-season shutout suffered by the Cowboys.

The next day, during a defensive players-only meeting, Jordan started the rallying cry, "We're are not going to let them in the zone," with Lilly vowing, "If we allow another point this season, they're going to have to crawl over our dead bodies."

After defeating the Redskins 45–21 the following week, the defense was simply impenetrable, not allowing a touchdown over the final 17 quarters of the regular season, including a 6–2 triumph in the freezing rain and wind at Cleveland on December 12, which led Landry to say, "Our guys were beside themselves with excitement after the game. We haven't had this kind of emotion. I thought our defensive performance was remarkable."

Two weeks thereafter, in what to this day remains the lowest-scoring postseason contest in NFL history, the Cowboys defeated the Detroit Lions 5–0. The following morning, one Dallas newspaper headline read, "Cowboys *Can* Win Big One."

49	Point differential in the largest margin of victory in franchise history, a 56–7 defeat of visiting Philadelphia on October 9, 1966.
12	Victories in the longest winning streak in franchise history, including postseason, which began on November 7, 1971, and was snapped with a 16–13 loss at Green Bay on October 1, 1972.
10.06	Seconds Bob Hayes needed to win the 100-meter dash at the 1964 Summer Olympics in Tokyo.
5	Combined points scored by Dallas and Detroit in the Cowboys' 5-0 postseason triumph on December 26, 1970, still an NFL record for fewest combined points in a playoff game.
2	Members of the NFL's 1960s All-Decade Team who played for the Cowboys: Bob Lilly and Ralph Neely.

MOST OF THE COWBOYS PLAYERS JUST SHAKE THEIR HEADS WHEN THINKING BACK TO THIS CONTEST, A FEW OF THEM SAYING THAT PERHAPS THE TEAM WAS CONTENT WITH JUST MAKING THE FINALE.

Next up was the NFC Championship Game at San Francisco, which was coached by Dick Nolan, a Cowboys assistant from 1962 to 1967. And while the defense finally allowed a touchdown in the third quarter, Dallas prevailed 17–10 behind 289 yards from scrimmage combined by Thomas and Garrison.

"That was the biggest game I ever played in," Garrison said. "No win meant more to me, especially because it meant so much to the guys who had been there longer—the Lillys, the Howleys, Coach Landry—and dealt with all that crap about 'Next Year's Champions.' I bet you a lot of guys think of that win as the most important of their careers, more than the Super Bowls even."

Among those teammates who concur with Garrison's assessment is Renfro, who secured the Lions win with an interception late in the fourth quarter and kept San Francisco wide receiver Gene Washington out of the end zone against the 49ers while returning another pick 19 yards.

"Absolutely, without question, those were my most memorable games and the highlight of my NFL career," Renfro said. "I remember a reporter asked me something after the San Francisco game, don't remember the question, and I replied, 'Finally, finally, finally. We've reached the mountaintop.' That's how we felt."

Super Bowl V resulted in a disappointing 16–13 loss to the Baltimore Colts, a game that was truly ugly. Most of the Cowboys players just shake their heads when thinking back to this contest, a few of them saying that perhaps the team was content with just making the finale. The two sides combined for a still-standing Super Bowl record 11 turnovers with Jim O'Brien kicking a 32-yard field goal as time expired to give Baltimore the title.

Afterwards, Renfro went on to earn Offensive MVP honors at the Pro Bowl. Yes, offensive, as the defensive back returned two punts for touchdowns.

Looking back on the first 50 years of the Dallas Cowboys, few, if any, seasons offer more historical meaning than that of 1971. There was the opening of the magnificent Texas Stadium, the first Super Bowl triumph, the initial glimpses of greatness from Captain Comeback, and perhaps most important in terms of comic relief, there was the debut of kicker Toni Fritsch.

Landry himself traveled to Europe during the summer in hopes of finding a soccer-style kicker. His first stop was Vienna, Austria, where he found Fritsch, who accepted an offer to come stateside despite speaking hardly a word of English.

RUNNING BACK AND ASSISTANT COACH
DAN REEVES

On making the team as an undrafted free agent in 1965:
"I was a quarterback at South Carolina, but the Cowboys were pretty well set there with Don Meredith, Craig Morton, and Jerry Rhome. I signed with them because they told me I could try a number of positions: running back, wide receiver, defensive back. There were a lot of injuries my first preseason, and I was fortunate to make the team as a running back. It was a new position, but I was just happy to be in the NFL."

On the similarities between Roger Staubach and John Elway, who Reeves coached:
"Both were extraordinarily talented. They were those rare quarterbacks who could beat you throwing and still hurt you running the football. Both were extremely competitive, as much as any two athletes I've ever been around. They were also great leaders; both of them worked harder in the offseason than any of their teammates, and when guys see the best player working that hard, they tend to give that extra effort. No matter the situation, no matter the stadium, they both thrived in tough situations. No football team with Roger Staubach or John Elway at quarterback was ever out of the game."

TEXAS
STADIUM

For the majority of his near-quarter-century ownership of the Dallas Cowboys, Clint Murchison Jr. let Tex Schramm, Tom Landry, and Gil Brandt make the football decisions, the lone caveat being an obligatory phone call from Schramm for sign-off on substantial financial matters.

Heck, Murchison didn't even attend the majority of the league's owner meetings, allowing Schramm to vote on the team's behalf. He also worked from his own downtown Dallas office rather than at the Cowboys headquarters.

When the time arrived to talk about constructing a new stadium, though, Murchison was front and center, for this was his area of expertise. The engineer from MIT wanted to construct a stadium beyond the realm of the highest expectations.

Unfortunately, Murchison first had to wage a bitter public battle with the powers that were in Dallas, primarily city planners and mayor Erik Jonsson, who was also the cofounder and former president of Texas Instruments. The talks started in 1965, with Murchison wanting to build a state-of-the-art stadium in West Dallas. The city had absolutely no interest in that idea, countering with simply renovating the Cotton Bowl.

Throughout his life, Murchison relied upon letters as his chosen method of communication, the back-and-forth with Jonsson during the stadium debate being no exception:

Dear Erik:
I noted in the morning paper your comment that until the Astrodome was built, everyone thought the Cotton Bowl was pretty good.
Of course, until the transistor was developed, people thought the vacuum tube was pretty good.

This gem was all the more genius considering Jonsson's greatest advancements with Texas Instruments involved the transistor.

"Dad felt the streets outside the Cotton Bowl were dangerous and felt like the Cowboys needed a better place," Burk Murchison, Clint's son, recently recalled. "Erik Jonsson was an egghead. He had no clue the impact a stadium downtown would've had. There were 90 acres where Reunion Arena was built that were available, in west downtown. That's where Dad wanted to build.

"He wanted to create the most fan-friendly stadium the world had ever seen. He wanted 55,000 capacity so there would be intimacy. When they finally built Texas Stadium, he literally studied where the first-row seats were built so that they would be 15 feet off the field. He wanted to enhance the view for the fans."

Much like Jerry Jones would turn to Arlington more than 30 years later when Dallas passed on housing the Cowboys, Murchison struck a deal with another neighboring suburb, Irving. The $35 million project was financed primarily by the city offering bond options to potential season ticket holders, the bonds selling for $250 for tickets outside the 30-yard line and $1,000 for those between the 30s. Murchison himself sketched the original plans, including, yes, the hole in the roof, which would shield fans from the elements, mainly the scorching Texas heat, yet leave the field itself exposed.

On a recommendation from a friend, Murchison enlisted the assistance of architect Warren Morey.

"He invited me to his office, and just like that, I was signing a contract," Morey recalled. "Clint never said much, but I sensed he liked the work we were doing. That was a long process, especially since the city of Irving owned the land, so its mayor and city council were also involved."

The Cowboys christened the new stadium on October 24, 1971, defeating the New England Patriots, 44–21. Reviews were favorable, although some felt the extravagance priced out many of the

diehard fans from the Cotton Bowl. But the bells and whistles were revolutionary, the stadium being the first to feature luxury boxes, which sold for $50,000 each.

"That was as happy as I ever saw my father," said Burk Murchison. "He was heavily involved in the architecture of the stadium, not to mention all he went through in trying to find a site for the Cowboys in Dallas. No one will ever fathom how badly he wanted to build a new stadium in Dallas, but some very stubborn political folks just weren't going to allow that.

"But he was very proud the day Texas Stadium opened."

LONGTIME TEXAS STADIUM GENERAL MANAGER
BRUCE HARDY

On his first memories of the Dallas Cowboys:
"That first year, 1960, my father used to take the family and a bunch of our friends to games. We'd sit in the end zone; adult admission was $1. My family was friendly with Bedford Wynne's, who bought the team with Clint Murchison. I also remember the Green Bay Packers and Vince Lombardi used to have training camp at SMU; we lived a few blocks from there in Highland Park. When I was old enough, I'd sell programs at SMU games. At 16 years old, I was driving Pat Summerall and other announcers from the airport to their hotel and the Cotton Bowl. The first time Pat was driving with me he asked, 'Do you even have a driver's license, kid?' Thing is, I'm not sure if I had one then."

On Randy White's pregame ritual at Texas Stadium:
"After he was taped, about an hour before they took the field for warm-ups, Randy would come into my office and lay on the couch. I'd get up to leave, and he'd just grunt. I would turn the lights off, and he'd lay there for however long, usually 30 to 40 minutes, and mentally prepare himself. This is when Randy White the man would transform himself into the football player we saw on the field. He'd walk out on his tiptoes, that's just how he walked, and his calves would be bulging, they were so big."

On Randy White's postgame ritual at Texas Stadium:
"[Defensive coordinator] Ernie Stautner and Randy would take a case of beer and have one of my guys drive them out of the Lot 10 tunnel. They would go out and thank the fans still in the parking lot for their support and sit around drinking beer with them. It was a different time."

On being diagnosed with multiple sclerosis at 42 years of age during the 1990 season:
"My life has been the Dallas Cowboys; I have literally eaten, lived, and breathed this franchise for 50 years. When that happened, when the doctor told me, I figured that was it. But Jerry Jones came and found me and said his family would search for the best doctors, and we'd beat MS. I was so worried about performing my job, but he threw his arm around me and said, 'You'll always have a job with the Dallas Cowboys. Let's go beat this thing.' And here I am 20 years later. I can't golf anymore, walking can be tough, but it's been the most wonderful of rides."

On his favorite memory:
"The last game at Texas Stadium, even though we lost. My family was there; my six-year-old grandson was driving around on the golf cart with me. I didn't want to go home. We left the field around 1 a.m. I was crying."

"So our first exhibition game in 1971, we're playing the Rams," Neely said. "He [Fritsch] points at one of the officiating crew and asks his roommate, Don Talbert, 'Name, name?' So Talbert tells him. We line up for the kickoff and one of the officials hands Fritsch the ball, and he says, 'Thank you, Mr. Son of a Bitch.'"

Then there was the time in training camp Landry wanted to practice onside kicks. The team lines up in proper formation, Landry blows the whistle, and Fritsch launches the ball toward the end zone. Calmly, Landry says, "No, no, no. Onside kick, Toni, onside kick."

Kickoff unit lines up again and sure enough, same result. This went on for about five minutes with some of the veteran players convinced Landry was enjoying himself watching the rookies sprint like maniacs downfield each kick.

Despite his stoic, almost robotic image, Landry was not without a sense of humor.

"One day in practice, Coach Landry has us running 110-striders, which is 110 yards in each direction," Neely said. "He's up in the tower, giving us maybe 10, 15 seconds between each one. Finally, Lilly is on his hands and knees, screaming at Landry, 'You're going to kill us you son of a bitch.' Landry blows his whistle for us to run another.

"The next day before practice, Coach says to the team, 'I'm sure yesterday afternoon all of you heard Bob expressing himself during sprints. If you play like Bob Lilly, you can express yourself that way, too.'"

Then again, Landry wasn't always amused during moments of levity.

"My father was a pilot, but I never liked flying," Rentzel said. "I would always sit up in the cockpit during flights, just made me more at ease for some reason. Most of the pilots knew my father, and I knew all the terminology, so we'd usually talk during the flights. So this one time, the pilot I guess just assumed I knew how to fly. He asks me if I wanted to handle the controls, and I decided why not. It wasn't as easy as it looked, and we dropped further than normal pretty quick, and Lilly comes down the aisle to see what the problem was.

"When he sees me at the control, he turns around and yells, 'Rentzel's flying the plane! We're all gonna die!' Took Coach Landry, who was a pilot, about 10 seconds to get up there, and he wasn't happy. Coach rarely raised his voice, but this was one of those times. That was the last of me in the cockpit."

The early stages of the 1971 campaign witnessed Landry struggling with his quarterbacks as much as ever, at least in deciding on who would start, Staubach or Morton. The dilemma

GUARD
JOHN NILAND

On playing guard in Tom Landry's offense:
"Playing guard in that era was so much more complex than nowadays, especially so in our offense, where 90 percent of the plays you were the lead blocker for the point of attack. Also, you were responsible on many plays for multiple blocking assignments, and we ran a ton of plays with the guard pulling, so you needed to know what everyone else was doing in terms of blocking assignments. I remember the Cowboys giving me an aptitude test before drafting me. They did that with all the college kids because Tom Landry needed smart guys to play in his system."

On kicker Toni Fritsch:
"He barely spoke English, so he's walking through the weight room, and someone asks him about lifting. He says, 'Toni kicks with foot. Not arm. No weights for Toni.'"

On being a six-time Pro Bowler:
"Back then, the players and coaches voted, so it meant a lot. People don't remember me these days, so I just tell them I blocked for Don Meredith and Roger Staubach, and that impresses them."

"WE LINE UP FOR THE KICKOFF AND ONE OF THE OFFICIALS HANDS FRITSCH THE BALL, AND HE SAYS, 'THANK YOU, MR. SON OF A BITCH.'"

—Ralph Neely

reached new heights in a 23–19 loss at Chicago on October 31 in which Landry had them alternate each play. After the defeat, which knocked the Cowboys to 4-3, Landry finally settled on Staubach, who guided the team to seven straight wins to finish the regular season. In terms of overall talent, this team that finished 11-3 probably ranks first among Landry's squads with eight future Pro Football Hall of Famers (Roger Staubach, Bob Hayes, Bob Lilly, Mel Renfro, Herb Adderley, Lance Alworth, Rayfield Wright, and Mike Ditka), not to mention Lee Roy Jordan, Cliff Harris, and Chuck Howley, each eventual Ring of Honor inductees.

Despite the roll call of Pro Bowlers, though, Staubach's presence behind center was the key cog, as he led the NFL with a 104.8 passer rating and threw just four interceptions. More than the numbers, though, he brought a presence, an unrelenting work ethic and a competitiveness bordering on obsessive. He wouldn't lose, he couldn't lose, and the thought of losing never entered his mind until well after defeat had taken place. No comeback was without possibility.

"Roger is as good of an athlete as any quarterback in NFL history," former Cowboys quarterback Eddie LeBaron said. "I remember we were in Las Vegas one offseason, and this is when Roger was playing and I was living there, and he asked me where he could work out. I arranged for him to work out at UNLV, so after he already played tennis, he got a ride there, which was four or five miles from the hotel, and worked out. Keep in mind it was 104 degrees or whatever. When he was finished, someone asked him if he needed a ride back to the hotel and he said, 'No, I'll just run back,' and sure enough, he did."

The path to Super Bowl VI, in New Orleans, offered stiff competition, but the Cowboys weren't to be denied, defeating Minnesota 20–12 on the road before returning home for a 14–3 decision against San Francisco in the NFC Championship Game. Entering the Super Bowl, the vaunted Doomsday Defense had allowed exactly two touchdowns in the last 25 quarters.

(See "Super Bowl VI" special insert.)

As defending Super Bowl champions, the Cowboys suffered a setback before the 1972 regular season even started when Staubach was sidelined with a separated shoulder. Morton was decent in his place, throwing for nearly 2,400 yards, although his 21 interceptions were less than desirable. The running game behind Hill, who became the first Cowboy to rush for 1,000 yards in a single season (1,036), and defense were enough to secure another playoff berth with a 10-4 finish.

Staubach orchestrated arguably his greatest symphony at San Francisco in the division round, coming off the bench late in the third quarter with the Cowboys trailing 28–13.

DEFENSIVE END
PAT TOOMAY

On moving from the Cotton Bowl to Texas Stadium in 1971:

"It was complicated. A lot of the older guys liked the Cotton Bowl. The end zone seats were fairly inexpensive, so a lot of folks who lived in the neighborhood could afford to come to games. They were great fans who sort of got priced out when the shift came to Texas Stadium.

"The new stadium, by comparison, was sort of austere with private boxes. Games took on a social ambiance that hadn't been present before. And there were a lot of jokes about the hole in the roof, the way it kept fans dry during storms while players got soaked. And, there was a lot of grumbling about the way the roof held heat during hot summer nights.

"In the end, though, the uniqueness of the stadium proved to be a great advantage for us. Opposing teams found it difficult to adjust to the conditions there. The play of light could be weird—the way the sun hit the field, the odd shadows. And the field was curved in a way that others weren't, more severe. There was just no stadium like it, and while we got used to its idiosyncrasies, opposing teams couldn't. They just didn't have the time."

STAUBACH ORCHESTRATED ARGUABLY HIS GREATEST SYMPHONY AT SAN FRANCISCO IN THE DIVISION ROUND, COMING OFF THE BENCH LATE IN THE THIRD QUARTER WITH THE COWBOYS TRAILING 28–13.

FULLBACK
WALT GARRISON

On making the team as a rookie in 1965:

"A lot of people assume I was excited about being picked by Dallas in the fifth round because I was from nearby Lewisville, Texas, but that wasn't the case at all. I never heard a single word from them, and as senior at Oklahoma State, I wasn't thinking about playing professional football.

"That first training camp, I was completely lost. If not for Dan Reeves and Don Perkins, I would've been cut. Our college playbook was maybe 6 pages; Tom Landry's was 600. Reeves was my roommate, and he spent hours with me every night going over the playbook. He taught me how to study, and Perk would teach me two or three new blocking techniques every practice.

"Every Friday, Coach Landry gave a test on that week's game plan. I failed a few of those the first few years, which meant a one-on-one visit from him. He said, 'Walt, you're not ready to play for me,' and that hurt my feelings. He was right, though, so I just studied all the time. I wasn't use to that, but I kept studying because I never wanted to let Coach Landry down. I respected him so much."

Outside of a field goal, he hadn't ignited the offense much himself until leading Dallas on two scoring drives in the last 1:53, the final strike a 10-yard bullet to Ron Sellers on a hook.

"I still don't know how we won that game," Hill recalled 38 years later.

But the 30–28 win didn't carry much momentum, and the Cowboys were blown out by the host Redskins 26–3 in the following week's matchup to decide the NFC crown.

Double-digit wins were again achieved in 1973, all the more impressive considering the 14-game regular season, the 'Pokes finishing at 10-4. Staubach was back behind center, throwing for 23 touchdowns, but it was unquestionably Hill who was the offensive catalyst, rushing for 1,142 yards while also leading the Cowboys with 32 receptions. This season, like the one previously, though, ended one win shy of another Super Bowl appearance, Dallas falling at home to Minnesota 27–10 in the NFC Championship Game.

The disappointment the team felt would indeed get worse before it got better, but oh how much better the Cowboys would soon be.

VERNE LUNDQUIST
POSTGAME REACTIONS

Bill Mercer was the Dallas Cowboys radio network play-by-play announcer, and Blackie Sherrod, the legendary sportswriter, was the color commentator when I arrived in Dallas in September of 1967. The Cowboys had played the Green Bay Packers in the NFC Championship at the end of the '66 season, and, despite the loss to the team from up north, they had captured the imagination of the nation.

I was invited to join Bill and Blackie as the pregame and postgame host during the '67 season that ended with the defeat in the Ice Bowl, and, because of subsequent assignments as Blackie's replacement as the color commentator and Bill's replacement as the play-by-play man, I was provided with a front-row seat as the Cowboys exploded in popularity and achievement.

Dallas, having lost twice to Green Bay in title games in 1966 and 1967, found, in the Cleveland Browns, a new playoff nemesis in 1968. They met the Browns in Cleveland's cavernous Municipal Stadium on December 21, 1968. The Browns were rude hosts. They dominated Dallas, so much so that Tom Landry changed quarterbacks in midcontest, yanking longtime starter Don Meredith and inserting backup Craig Morton.

> **GENERAL MANAGER TEX SCHRAMM APPROACHED DON, EMBRACED HIM FOR PERHAPS TEN SECONDS, AND THEN BACKED AWAY. NEITHER SAID A WORD. IT WAS THE LAST TIME DON MEREDITH WOULD WEAR A COWBOYS UNIFORM.**

With no more than three minutes remaining in what was to become a 31–20 defeat, I was standing near the 30-yard line, adjacent to the Cowboys bench, preparing for the postgame interviews. Meredith stood atop the bench, maybe two feet above the almost frozen ground, alone, 20 feet away, his cape draped about his shoulders to shield him from the cold, staring into the distance. General manager Tex Schramm approached Don, embraced him for perhaps ten seconds, and then backed away. Neither said a word. It was the last time Don Meredith would wear a Cowboys uniform.

Later, aboard the Cowboys charter, Meredith sat in the very back row across the aisle from tight end Pete Gent and immediately next to the long staircase from which one could enter and exit the plane. Five minutes before that staircase was raised for departure, Meredith indicated to Gent that he wanted to get off the plane. The two of them descended the steps and, ultimately, made their way to New York City where they hung out in Frank Gifford's apartment for a couple of days. Don just wanted to get away from it all and asked Gent to come along as a friend. Six months later, Don Meredith announced his retirement. He was 31 years old.

The 1970 season had a much brighter finish. After a 5-4 start, including a humiliating 38–0 loss to St. Louis at home, the Cowboys ripped through the rest of the regular season and the playoffs and, with a win at San Francisco in the NFC Championship game, earned a spot in Super Bowl V in Miami. That they lost to Baltimore 16–13 on a last-second field goal took some of the luster off the year, but it ultimately did not diminish the enthusiasm for the Cowboys postgame party at the Galt Ocean Mile Hotel on the beach in Ft. Lauderdale.

The late Clint Murchison was the much-admired owner of the team. The late Bedford Wynne had a minority financial interest in the team and a majority emotional interest in making sure that everyone had a good time. He was in charge of the postgame party. He contacted a friend

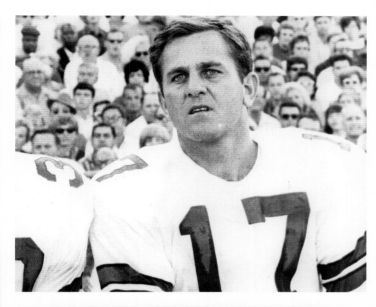

▲ (clockwise from top left): Pete Gent; Don Meredith; Cowboys' training camp lockers; Clint Murchison.

about providing entertainment for the event, win or lose. The friend, a then relatively unknown presence in the music world, said, "Sure, I'll be there. If you can get some extra tickets, I'll bring some other guys with me." Tickets back then were "gettable."

Shortly after dinner had been served, Willie Nelson, Waylon Jennings, Jerry Jeff Walker, and the band began to play. They played past midnight. Well past. They helped ease the sting of defeat for a team that had come oh so close. They provided a memory for the ages for all of us who were lucky enough to be there.

And, of course, Dallas defeated Miami 24–3 in Super Bowl VI and began its run, which continues, as America's Team. It was a privilege to witness it from close range.

Verne Lundquist is the lead play-by-play announcer for CBS Sports' college football broadcasts. He also provides play-by-play coverage of the NCAA Men's Basketball Championship and commentary for the Masters.

(left to right) Charlie Waters and Rafael Septien; Rayfield Wright; Jackie Smith drops a touchdown pass in Super Bowl XIII; Randy White; Larry Cole; Drew Pearson; Bob Hope and Roger Staubach.

3

AMERICA'S
TEAM

1974–1982 ★★★

Tom Landry's 20 consecutive winning seasons are nice, an NFL record and all, but for whatever reason, history has overlooked the more impressive mark. The Dallas Cowboys qualified for the post-season 17 times in 18 seasons during an era when there were far fewer playoff berths.

★ ★ ★

For example, in 1966 the Cowboys played just one postseason contest, that being the NFL Championship Game.

From 1960 to 2009, the longest run of consecutive playoff appearances in the NFL belonged to the Cowboys, with nine from 1975 to 1983. There were five teams tied for second with eight appearances, including, yes, the Cowboys from 1966 to 1973.

"Any team can achieve that magical equation for a season or two, catch a few bounces of the ball, a few calls from the officials, the fluke play," Roger Staubach said. "You make the playoffs that many times, that's no accident. That speaks for itself."

The lone interruption came in 1974 when the 'Pokes finished 8-6 despite winning seven of eight games down the stretch before a 27–23 loss at Oakland in the season finale. In many ways, the year was that magical equation of which Staubach spoke—just in reverse—as the Cowboys lost four games by four or fewer points. The greatest deficit was an eight-point setback against the Giants on September 29. They led the NFL in total offense and placed second in rushing defense, concluding an incredible three-year run of allowing just 3.6, 3.4, and 3.2 yards per carry, respectively.

"Great players playing a great defense, which was designed to stop the run," defensive end Pat Toomay said. "Landry's Flex was unique, unlike any other pro defense, so opposing teams had to spend extra time preparing. For them, nothing they routinely did carried over when they played Dallas. Everything was different. And a lot of opposing coaches didn't truly get what was going on, the elegance of it.

"Often, as I discovered when I played for other teams [after leaving Dallas], opposing coaches would mock it, especially the odd stances defensive ends had to assume when play-

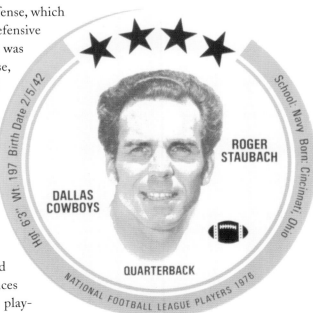

▲ Clint Longley rattlesnake hunting.

ing the Flex. It struck them as being froglike and funny. As the stats show, however, the joke was on them."

Looking back, few seasons produced more poignant developments than 1974 and its postscript.

Bob Lilly retired. Among the most disruptive forces the sport has ever witnessed, he was, and remains, the most gentle and humble of men, never fully accepting his iconic place with the franchise or the game.

Several former teammates and even opponents have wondered what Lilly might have been capable of if he had possessed the anger and rage of many of his contemporaries, such as Deacon Jones and Mean Joe Greene.

"I was never angry; I was competitive," Lilly said. "I watched a ton of film, tried to learn the tendencies of the offensive linemen, even down to how red their knuckles were, which told me whether they were going to pull based on that little extra pressure. I just wanted to win. I was never angry."

Neither was Howard Clinton Longley Jr. Well, at least the Thanksgiving afternoon of November 28, 1974, he wasn't. Some 35 years later, Pat Summerall, who was announcing the game against the Washington Redskins for CBS, remembers Cowboys president Tex Schramm pulling him aside during the pregame and raving about Longley's arm strength, which had earned him the nickname the Mad Bomber among teammates. When Staubach was sent to the sidelines with a concussion early in the third quarter, the 22-year-old from Abilene Christian University led the Cowboys back from a 16–3 deficit, highlighted by a 50-yard touchdown pass to Drew Pearson in the final 30 seconds.

"It was the triumph of the uncluttered mind," Cowboys guard Blaine Nye famously said.

By no means was this an isolated injury for Staubach in 1974. He took an absolute physical pounding, including a career-high 45 sacks. He tossed 15 interceptions against 11 touchdown passes, far and away the worst ratio of his career as a full-time starter.

"I couldn't run that season because of an ankle injury in training camp," Staubach said. "Those first four losses

WIDE RECEIVER
DREW PEARSON

On his first training camp as an undrafted free agent:
"I was literally intimidated by just Tom Landry's presence. Here's this icon telling me what to do and how to play. Listening to his words, you almost want to pinch yourself, just make sure you're really there. That first practice ends, and I want to run to the nearest phone and tell somebody, anyone, that Tom Landry is my football coach."

On the Pro Football Hall of Fame:
"I really don't understand. It's baffling, really. Every offensive and defensive member of the NFL All-Decade 1970s first team is in the Hall of Fame except Cliff Harris and me. I remember thinking at the time, when I was named to the team, that this was my ticket to Canton. That this meant Cliff and I were guaranteed a spot. Cliff came so close a few years back, too. I felt terrible when he didn't make it. It's a difficult situation for me because while I don't want to bad-mouth anyone, it's frustrating to ask yourself, 'Why aren't I included?' There are four wide receivers in the Hall that played the majority of their careers in the 1970s that weren't named to the first team."

"I NEVER CARED ABOUT THE PASSING YARDS, THE TOUCHDOWN PASSES. I JUST CARED ABOUT THE WINS. THAT'S ALL FOOTBALL GAMES WERE ABOUT FOR ME, WINNING."

—Roger Staubach

were close. We should've beaten the Eagles; we fumbled on the 1-yard line. We missed a field goal against the Vikings. I never cared about the passing yards, the touchdown passes. I just cared about the wins. That's all football games were about for me, winning.

"I was only at Coach Landry's house once during my playing career, and that was during the 1974 season after the Thanksgiving win. He knew I was down in the dumps, almost despondent, and he just talked about how the season wasn't my fault."

This also marked the final season of Calvin Hill, who earned his fourth Pro Bowl nod in six years before departing for the short-lived World Football League. The Yale graduate later played six seasons with the Washington Redskins and Cleveland Browns.

"Our first offensive meeting each training camp with Coach Landry, we'd spend two, three hours going over rules. He'd read every one himself and all the offensive situations," Hill said. "Then he'd read our goals for every situation imaginable: rushing average on third down and less than two yards, completed passes on first down, everything. After each goal, he'd read where the average team, the Super Bowl winner, and the Cowboys finished the previous season. I never knew where he found these statistics, but they were so in-depth.

"The focus from the first day of practice was winning the Super Bowl. There was nothing worse than Coach Landry signaling you out when watching film and saying, 'Look at the way you executed this play. You can perform at that level and have a long, productive career in the NFL, but that's not good enough for the Dallas Cowboys.'"

At the time, the majority believed Dallas was headed for a transition, one that would likely take several seasons before the team was once again ready to compete for a conference championship. Among those departing along with Lilly and Hill were Cornell Green, Bob Hayes, John Niland, and Walt Garrison. However, buoyed by an infusion of young talent tabbed the Dirty Dozen, the rebuilding—reloading?—process lasted about 48 hours, or whatever the elapsed time was of the 1975 NFL Draft. While offensive coordinator Dan Reeves and the majority of the coaching staff pleaded for the brass to take Walter Payton with the No. 2 overall pick, which was obtained via the Giants for Craig Morton, Gil Brandt selected Maryland All-American defensive end Randy White. He was among the 12 draft picks to make the squad, including linebackers Thomas "Hollywood" Henderson and Bob Breunig, and offensive linemen Pat Donovan and Herb Scott.

"The rookies certainly brought an enthusiasm that we were lacking the year before," linebacker D. D. Lewis said.

Another key addition was veteran running back Preston Pearson, who was released by the Steelers late in training camp. He would rack up nearly 3,500 yards from scrimmage over the next six seasons while emerging as football's first third-down specialist.

This wasn't a dominant Cowboys team—10 of their first 11 games were determined by 11 or fewer points—but Dallas won the majority of the close outcomes, finished 10-4, and headed to Minnesota for a divisional playoff matchup against head coach Bud Grant and the Vikings as eight-point underdogs.

Trailing 14–10 late in the fourth at frigid Metropolitan Stadium, Staubach, starting from his own 9-yard line, completed four straight passes to Drew Pearson, including a 22-yarder on fourth and 16. Following an incomplete pass, Staubach, taking the snap out of the shotgun from midfield, drifted back and pump-faked to his left, which kept safety Paul Krause from doubling Pearson down the opposite sideline, before launching a high-arcing throw toward the end zone. At the

208	Points allowed in 1978, the fewest in team history for a 16-game regular season.
37	Interceptions recorded by the Cowboys in 1981, a single-season franchise mark.
22	Players who have worn No. 81, a team record. The roll call includes Billy Howton, Jackie Smith, Raghib "Rocket" Ismail, and Terrell Owens.

TIGHT END
BILLY JOE DuPREE

On the lineage of Cowboys tight ends:
"It's been like *The Naked City*; only the names have changed. I think they've gone more to passing and less running since the year I retired. [Doug] Cosbie came after me and became a primary target, and after Doug the next productive individual was [Jay] Novacek, and now they've got Jason [Witten]. It's just the scheme of how things are put together offensively. During the time I played, tight end was a focal point, but the way the system was structured didn't allow the tight end to have the exposure. My position was one that was utilized to send plays in and out of the game. So, theoretically, for 10 years I played half the game. And it's a little scary for me to think how, if I had played the whole game, what else could I have done?"

On how the tight end position has changed:
"The biggest change I've seen is that the defender can't beat up on the receiver past certain yards. Five yards is all they have. In the years I played, if you were off the line of scrimmage, the defensive back could beat up on you until the whistle blew."

5-yard line, Pearson, after initially juggling the ball, corralled the pass against his right elbow and hip before taking a few steps backward for the game winner. The Vikings screamed that Pearson pushed off corner Nate Wright, who fell down as the catch was made, but no flag was thrown.

In the locker room afterward, Staubach said of the pass, "I closed my eyes and said a Hail Mary."

Behind four Staubach touchdown passes, three to Preston Pearson, and two interceptions from Lewis, the Cowboys pummeled the host Los Angeles Rams 37–7 in the NFC Championship Game and advanced to Super Bowl X against the Pittsburgh Steelers.

In the Big Game, Dallas led 10–7 entering the fourth quarter. But Pittsburgh added two field goals before Terry Bradshaw found Lynn Swann for a 65-yard score to take the lead. Despite a late touchdown catch by Percy Howard, his lone career reception, the Steelers prevailed, 21–17.

The training camp of 1976 in Thousand Oaks, California, was the setting for one of the more bizarre and uglier moments in franchise history. Longley was difficult from the start of camp, upset that the Cowboys had brought in Danny White, their third-round pick in 1974, after the World Football League folded. Eventually, according to his book, *Time Enough to Win*, Staubach confronted Longley: "Clint, I'm getting tired of you talking behind people's backs. Somebody is gonna knock those Bugs Bunny teeth of yours in." He said, "Are you going to be the one?" and I said, "Yeah, I'd love to do it." The two headed for a nearby baseball field with White recalling, "Clint threw the first punch, then Roger cleaned his clock."

Three days later, in the locker room on the final day of training camp, Longley blindsided Staubach when he was adjusting his shoulder pads. The players were separated before Staubach could retaliate, and by the time he had returned from the hospital, having received nine stitches over his left eye, Longley was long gone. Immediately driven to the airport, he was traded to San Diego, his once-promising NFL career all but finished.

"Clint and I sat together every trip in 1974. We would talk, he would ask me questions, I kind of thought he looked up to me in a way," Staubach recalled. "When Danny arrived for quarterbacks camp in the spring of 1976, that's when Clint started to unravel. I think it was the threat of losing his job as the backup. If you have an axe to grind, let's fight like men. His sucker punch was as dirty as dirty could be. I didn't start it."

Years later, Staubach is still bothered by the incident, but says he has forgiven Longley and would be willing to meet with him. That is easier said than done.

12 — Selections from the 1975 NFL Draft who played for the Cowboys, a team record: Randy White, Thomas Henderson, Burton Lawless, Bob Breunig, Pat Donovan, Randy Hughes, Kyle Davis, Rolly Woolsey, Michael Hegman, Mitch Hoopes, Herb Scott, and Scott Laidlaw.

6 — Members of the NFL's 1970s All-Decade Team who played with the Cowboys: Cliff Harris, Bob Lilly, Harvey Martin, Drew Pearson, Roger Staubach, and Rayfield Wright.

0 — Career regular-season receptions by wide receiver Percy Howard. However, the undrafted free agent from Austin Peay caught a 34-yard touchdown in the fourth quarter of Super Bowl X, beating Pro Football Hall of Fame cornerback Mel Blount in the process.

▼ (clockwise from top left) 1976 Pro Bowl players Billy Joe DuPree, Rayfield Wright, Harvey Martin, Cliff Harris, Charlie Waters, Drew Pearson, and Roger Staubach. Not pictured: Blaine Nye.

By all accounts, the lone Cowboys player to see Longley since "The Punch" is Lewis, who hooked up with him while on a fishing trip with clients in Corpus Christi, Texas, in 2003. The two ate dinner at a local Italian restaurant before Lewis pleaded with his former teammate.

"I urged him to reach out to Roger, to make amends," Lewis said. "Clint's a strange guy. It's so sad. Who knows how the human mind works? He seemed healthy for the most part. I told him that we've all made stupid mistakes, but he didn't want any part of getting back with the team or Roger."

Behind a franchise-best 9-1 start, the 1976 Cowboys were heavy favorites to represent the NFC in another Super Bowl, but a stunning 14–12 loss to the Rams at Texas Stadium ended those aspirations in the playoff opener. Among the more balanced of teams, Dallas didn't have a single player reach 600 rushing yards or 60 receptions yet sent eight to the Pro Bowl, including offensive linemen Rayfield Wright and Blaine Nye, tight end Billy Joe DuPree, safeties Charlie Waters and Cliff Harris, defensive end Harvey Martin, wide receiver Drew Pearson and quarterback Roger Staubach.

Brandt and Landry were convinced the team needed an explosive threat. The expansion Seattle Seahawks were in equally dire need of players, making them prime targets for a trade. Dallas dealt its first-rounder and a trio of second-round picks to the Seahawks for the No. 2 overall selection in the 1977 NFL Draft. If need be, the Cowboys would've secured the first pick, but everyone knew the Tampa Bay Bucs were taking Ricky Bell, who played for their coach, John McKay, at USC.

"We wanted Tony Dorsett more than we ever wanted a collegiate player, before or since," Brandt recalled.

RING OF HONOR LINEBACKER
LEE ROY JORDAN

On Paul "Bear" Bryant and Tom Landry:

"Both were completely dedicated to their profession, their teams, and their players. Also, I believe both truly loved what they were doing. Coach Bryant was a fiery kind of guy. He was the absolute best during pregame speeches. He would have us so emotionally excited, we would run onto that field with an energy you didn't even know existed. He also possessed an underrated knack for bringing along young players.

"Coach Landry led more by example; he wasn't going to tell you how to live your life. He was, obviously, much quieter than Bear. I think, at first, Coach Landry thought that professional athletes should motivate themselves, but he learned to inspire as he went along. He would sometimes quote Bible verses during pregame speeches, but for the most part they were more strategic and analytical than inspirational."

On his own legendary leadership:

"It was a gift for me, just knowing how to read people. Early on I realized you can't deal with everyone the same way either. Maybe this teammate needed an arm draped around him in private, while this next guy needed a kick in the butt on the practice field."

The reigning Heisman Trophy winner from Pittsburgh, Dorsett rushed for an NCAA-record 6,082 yards, a mark that stood for 22 years.

"I was absolutely the little kid in the candy store when Dallas traded up and picked me. I was shocked and surprised," Dorsett remembered. "Back then, expansion teams didn't have the pick of the litter. They weren't going to conference title games like Carolina and Jacksonville did in the 1990s. We were trying to discourage Seattle from taking me. We even threatened playing in Canada, although in reality that would've never happened. All my worrying, and I ended up with a great organization on draft day."

Landry decided to bring Dorsett along slowly, giving him just 21 carries the first three games behind Preston Pearson. The rookie saw more action thereafter, sharing attempts with Pearson and fullback Robert Newhouse, but as the calendar approached Thanksgiving, Dorsett was still coming off the bench.

"I was really down on myself not starting," Dorsett recalled. "I always thought of myself as a game player. Honestly, football just came so easy to me in high school and college. This was new. I had to learn the system and prove myself in practice. I had always practiced hard. At Pitt, I would run to the end zone every handoff in practice because that's where I expected to finish my runs during games.

"I made up my mind in week 10, when ironically enough we were going to Pittsburgh, my home-town. I was going to wait until next year, come back in the best shape possible, and win the starting job. The day before the game, Coach Landry calls me in for a one-on-one meeting. At that point, I had written off my rookie year, and Coach says, 'We expected you to be a starter by now.' I said, 'Me, too,' and I told him about my mind-set for the following season. He said he had been impressed by my ability to do a little of that and a little of this, and that I was ready to start."

Two weeks later, on December 4, Dorsett rushed for a then-team-record 206 yards against Philadelphia en route to a still-standing rookie mark of 1,007 yards for the season.

But Dorsett was by no means a one-man show. No NFL offense tallied more yards than the 1977 Cowboys, while no defense allowed fewer, an amazing feat considering Landry was calling the plays on both ends.

"In my 39 years in the league, I never saw or even heard of anyone else running the offense and defense," said Dan Reeves, a Cowboys assistant from 1970 to 1980. "When I became a head coach [with Denver], I remember having even more of an appreciation for what he did. There is no way to properly explain Tom

RING OF HONOR QUARTERBACK
ROGER STAUBACH

On his style of play:

"If Coach Landry could have designed his perfect quarterback, it certainly wouldn't have been me. I was creative, and he hated creative. He wanted to call a specific play and have that play run the way it was designed. My arm was strong, more so than people realize. I made the most out of my arm, could throw as hard as any quarterback of my era, but at times I would run. Defenses hate running quarterbacks, especially if they know how to run. I wasn't Marion Barber out there initiating contact. Most of my injuries occurred sitting back in the pocket."

On Tom Landry:

"You will not find a better human being. He spoke the message and lived it. There are not many people in this world you would trust unequivocally in the foxhole. Tom Landry was one of those men. We weren't close when I was playing—no one wants to kiss up to the coach—but after I retired, we became very, very good friends. Coach Landry was also fiercely competitive; guess we were alike in that way."

On Walt Garrison's practical joke on Tom Landry:

"One day, Walt parks his car in Coach Landry's designated spot at our practice field. It was a God-awful car with a lawn mower on the roof, rubber chickens on the hood. He got it from his buddy Goss, who owned a used car lot on nearby Ross Avenue called 'Goss on Ross.' So Coach shows up, calmly and politely asks Walt to move his car, and Walt starts telling him what an incredible engine it has and how he has to try it out. So Coach being a good sport agrees and gets into the driver's seat with the door open while Walt slides into the passenger side and lights up a cigar. As Coach starts the ignition, Walt flicks the cigar toward the floorboard, which has an iron pipe below it with a cherry bomb. As it went off, Coach Landry jumped six feet sideways, literally in a singular motion, from the seat to standing upright adjacent to the car. As everyone is laughing hysterically, Coach starts to walk away as if nothing happened and says, 'Very funny, Walt.' We were pretty sure he even smirked."

Landry's football knowledge and attention to detail. He was an amazing man."

Dallas won its first eight decisions, eventually taking the NFC East with a 12-2 record. The pass defense was of another world, allowing just 1,562 yards, barely 111 per game, which was all the more incomprehensible considering teams were often trailing late and throwing the football. Having been moved from linebacker to tackle before the season, Randy White created havoc and a plethora of double teams, while Harvey Martin earned NFL Defensive Player of the Year honors with 23 sacks. Ed "Too Tall" Jones and Jethro Pugh rounded out the potent front four of the Doomsday Defense.

The path to Super Bowl XII was almost routine, with the Cowboys outscoring Chicago and Minnesota by a combined 60-13 in home playoff wins.

Destiny awaited in New Orleans. *(See "Super Bowl XII" special insert.)*

For those members of the Dallas Cowboys involved, the end result of the 1978 season was without debate the most frustrating, bitterly disappointing experience of their careers. The pain of the 35–31 Super Bowl XIII loss to the Pittsburgh Steelers is still vivid, the anger definitely present.

There were several controversial calls, none more so than the inexplicable pass interference penalty against Benny Barnes on Lynn Swann, a 33-yard infraction that even NFL commissioner Pete Rozelle later publicly admitted was wrongly flagged.

There was the dropped touchdown pass by future Pro Football Hall of Fame tight end Jackie Smith, and the corresponding renowned call by Cowboys radio broadcaster Verne Lundquist: "Roger back to throw, has a man open in the end zone . . . caught, touchdown . . . dropped. Dropped in the end zone. Jackie Smith all by himself. Aw, bless his heart, he's got to be the sickest man in America."

The near-five-month journey included a 12-4 regular-season, a 27–20 home defeat of Atlanta in the divisional round, and a 28–0 rout of the Rams in Los Angeles. Staubach, now 36 years young, was his sensational self, while Dorsett showcased speed and vision previously not witnessed. The defense, anchored by Pro Bowlers White, Martin, Henderson, Waters, and Harris, allowed 10 or fewer points an incredible nine times including the playoffs.

In the end, though, Pittsburgh laid claim to Team of the Decade honors for the 1970s with a third Super Bowl title. The Steelers added a fourth the following season.

When the doors closed at Texas Stadium following the 2008 campaign, this much was abundantly clear: There was no greater game played there than the regular-season finale between the Cowboys and Washington Redskins on December 16, 1979. The fierce rivals didn't like each other, plain and simple, and this contest held the highest of stakes—the NFC East title. The Friday before the kickoff, a wreath was delivered to Harvey Martin at the team's practice. It read, "With Deepest Sympathy, For the Sympathy You Will Need on Sunday."

No one has ever been sure who sent the wreath, although the *Washington Post* ran a story the following week claiming a Redskins fan was responsible. Thirty years later, then Cowboys

Harvey Martin delivers a wreath to the Redskins'
locker room after the Cowboys defeated their rivals
in the season finale. ➤

LINEBACKER
D. D. LEWIS

On Tom Landry saying he was the most underappreciated player he ever coached:

"I always appreciated that, especially coming from Coach Landry. Over my years playing for him, I don't remember him saying anything like that, so when I read that after he retired, just, wow, those words blew me away. There was nothing more than a pat on the behind after a game from Tom, which also meant the world to me at the time. I guess looking back, I never promoted myself or anything. I just wanted to play football. I didn't care about all that other stuff. I was just a regular working stiff, a cog in the wheel."

On playing in a Cowboys' record 27 playoff games:

"My daughter comes home one day, this is a ways back, and tells me, 'You're in Trivial Pursuit; you played the most playoff games in the history of the NFL.' I had no idea. Guess it's one of those things that come with playing long enough. Jerry Rice has since passed me, but I'm still second, which isn't bad."

owner Clint Murchison's youngest son, Robert, offered that his father sent the wreath in hopes of motivating the team, an entirely plausible scenario. Regardless, both sides were primed and lathered for kickoff.

"Win or lose, we weren't shaking hands after the game," Staubach said.

The Redskins took an early 17–0 lead, only to watch the Cowboys score the game's next 21 points. Sure enough, the Redskins responded with another 17 unanswered points and led 34–21 with four minutes remaining and the ball.

"Fans were leaving. I remember looking around and thinking, 'Just get the football back,'" Staubach said.

White answered his wishes by recovering a fumble, and Staubach quickly connected with Tony Hill for 14- and 19-yard strikes. He then found rookie running back Ron Springs across the middle for a 26-yard touchdown with 2:20 remaining. Landry chose to kick off, and sure enough, defensive end Larry Cole proved his faith with a tackle for the ages on Redskins rusher John Riggins on third and two following the two-minute warning.

After a 44-yard punt, Dallas took over at its 25 with 1:46 remaining. Staubach quickly found Hill for 20 yards, and after an incompletion, he avoided an outside blitz before launching a frozen rope to Preston Pearson for 22 yards. Two plays later, it was Preston Pearson again for 25 yards down to the Washington eight. He finished the game with five grabs for 108 yards.

"That was a special game. It really typified who Staubach was as both a quarterback and a person," Pearson said. "A lot of people remember me for that game, but Roger was hitting me with perfect passes. It wasn't like I was making diving catches at the end.

"In my years with the Cowboys, that was as locked in as I've ever seen him. That was as locked in as I've ever seen any quarterback. Every pass was right there, in stride, right where the receiver wanted the football. There was one play I stopped my route a few yards early because there was a soft spot in the defense, and sure enough, as I turned, the ball was coming at me. I've never seen anything like it, before or since."

On second and goal, Staubach found Hill's fingertips from eight yards out. Game, set, and match, Cowboys win 35–34. After the game, Martin opened Washington's locker room door and threw the wreath in, saying, "The Redskins deserved what they got. Nothing. Now they can shop tomorrow for Christmas."

Perhaps drained from the dramatic comeback the week before, Dallas then fell at home to the visiting Rams, 21–19, in the Divisional Playoff.

On March 31, 1980, at a press conference with nearly 200 members of the media, Roger Staubach retired, battling his emotions in saying, "The nuts and bolts of the Cowboys is the man who wears the funny hat on the sideline, Tom Landry."

Also hanging up the shoulder pads was Cliff Harris, the undrafted free agent from nowhere who reinvented the safety position. The kid who had never played in front of more than 7,000 fans before arriving at Cowboys training camp in 1970 was later named to the All-Decade Team by

> ## "I JUST ALWAYS PLAYED WITH THAT SAME INTENSITY; IT WASN'T A CONSCIOUS EFFORT. IT WAS AN EFFORT OF LOVE: I LOVED PRACTICE, I LOVED TRAINING, I LOVED THE GAME, I LOVED THE COMPETITION."
> —Cliff Harris

the Pro Football Hall of Fame. While free safety was previously considered one for ball hawks, a centerfielder of sorts, Captain Crash transformed the position to one of intimidation and fear.

"My college teammates later told me I practiced like I played, and that I was pretty rough on them," Harris said. "I just always played with that same intensity; it wasn't a conscious effort. It was an effort of love: I loved practice, I loved training, I loved the game, I loved the competition. I was able to release my inner being completely and totally. I would have to leave Dallas a week early for training camp after that first year just to transform myself into attack mode.

"I wasn't mouthy on the field. There were selective words I'd say to wideouts after a hit to impose that fear into them, but I wanted to let my actions speak for themselves. If a receiver saw or heard about me knocking a guy out the week before, that was an intimidating factor now in his mind."

Of the 11 players on the All-Decade 1970s first-team defense, only Harris isn't also a member of the Pro Football Hall of Fame, this despite having the second-largest lead in votes for any position. His nearest counterpart, Miami safety Dick Anderson, was named on only three ballots, while Harris claimed 15 of the possible 25 tallies.

"It's a shame. I'm not going to lie, I'd like to be in the Hall of Fame," Harris said. "Maybe I didn't stand out as much. To me, my strength was as a team player and maximizing the abilities of those around me. I'm not going to dwell on (induction) or get angry, but I hope my time comes."

Danny White, he of the toughest gig in football—replacing Captain America—threw for 3,287 yards and 28 touchdowns in 1980 and led the Cowboys to an impressive 12-4 mark. The magical run ended in Philadelphia with a 20–7 setback in the NFC Championship Game.

Almost exactly 12 months later, Dallas found itself in another title tilt, this time in San Francisco. The game has become legend in the lexicon of NFL lore, with the 49ers prevailing, 28–27, thanks to a late touchdown connection from Joe Montana to Dwight Clark, later known simply as the Catch.

"That was the last play of my football career," Lewis remembered. "Few days pass without me thinking of Montana drifting back, how different it all would've been if one of us could've made a play to prevent that touchdown, or maybe he throws the ball a few inches higher. I've seen that play a million times.

"My first start came in the 1972 regular-season finale against the New York Giants at Texas Stadium. The next week we played in San Francisco in the playoff game with the incredible Staubach comeback the last 90 seconds. Anyway, from the first play of that game, there's this 49ers fan in the first row behind our bench just ripping me apart. I'm no good, I'm going to get my ass beat, I'm completely

QUARTERBACK
DANNY WHITE

On serving as Roger Staubach's backup from 1976 to 1979:

"If it was anyone I felt like I was better than, I would've wanted to compete for the starting job. I never would've lasted four years if it was anyone else but Roger. I wasn't going to compete with him, yet he always made me feel like we were competing. He would always tell me he couldn't afford to get hurt because he'd end up the Wally Pipp of football and never get his job back. That gave me such an ego boost; this was one of the all-time legends of football.

"I wanted to be like Roger. There are not many people in this world that admire another human being so much and are allowed the opportunity to be around them for four years. I was so lucky. Roger came along at a critical time of my life, and his guidance benefited me as a father and husband as much as a quarterback. You could offer me 13 years with the Chicago Bears and every passing record in NFL history, and I wouldn't trade it for those four years behind Roger Staubach. He is the best of men."

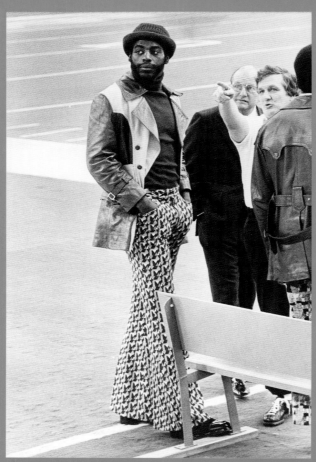

▲ Billy Joe DuPree in the 1981 NFC Championship Game against San Francisco.

RING OF HONOR SAFETY
CLIFF HARRIS

On cracking the starting lineup as an undrafted free agent:
"I was sometimes in awe during training camp. I had never even seen an NFL game in person. It was surreal to be playing for the Cowboys. But once we started practicing and scrimmaging, I was so immersed in the competition, so intent on proving I belonged on that level, it was just football. And I gradually realized they were human beings just like me."

On his surprising retirement at 31 years of age after the 1979 season:
"I knew it was my last year before the season started but kept it to myself. There were a lot of different factors in that decision, first and foremost, my style of play. The equation that worked for me was to attack the run, cover deep, and play on edge every snap. If I was a little hurt, I couldn't do that. My neck was worse than anyone realized, and it would've continued to become worse if I didn't retire. That would've taken away my ability to hit like I needed to. I had to live up to my reputation, and I didn't want to become one of those players who were more reputation than action. Coach Landry, my teammates, and the fans deserved better than that."

worthless, the works. I have no idea what his deal was with me. Heck, I'm not even sure how he knew who I was. When we won that game, I went over and kind of gloated; we jawed a little bit.

"Every time we went back there for 10 years, the same guy, same seat in the front, and he just rode me every which way. He used words on me I didn't even know existed, and I thought I knew them all. So, after that last game, I start walking off, and this same guy calls me over. Not even sure why I went, but I did, and he says, 'D. D., I know we've had our differences and exchanged some words over the years, but I really enjoyed watching you play. You're a great linebacker.' I remember that 30 years later so clearly. I appreciated him taking the time, at that moment, to say that."

For Danny White, a different life lesson was learned.

"I learned the hard way about just how high the expectations were," White said. "No one expected us to win the division or play for the NFC Championship in 1981. I was hurting more than anyone after the San Francisco loss. We still should've won that game after Clark's catch. I fumbled the last play after being hit while throwing.

"The next morning, I'm taking the elevator at the Cowboys headquarters. I look up and written on the wall is, 'Danny White sucks.' I realized that conference title games weren't enough. At the very least, we had to play in the Super Bowl for the season to be considered acceptable. Success was achieved only if we won a ring."

STEVE SABOL

HOW THE COWBOYS BECAME AMERICA'S TEAM

The facts are simple enough. The Cowboys' famous tagline didn't come from them, it came to them, courtesy of Bob Ryan of NFL Films. Some three decades ago, he was producing their annual highlight film. His script opened with this: "They appear on television so often that their faces are as familiar to the public as presidents and movie stars. They are the Dallas Cowboys, America's Team."

Good stuff. So good, it found its way not only into the highlight reel but also onto the lips of network TV announcers and into the hearts of the Dallas Cowboys management.

Those are the facts. Of course, facts alone never answer a really good question, and they don't answer this one. They just lead to other questions, such as Where did Bob Ryan come up with the line "America's Team"?

Bob has always said he noticed that wherever Dallas played, the stands were filled with Cowboys' pennants and jerseys, plus they were always the national game on television. "Hey, they're the most popular team in the country. How can I use that? Why don't we call them 'America's Team'?"

He did, and it stuck.

But Bob Ryan's eye, his feeling for phenomena, and even his gift for language don't drill down to the deepest level. Why all those Cowboys fans in places other than Dallas? What drew fans to the Cowboys? Perhaps it was the idea of the cowboy.

> **COWBOYS, THE REAL KIND, WITH SADDLE PONIES, LARIATS, AND 10-GALLON HATS, HAVE ALWAYS BEEN BIGGER THAN LIFE FOR AMERICANS. THEY RIDE TALL IN THE SADDLE. THEY ARE MEN OF FEW WORDS, BUT MEN WHO MEAN WHAT THEY SAY.**

Cowboys, the real kind, with saddle ponies, lariats, and 10-gallon hats, have always been bigger than life for Americans. They ride tall in the saddle. They are men of few words, but men who mean what they say. They fight, maybe, but only on the side of right. They travel heroically. They move where the winds and their wills take them. They are self-made. They are the best of what we hope we are and want to be. They are cowboys.

No boy who lived at any time in the 20th century could fail to understand what that word means. Cowboys are not only heroic, they are free from the constraints that chafe us in modern life. They live in the West of our dreams, where skies are endless and the horizon is not a limit but a waypoint to adventure.

Other teams have names that let you root for fur or fangs or feathers, but the Cowboys are different. A Cowboy is something you could be, and probably wanted to be. At least when you were young and your world had no fences.

Cowboys are not just America's team, they are America itself. All the good things we stand for, the men we are, or feel we will be. Someday.

Of course they are America's Team. After all, they're us.

Steve Sabol is currently president of NFL Films, having won 27 Emmy Awards for his writing, editing, producing, and cinematography.

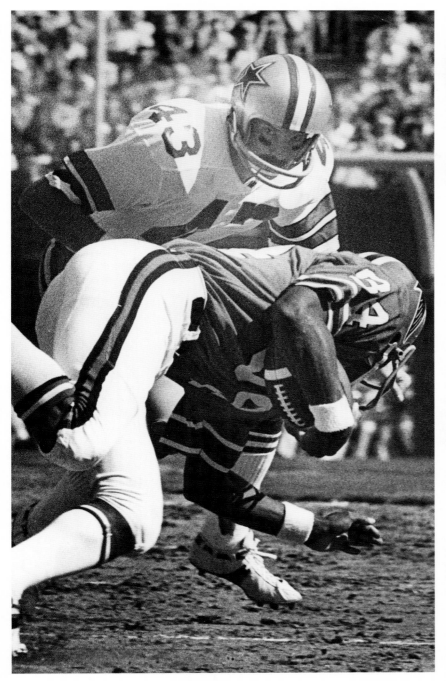

▲ (clockwise from top left) Cliff Harris; Roger Staubach and Tom Landry; Charlie Waters; see no evil, say no evil, hear no evil; Robert Newhouse.

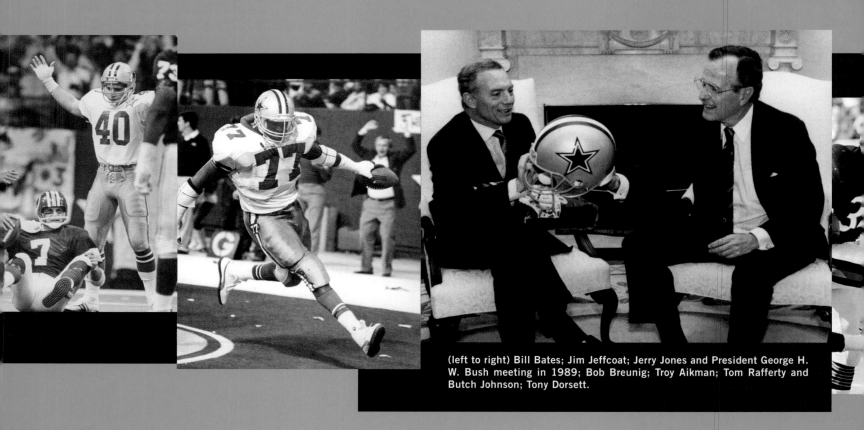

(left to right) Bill Bates; Jim Jeffcoat; Jerry Jones and President George H. W. Bush meeting in 1989; Bob Breunig; Troy Aikman; Tom Rafferty and Butch Johnson; Tony Dorsett.

4

A FRANCHISE
IN FLUX

1983–1989 ★★★★

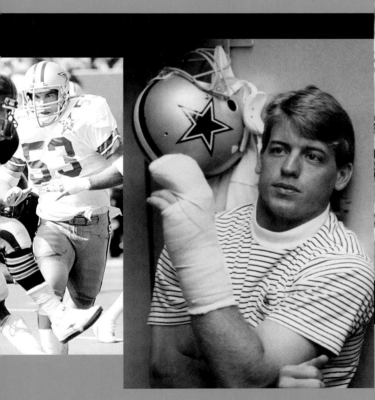

The NFC Championship Game in San Francisco on January 10, 1982, would be the final occasion for Charlie Waters to take the football field, at least as a player, a chronic knee injury forcing his retirement.

★★★★

A quarterback and wide receiver at Clemson, Waters was asked on draft day, back in 1970, if he could backpedal, and sure enough, the third-round selection eventually became a three-time Pro Bowler as a strong safety.

An exceptional athletic talent and dedicated in the weight room, Waters seemingly forced himself to succeed. A brilliant football mind who later became the defensive coordinator for the Denver Broncos, he helped the Cowboys win two Super Bowls. His 41 career regular-season interceptions are third in team history, while his nine postseason picks are tied for the NFL record along with the likes of Ronnie Lott.

Honestly, among the 415 other players Tom Landry coached in his 29 seasons with the Dallas Cowboys, there were better athletes, quicker defensive backs, and harder-hitting safeties. Perhaps even those who worked harder, although the list is short, if even existent.

Yet few, if any, shared a more profound relationship with Landry during their playing careers than Waters.

"The only redeeming qualities I have, they're because of Coach Landry," Waters said. "His influence on my life is beyond any description my mind possesses."

When a reporter asked Waters toward the end of his playing days if Landry had ever made a mistake, he replied, "No, he's a lot different than us mortals."

There are a plethora of assumptions about Landry that are pure fiction. The legend may be a statue, but the man wasn't. Sure, he didn't yell and scream, rant or rave, and yes, he took the business of football with the utmost of seriousness. The practice field was not the time or place for sarcasm or wasted energy, nor was the cathedral that was Sunday afternoons.

However, Landry wasn't devoid of a sense of humor; he had both a dry wit and the ability to take the occasional innocent prank from his players, say when they tossed him in the pool fully dressed at a team function in 1980.

Tom Landry was from a different era than those who played for him. In 1941, as a senior at

▲ Tom Landry overseeing his troops during practice.

Mission High School, in Mission, Texas, he was a member of the National Honor Society, senior class president, and captain of the football team, which finished 12-0 and outscored opponents 322-7. In the week before his team's championship game, though, the world changed forever on December 7, when Japan attacked Pearl Harbor, killing 2,403 Americans.

Less than a year thereafter, Robert Landry, Tom's older brother who had joined the air force, died when his B-17 exploded while flying over Iceland. After a year at the University of Texas on a football scholarship, Tom Landry was called to active duty in the spring of 1943. He would fly 30 missions and survive two crashes over Germany and other occupied territory, often volunteering for extra missions, later saying, "We were a country of patriots. If we hadn't been, there's no telling what might have happened."

As a football player, Landry, who spent six seasons in the secondary with the New York Giants, saw himself in Charlie Waters. They were the exact height and weight, six foot one inch and 195 pounds; each had played quarterback and another offensive skill position in college. They were even born a date apart on the calendar—Landry on September 11, Waters a day earlier.

"After three seasons at safety, they moved me to corner, and that just wasn't my position, just a different animal than safety. But I think Coach Landry respected me for making the switch. He knew what I was going through, as he did the same thing with the Giants," Waters said. "This one game, I was beat for three touchdowns by Harold Jackson of the Rams. I lost the game for us, without a doubt, and Coach Landry says in front of the entire team, 'Charlie had a tough day, but if I had 45 guys try as hard as him, we wouldn't lose a game.' That set the hook in me. Tom Landry had me for life at that point.

"I think we developed a father-son-type relationship. We'd been through so much together. He called me Charles when he was angry or disappointed, just as a parent would. There were days when we as players loved him and others when we hated him."

During one training camp, which was held for 27 straight seasons in Thousand Oaks, California, Waters was in the audience as Landry gave a speech at nearby Crystal Cathedral. He took questions, among them, "Coach, what should your tombstone say when you pass away?"

Landry paused, obviously not prepared for the question, before answering.

"I'm not sure, but I'd like my players to say, 'Coach was right about what's most important in life: faith, family, and football, in that order.'"

In February 1969, *SPORT* magazine, ran a cover story titled "Tom Landry: God, Family, and Football." The subtitle read "That is the

---

SAFETY
CHARLIE WATERS

On his favorite Tom Landry story:
"He calls me for a meeting, and I'm thinking it was for something bad. At the time, I had long, wild-looking hair. So he says, 'I wanted to let you know what a great example you've been setting in the weight room. And, well, I've been talking to my therapist, and I'm not going to judge people by the way they look any longer. I've always had this thing about men with long hair, but no more.' Three days later, I arrive at our practice facility around 7:30 a.m. and run into Coach Landry as he was walking from the shower to the coaches' room. I hadn't shaved in three days and was wearing a cowboy hat. Coach Landry says, 'Well, Charles, hey, when are you getting a haircut?' He immediately remembered what he told me three days previous and tries to tell a joke, saying, 'Oh, I know what this is, Samson [from the Bible] loses his hair and he loses his strength.' So I say, 'Yeah, you lost your hair and your knee went gimpy.' And Coach says, 'The functionality of my right knee was not directionally proportional to the loss of my hair,' and walks away."

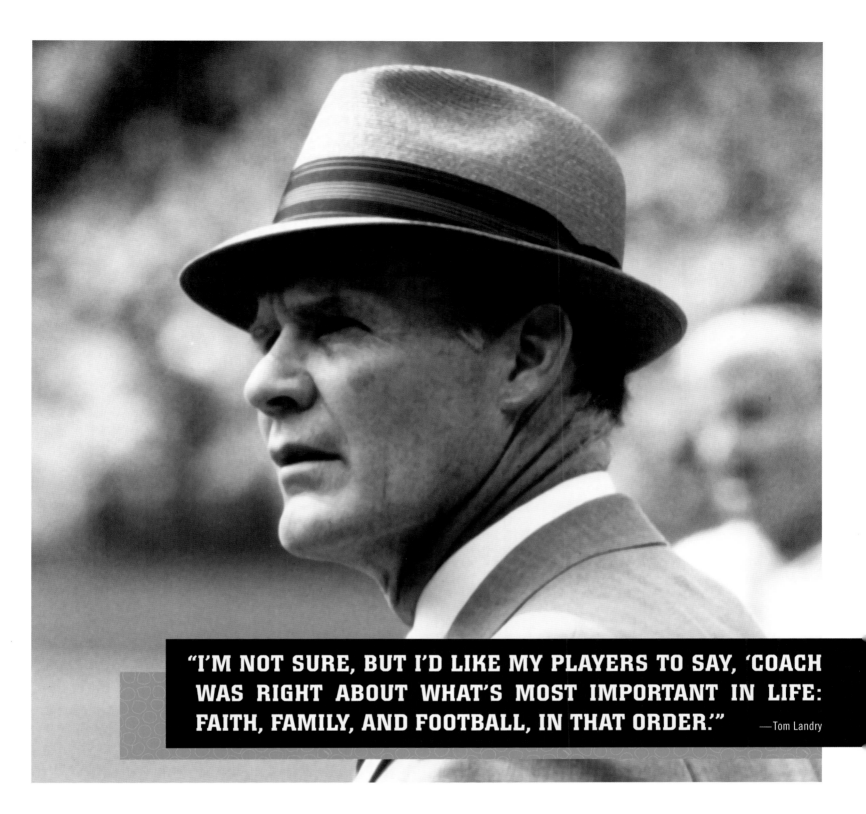

"I'M NOT SURE, BUT I'D LIKE MY PLAYERS TO SAY, 'COACH WAS RIGHT ABOUT WHAT'S MOST IMPORTANT IN LIFE: FAITH, FAMILY, AND FOOTBALL, IN THAT ORDER.'" —Tom Landry

priority for the brilliant coach who has built the Dallas Cowboys into one of the NFL's great teams. 'I pray . . .' he says, 'that I'll make the right decisions.'"

Admittedly, of the team's 20 consecutive winning seasons, the one least enjoyed by Landry was 1982, as seven games were canceled because of the 57-day players' strike. After starting 1-1 before the stoppage, the Cowboys returned with a fury, winning five straight and eventually landing in their third consecutive NFC Championship Game. As in the two previous, though, Dallas failed in its quest for another Super Bowl dance, losing at Washington, 31–17.

While no one could've envisioned the team's decline on the horizon, this would mark the 14th and final conference title game of Landry's career. What's more incredible is that he didn't coach in one before 1966 or after 1982. That's 14 conference championship games in 17 years, the lone exceptions being 1974, 1976, and 1979.

Then there's Danny White, among the more misrepresented of quarterbacks. Through his first 52 starts, he posted a 39-13 mark, which through the 2009 season ranked as the second-highest winning percentage in the last 60 years for the beginning of a player's career. Only Ken Stabler, at 42-9-1, won more often. White also threw for at least 3,000 yards in 1980 and 1981 and set a franchise record with 3,980 yards in 1983, a mark that stood for 24 years. Not to mention he remained

RING OF HONOR RUNNING BACK
TONY DORSETT

On his 99-yard touchdown at Minnesota on January 3, 1983:

"A couple of days have passed without me being asked about that run, but definitely not a week. People still remember where they were watching. More than the run itself, that's because of the platform that was *Monday Night Football* back then. Everyone was watching. Thing is, in my opinion, it wasn't my best run. I knew we were at the 1-yard line. I remember tightening my chinstrap because Minnesota knew we were going to run and I was preparing myself for a pretty good shot.

"There were two great blocks on the play from Tom Rafferty and Herb Scott, and I was able to make a few cuts, force a couple of missed tackles. Around midfield, Drew Pearson was in front of me, and I noticed his legs were going every which way. I remember thinking he was tired, so it was time to make a final move. When I was sucking the oxygen on the sidelines, Gil Brandt came over and told me it was an NFL record. At that moment, I regretted not keeping the ball. I really wish I kept that football."

the team's primary punter while posting those prolific aerial numbers.

Still, for the somewhat spoiled, always fickle fan base, White was more or less the focus of its frustration. In truth, as White understood, his greatest crime was simply not being Roger Staubach, although statistically speaking, his numbers those first four years as a starter were better than his predecessor's.

"Danny White was probably as fine a winner as we ever had," Landry once said. "He didn't have the natural gifts of some of the other quarterbacks, but he knew how to win. I don't think anybody could have followed Roger and done as well as Danny. If we had beaten San Francisco that year and gone to the Super Bowl with Danny, I think we might have gone a couple more times with him. He was an excellent quarterback, but a lot of people were critical of him and just didn't recognize that."

The Dallas Cowboys and Washington Redskins were the class of the NFL the first 14 weeks of the 1983 campaign, with the Men of Landry winning 12 of 14, their two setbacks by a combined three points. Led by Danny White, who broke his own single-season team mark with 29 touchdown tosses; All-World tailback Tony Dorsett's 1,321 rushing yards; and a potent defense anchored by Randy White, Ed "Too Tall" Jones, and Everson Walls, the Cowboys had outscored their opponents 452–287 when Joe Gibbs, Joe Theismann, and John Riggins visited Texas Stadium on December 11 for the most anticipated regular-season game on either side since the iconic 1979 finale.

And . . . thud. Absolute nightmare. Little girls' heads spinning, hockey masks, chainsaws, Kathy Bates may have even showed up at one point. Either way, misery was most definitely front and center following the 31–10 loss.

In many ways, this was the official end to the reign of Tom Landry's Dallas Cowboys. The streak of winning records survived another two years, at 9-7 and 10-6, respectively, but the swagger was gone; the expectation of success, even dominance, long forgotten the remainder of the decade. The following week, San Francisco removed the door from the hinges and blew said door about 500 miles into the Pacific Ocean, destination unknown, after a 42–17 massacre on *Monday Night Football*. Dandy Don didn't need to wait long on this night for his classic serenade as the lights were already off and the party was indeed over.

The Rams mercifully ended the season of seemingly limitless promise the day after Christmas in a wild-card matchup, defeating Dallas 24–17 at Texas Stadium for a one-and-done postseason departure.

When the Cowboys opened the following year's schedule on *Monday Night Football* in a rematch with the Rams, Gary Hogeboom was now the one taking snaps from center Tom Rafferty. Over the remainder of his career, Danny White split time with Hogeboom and Steve Pelluer.

"My performance on the field definitely wasn't enough for the fans," White recalled. "Roger set the bar so high, success was only measured by Super Bowls. I kind of accepted that at some point; guess I learned the hard way.

Following pages (left to right): Gil Brandt, Tom Landry, and Tex Schramm on draft day.

107

714 Days spanned between victories by America's Team in any of the 50 states. From September 25, 1988, through September 9, 1990, the Cowboys' only two wins came in the District of Columbia against the Washington Redskins.

62 Sacks registered in 1985, a single-season franchise record. Three players, Ed "Too Tall" Jones (13.0), Jim Jeffcoat (12.0), and Randy White (10.5) tallied double digits.

44 Point differential in the largest margin of defeat in franchise history, a 44–0 loss against Chicago on November 17, 1985.

16 Eugene Lockhart's team record solo tackles vs. Phoenix on October 29, 1989.

"Coach Landry called me into his office during training camp in 1984 when he decided to go with Hogeboom, and I knew it was a hard thing for him. He said he thought it was the best thing for me at that point, and I told him, 'I disagree with you, but you're the coach, and I'll honor and respect your decision.'

"As I started to walk out, he said, 'Danny, don't ever change the way you play football.' That was Tom Landry. He took the most negative experience of my life as an athlete and turned it into a positive with a single sentence."

White retired following the 1988 campaign with a 62-30 record as a starting quarterback, better than 67 percent, and a career quarterback rating of 81.7. At the time, the lone signal callers in the history of the National Football League (minimum 2,000 passing attempts) with both a higher winning percentage as a starter and a better quarterback rating were Otto Graham, Joe Montana, and, yes, Roger Staubach.

While the Cowboys were still clearly America's Team through the mid-1980s, there were fewer and fewer marquee names remaining, if not performing within the prime of their careers.

Drew Pearson, a three-time, first-team All-Pro selection, was forced to retire after a tragic car accident on March 22, 1984, which killed his younger brother, Carey Mark Pearson. Driving home from a charity basketball game in Oklahoma, Drew fell asleep at the wheel and hit the backside of a tractor-trailer. When he woke up following emergency surgery to stop bleeding from his liver, the first person he saw was Landry, who visited him daily throughout his recovery process.

"I was raised by the most wonderful parents, just great, great people," Pearson said. "And no one has been more of an influence on my life than Tom Landry. He talked the talk and walked the walk. My discipline in life, the ability to treat people fairly, learning to say no when need be, that's all because of Coach Landry and how he made it his mission to develop us as men. I love him so much."

Through the first 50 years of the Dallas Cowboys, only Michael Irvin and Jason Witten have had more catches than Pearson, with just Irvin and Tony Hill owning more receiving yards.

While players, even the great ones, come and go, the organization itself experienced a dramatic change during this time as well. In 1983 Clint Murchison Jr., patriarch of the franchise, suffering terribly from a vicious neurological disorder since the late 1970s, informed president Tex Schramm that he was selling the team. On March 19, 1984, NFL owners approved the purchase of the Cowboys for $60 million by local businessman/oil mogul H. R. "Bum" Bright and 10 limited partners. They paid an additional $20 million for Texas Stadium.

A somewhat peculiar man, Murchison was nonetheless equal parts brilliant, hilarious, and selfless. His legacy is oftentimes overlooked with contemporaries like Lamar Hunt and those Murchison hired, Schramm and Landry, rightfully enshrined in the Pro Football Hall of Fame as titans of professional football. Yet, there was Murchison landing an NFL franchise for Dallas; there was Murchison willingly losing millions of dollars the first few years to compete with Hunt's AFL Dallas Texans; there was Murchison putting aside his own ego and hiring Schramm on the advice of Chicago Bears owner George Halas and NFL commissioner Pete Rozelle; and when every sportswriter in the country was calling for the firing of Landry after his 13-38-3 record through four seasons, there was Murchison signing him to a never-before-seen 10-year contract.

He was almost a man on an island in his quest to build Texas Stadium, convinced that the fans of his franchise deserved only the ultimate in luxury. The man also raised two Super Bowl trophies. Not a bad run.

Murchison left this world on March 30, 1987, at just 63 years of age. During his funeral, Landry said, "He probably had the greatest impact (on my life) of anybody that I know. But I think in his contributions to the Cowboys and their winning seasons, he made even a greater contribution to Dallas, Texas. The '60s were tough times for Dallas. With the assassination of John Kennedy, we were known worldwide as the City of Hate. Nobody had a good image of us. Our pride was down as a city. But because of the Cowboys, and because of our winning tradition, we changed that. And we became America's Team, which was hard to live down, but it was kind of true. And it changed the vision that people have for us in Dallas.

"I guess the thing that I'm sorriest for, right now, as Clint has gone away from us, is that he wasn't recognized by the city of Dallas for the great contribution he made to the welfare of our city."

As for Bright, he was a businessman more than a football fan, so little changed in terms of the status quo; Schramm remained in control of the day-to-day operations of the club.

Unfortunately, the Bright era got off to an unsatisfying start. While the team was able to keep its streak of consecutive seasons with a winning record alive in 1984, they failed to make the playoffs after finishing fourth in the NFC East with a disappointing 9-7 record. Still, there was no bigger draw on Sundays.

"The two most important people to CBS are J. R. Ewing and Tom Landry," former CBS commentator Beano Cook said in 1984. "We have a rule we go by when planning NFL telecasts. Give people the best game possible.

GUARD
NATE NEWTON

On playing for the Cowboys:

"Growing up in Orlando, I was a huge Cowboys fan. Everyone else was a Miami Dolphins fan, but the Cowboys were my team. Duane Thomas, Robert Newhouse, Cliff Harris, Charlie Waters, watching them play on television was such a big thing for me. So when I went to training camp out in California in 1986, I didn't expect to make the team, but I was living my dream. I had someone take my picture with Coach Landry. I met Randy White, which was unreal. He was nothing like his image; he was calm, stoic, just a nice guy."

On Jimmy Johnson:

"So Michael Irvin calls me during the offseason and says we're playing in this charity golf tournament. We had volunteer workouts that day, so I call Jimmy and let him know I'm playing with Michael. That man cut me no slack. He says, 'Charity? You go tell your wife right now that you're not going to have a job this season if I don't see you here for that workout. They're going to need to have a charity golf tournament for your sorry ass to pay the bills.'"

And when in doubt, give them the Cowboys. Generally, when our ratings are up, there's only one reason: the Dallas Cowboys."

The Cowboys made their final playoff appearance under Landry in 1985, a surprising NFC East Division crown at 10–6. They were led by Dorsett's final 1,000-yard campaign and a superb Pro Bowl effort from the vastly underappreciated wide receiver Hill. This would also mark the final of nine straight Pro Bowl nods for Randy White, one of the greatest defensive tackles the gridiron has ever witnessed.

The No. 2 overall pick of the 1975 NFL Draft, White, a defensive end at Maryland, spent his first two seasons like a ball in tall grass—utterly and completely lost—at middle linebacker.

"Coach Landry called me into the office during training camp in 1977 and asked me—didn't tell me, asked me—if I was interested in moving to defensive tackle," White said. "I said, 'Coach, I just want to play football and help this team win football games.' He just nodded his head and that was that.

"Those first two seasons were very frustrating. I loved the game so much. I knew how to play middle linebacker in the Flex. I knew the plays, but I was always thinking and was a beat off making the play. Maybe if we were playing a textbook 4–3, where the lone middle linebacker roamed the field always running toward the football, that might have been a little different. But the Flex, despite being a 4–3 scheme, wasn't like that.

"The middle linebacker had a lot of responsibility in pass coverage, which went against my natural instincts. I never felt freedom at middle linebacker, almost as if I was handcuffed. When I moved to tackle, the handcuffs were taken off."

Asked if he was a reactionary defender, White said, "I enjoyed freedom playing defense. As a tackle, I could run sideline to sideline, so yeah, I guess I was a reactionary defender."

While his 111 career sacks rank second in team history, White was so much more than a pass rusher at tackle, even dropping back into pass coverage on occasion when he recognized the play/formation via his diligent film study when playing linebacker.

For the majority, the debate over most accomplished defensive player in franchise history begins and ends with Bob Lilly and Randy White. That's the list.

While the selection of White in the NFL Draft 10 years earlier was a relatively easy decision like their 10th-round pick of Staubach back in the day, the Cowboys outsmarted the competition, or perhaps were just fortunate, in grabbing 1982 Heisman Trophy winner Herschel Walker in the fifth round of the 1985 NFL Draft. At the time, the physical specimen, who as a senior in high school captured Georgia state titles at the highest classification in the 100-yard dash and the shot put, was running wild for the

CORNERBACK
EVERSON WALLS

On growing up a block from the Cowboys' practice facility in Dallas:
"I would ride my bike and watch over the practice field fence. I had outlandish dreams about being a Dallas Cowboy just like any other kid. My dreams just happened to come true."

On not being selected in the 1980 NFL Draft:
"I led the nation with 11 interceptions at Grambling State, a school notorious for playing man-to-man. To me, it was beyond logic, especially when you look at some of the cornerbacks taken. When I wasn't drafted, three teams approached me with free agent contracts: Buffalo, [which] was too cold; the New Orleans Saints, who at the time were the Aints; and my hometown Cowboys. The choice was pretty obvious. Couple that with the fact the Cowboys had big problems at corner."

On his funniest memory:
"In the locker room, tight end Jay Saldi got into a fight with another player and was quickly body slammed. Ron Springs treated the fight location as a crime scene and took some baby powder and promptly made an outline of Jay's body. If that wasn't funny enough, Jay wore a toupee, and Ron outlined that as well."

> ## "I FINISH THE INTERVIEW, I WAS LIVING IN NEW JERSEY AT THE TIME, AND BEFORE I MADE IT OUT TO MY CAR, SOMEONE TELLS ME THE COWBOYS HAD JUST DRAFTED ME."
>
> —Herschel Walker

New Jersey Generals of the USFL. He would finish that season with a professional football record of 2,411 rushing yards in 18 games.

"I never really followed the NFL, not when I was with the New Jersey Generals, not when I was at Georgia, not really even when I was growing up," Walker said. "But my two older brothers always loved the Cowboys. They even still loved the Cowboys when I was with New Jersey.

"So this guy from ESPN is interviewing me and asks if I could play for any NFL team, who would it be? And without really thinking, I said the Cowboys in one sense because I never thought it would happen.

"I finish the interview, I was living in New Jersey at the time, and before I made it out to my car, someone tells me the Cowboys had just drafted me."

After the USFL folded, Walker signed a five-year, $5 million deal with Dallas and joined the team for the 1986 campaign.

The dream backfield of Dorsett and Walker never materialized, although the Cowboys started the year 6-2, including a thrilling 31–28 triumph over the New York Giants on *Monday Night Football* in the season opener. Walker rushed for the game winner, from 10 yards out with 1:16 remaining. The victory became all the more impressive when Bill Parcells and the G-men secured 17 of their ensuing 18 games, culminating with Super Bowl XXI.

The offense sputtered midseason, Dallas scoring more than 14 points just twice in its final eight games. Losers of seven of their last eight, the Cowboys' incomprehensible run of 20 consecutive winning seasons had finally come to an end at 7-9.

For Landry, the dean of NFL coaches since 1969, the finish was nearly identical to the beginning as the Cowboys continued their downward spiral over the next two seasons, finishing 7-8 in 1987 and a paltry 3-13 the following year, the team's fewest victories since their winless inaugural campaign. Not including three ties, Landry's record his first three seasons was 9-28. Minus two wins during the 1987 players' strike, Landry concluded his head-coaching career at 9-28. In between, he won 232 regular-season games against 106 defeats.

In the offseason of 1988, Bright announced he was putting the Cowboys on the market for $180 million. Later, in January of 1989, Landry, Schramm, and Gil Brandt watched Super Bowl XXIII between the San Francisco 49ers and Cincinnati Bengals from a luxury box at Joe Robbie Stadium in Miami. This, in and of itself, is hardly fascinating.

RUNNING BACK
HERSCHEL WALKER

On "The Herschel Walker Trade":
"If I owned an NFL franchise, I would want to get Jimmy Johnson to run my football team. He knows how to win and what it takes to win. The trade was a smart business move, but at times I think people tend to forget that the success the Cowboys had under Jimmy wasn't just because of that trade. He brought an attitude that we were going to win. I never think that much about the trade itself unless someone brings it up. If people want to say it was the biggest trade there ever was and ever will be, I'm okay with that. It's always good to be a part of history, no matter what the reason."

On leading the Cowboys in rushing and receiving yards in 1987:
"When I first came out of college, and maybe even with the New Jersey Generals, I think people thought of me as a power back, maybe a little one-dimensional. I think that surprised some people. I led the Cowboys in receiving two straight years, showed people that I could do some different things on the football field."

DEFENSIVE END
ED "TOO TALL" JONES

On sacks:

"While sacks didn't become an official NFL statistic until 1982, we were definitely familiar with the terminology. Harvey Martin and I would make a little side wager before every season for which of us would finish with the most sacks. The team kept track of them. Coach Landry had someone keep track of all those defensive statistics you hear about today—quarterback hurries, forced fumbles, passes blocked. Every season, at our first meeting, Coach would read all these statistics, and we're all looking around wondering where he got them and what half of them were. But Harvey and I just bet on sacks."

On Harvey Martin:

"When I'm talking to kids, high school and college players, I always use Harvey as an example. He didn't have the best technique, but he had wheels. Give me a guy with heart, one that'll crawl, kick, jump, whatever it takes to get to the quarterback. That was Harvey. Poor Ernie Stautner, our old defensive coordinator. He'd work with Harvey all day and night on technique, and come Friday, he was ready, had it all down. And then we'd watch the game film, and it was impossible to tell that Ernie spent any time with him. Harvey was all over the place."

When asked recently if he had ever met Landry, Jimmy Johnson shared this stunning account:

"Well, I was probably closest with Gil Brandt and Tex Schramm, but Tom invited me, and I sat in the box with them at Super Bowl XXIII. They actually had thoughts about me coaching the Cowboys when Tom was ready to step down, but yes, I sat with the three of them for the game."

Some 33 days prior to being named the second head coach in the 30-year history of the franchise, Johnson, then the head coach of the University of Miami, was attending the Super Bowl with the very people he would replace, not to mention openly discussing the possibility of eventually taking over the team once Landry retired.

"We were interested in Jimmy joining the staff as defensive coordinator. I know we offered him that position at that time," Brandt said recently. "I wasn't privy to the private conversation after that initial discussion between Tex and Jimmy; they spoke by themselves.

"Tex and I helped Jimmy get his first head coaching job at Oklahoma State, and then I was responsible for him landing the Miami job in 1984."

When Howard Schnellenberger left Miami for the USFL in June of 1984, fresh off winning a national championship, Hurricanes athletic director Sam Jankovich turned to Brandt, maybe the most influential voice in college football at the time, for advice. This took place at the College Football Association convention in Dallas, and sure enough, Johnson was at the top of Brandt's recommendation list. The next day, Jankovich bumped into Johnson and promptly asked him if he knew of anyone who might be interested in the gig. Jimmy being Jimmy smiled and said, "What about me?"

From 1986 to 1988, Johnson went 34-2 at Miami and won a national championship himself in 1987. His defensive coordinator during that stretch was Dave Wannstedt, who was also with Johnson at the aforementioned Super Bowl.

"I remember being in the luxury box with Tex, Gil, and Coach Landry during the pregame stuff, but my wife and I left before the game started," Wannstedt said. "Jimmy and I were hitting all the parties that weekend. Gil was our contact with the Cowboys. I know he invited us up to the box, but I wasn't around when Jimmy spoke with them."

On February 25, Jerry Jones reached an agreement with Bright to purchase the Cowboys, the final $300,000 negotiated by a coin flip, for which Jones called "tails" and lost. A day earlier, word had leaked of the likely purchase, and the rumors were all but solidified when a photo of Johnson and Jones appeared on the front page of the *Dallas Morning News*.

The two men had been roommates at the University of Arkansas, both playing for the legendary Frank Broyles on football scholarships. The Razorbacks won the national championship in 1964, with Jones serving as co-captain and a starting guard at just 184 pounds.

While Jones has always been the most instinctive and savvy of businessmen, buying the Cowboys wasn't about dollars and cents; it was more about a lifetime passion for the game of football.

"This is how much I wanted to own the Dallas Cowboys," Jones said in 2010. "People don't make mistakes knowing they're making a mistake at the time, right? I mean, give those people credit for coming around eventually; maybe they didn't see the error of their ways, or maybe it's a lack of knowledge. Here's my point: I knew it. I knew buying the Cowboys was not a good business decision. I knew, in fact, it was a bad decision. They were losing $1 million a month. No one was coming to home games. It was a mess. And we didn't exactly inherit Vince Lombardi's Packers either, in terms of players."

There was also the issue of Tom Landry.

Before addressing the media throng about his impending ownership, Jones flew to Austin and informed Landry of the situation face-to-face. The majority of the media vilified Jones for how he handled the situation, but in reality, he was trying to act honorably, even if he later admitted he could've dealt with matters differently.

"I don't agree, I think Jerry went out of his way; I should know, as I was part of the negotiations," Johnson said. "Bum Bright said, 'Hey, I'll tell Tom,' and Jerry said, 'No, I will,' and so they say we'll call up Coach Landry. I was standing next to Tex Schramm, and Tex called Tom and said, 'Hey, this is going to happen.' I could only hear one side of the call, but he said this is going to happen.

"Tom evidently told him he was going to go play golf in Austin, and Tex said, 'No, you'd better hang around because I think this is going to happen.' So Tom knew he was going to get let go, and he went down to Austin to play golf.

"Bum just said to make the announcement that Coach Landry was fired, but Jerry told him point-blank, 'No, I can't let anyone else do this. I've got to do it in person.' And he got on a plane, flew down, went to the golf course, and told him. So I think Jerry did all he could've done, and Jerry has gotten beat up over the way he handled it, but I don't know what else he could have done."

Shortly thereafter, after 29 years as team president and general manager, Schramm resigned.

RING OF HONOR DEFENSIVE TACKLE
RANDY WHITE

On Tom Landry:

"He didn't just teach us football, he taught us life's challenges and the right way and the not-right way to deal with them. I paid a lot of attention to whatever he said, and I find myself falling back on his words and guidance all the time. The one thing that really amazed me about Coach Landry is that not once, not a single time, in 14 years did I see him lose his temper. I saw him angry and upset, but he never raised his voice. And it's not like we were playing badminton. We're out there trying to rip heads off, but Coach Landry was always in control."

On drinking a few beers after games in the parking lot at Texas Stadium:

"[Defensive coordinator] Ernie Stautner and I were out there win or lose, every game. I don't remember how the tradition started; it just happened and became a ritual. The fans were always respectful. If we had won, they were jovial, and if we had lost, they felt as bad as we did. We enjoyed hanging out with the fans. We wanted to say thanks for supporting us, let's have a beer."

Following pages: Jerry Jones (speaking) announces he has purchased the team from Bum Bright (left) on February 25, 1989.

"The plane ride down to Austin to fire Coach Landry almost killed my father," daughter Kandy Schramm Court recalled. "You could see the shock in his face at the press conference. Everything happened so fast; what could he have done? His whole professional life was gone in about 48 hours. That's not easy to put your hands around."

Fans, players, and more or less the football universe were in stunned disbelief at Landry's dismissal. Even Rozelle said, "This is like [Vince] Lombardi's death."

When asked of Landry's dismissal some 21 years after the fact, Walker said, "I was shocked and disappointed when Coach Landry was fired. I loved the man. I will always love him. We would talk in his office sometimes about life, and those conversations meant a great deal to me. I find myself talking about Coach Landry and the lessons he taught me in speeches all the time. He once told me, 'Herschel, you can't just take a good football player and make a man of him without integrity.' A day doesn't pass without me thinking of those words."

As for whether or not the game had passed Landry by, Walker responded, "That is complete and total BS. We didn't have the players. We had a lot of decent players, but that doesn't win football games."

DEFENSIVE END
JIM JEFFCOAT

On Jimmy Johnson saying no one played harder during the 1989 season:
"Honestly, first of all, it was being professional. My rookie season was 1983, with Randy White, Ed Jones, John Dutton on the line, Ernie Stautner the defensive coordinator—they didn't accept any less. I knew what they expected of me, and even if they weren't around any longer, I wanted to honor them by playing every down with all my intensity and passion. They showed me how the game was supposed to be played, and I never forgot that. Also, there was a new coaching staff, and I knew they were going to make a lot of changes, and I wanted to be included in what Jimmy Johnson was building."

On the differences in Tom Landry's and Jimmy Johnson's defensive philosophies:
"Completely different schemes and mindsets. With Coach Landry's Flex, we were reading and reacting as opposed to Jimmy's attack, attack, and attack some more. With the Flex, the only time we were attacking was third down, and if you look back, we had some success pressuring the quarterback. Jimmy wanted to put pressure on the quarterback every chance possible."

The Cowboys didn't win many football games in 1989, either, finishing 1-15 with rookies Troy Aikman and Steve Walsh sharing the quarterback duties.

"I was really shocked that first season was so difficult," Johnson said. "My ego was such that I thought I was a pretty good coach. We only lost two regular-season games in four years at Miami, but after that first year with Dallas, I realized we won at Miami because we had better players."

If nothing else, Johnson and his coaching staff brought a new sense of urgency, an attitude of his way or the unemployment line, perhaps highlighted at the team's second mini-camp when Johnson had the team run sixteen 110-yard sprints. After running 10, free-agent kicker Massimo Manca collapsed, saying, "Coach, I got asthma," to which Johnson memorably replied, "Asthma, my ass. This isn't the asthma field. The asthma field is over there."

Reminded of the story in 2010, Johnson laughed.

"Once that story came out, we were flooded with phone calls and faxes from health organizations. Thing is, I've got a little touch of asthma myself, and I caught some flak for it," Johnson said. "Our responsibility was to win games, and if they couldn't perform, then don't give me excuses. You just need to get the job done to be a part of the team."

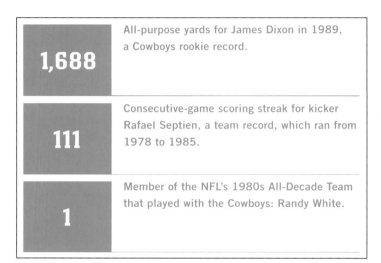

1,688	All-purpose yards for James Dixon in 1989, a Cowboys rookie record.
111	Consecutive-game scoring streak for kicker Rafael Septien, a team record, which ran from 1978 to 1985.
1	Member of the NFL's 1980s All-Decade Team that played with the Cowboys: Randy White.

After a 0-8 start, the team secured its lone win at Washington on November 5, 13–3.

"I've had so many people say over the years that if you were going to win one game that year that we sure did pick the right one to win—at RFK, the rivalry," said fullback Daryl "Moose" Johnston, a rookie that season. "And it also came at the perfect time, right in the middle of the year. No one wants to endure a 13- or 14-game losing streak."

Two weeks previous, following a 36–28 setback at Kansas City, Wannstedt admitted reaching rock bottom.

"As the season went on, there were a lot of conversations between Jimmy and me. I was so disappointed; we couldn't throw anyone down on defense," said Wannstedt. "We weren't a good football team. It's human reaction to allow self-doubt. We were getting beat up in the newspapers. I remember sitting there a few days after the Kansas City loss, watching tape with Jimmy, and I said, 'Should we rethink what we're doing with the defense?' And he said, 'I know it's frustrating, but I told you at Miami we'd win a national championship, so just hang in there with me because we're going to win a Super Bowl. We're not going to cave in and change philosophy. We're going to be just fine when we get some players in here.'"

The Cowboys soon took a major step in doing just that when Johnson and Jones completed the most important transaction in franchise history on October 12, 1989. They sent Walker, considered their best player, to the Minnesota Vikings for linebackers Jesse Solomon and David Howard, cornerback Issiac Holt, running back Darrin Nelson, defensive end Alex Stewart, and Minnesota's 1992 first-round pick. However, there were also six conditional draft selections that were directly tied to the players the Cowboys acquired and whether they were among the team's 37 protected roster players on February 1, 1990.

Many consider it the biggest and perhaps most impressive deal in the history of the NFL.

"One of the greatest coaches of all time, Tom Landry, was last in the NFL with Herschel Walker, so what makes me think losing our first six games that I was any better. So that's why I didn't mind trading him," Johnson said.

"It wasn't near as popular a trade then as what people think. He was our only Pro Bowl player. Well, I even made the comment at the press conference that you aren't going to realize it now, but years from now you'll look back and say this is like the great train robbery, and people laughed at me. They didn't understand my strategy. They thought I was getting a bunch of cast-offs, injured, and malcontents. I wouldn't let our coaches start these players, even though they were the best we had. David Howard and Jesse Solomon, Issiac Holt—they were the best players we had, but I wouldn't let our coaches start them because if they started them, they would fall in love with them, and that would screw my plan up.

"Some people still don't fully understand that trade."

For Jones, that first season was, admittedly, both miserable and exhilarating. He loved being an owner and general manager in the NFL. This was his dream from nearly the moment he stopped playing football at Arkansas on January 1, 1965. But while he never envisioned the on-field product

▲ Tom Landry and Jimmy Johnson.

as a short-term reclamation, he also wasn't planning on being vilified by the media. The same media, for the record, that was calling for Landry's retirement a mere months previous to his dismissal.

"The media needs to be controversial, and I understand that," Jones said. "There was no question from the day I bought the team that the expectations were for success or I would be held responsible. That was definitely a stressful time.

"However, while Jimmy was thinking six or seven wins, I didn't think we'd come in guns a blazin'. My view was more long-term for the Cowboys, but as the season went along, I could see Jimmy's disappointment. Another factor, looking back, was Jimmy was a college coach and he brought with him most of his staff, so although they were extremely knowledgeable about the college game, there was a transition period to the NFL."

After the season-ending 20–10 loss to Green Bay, in front of the sparest of home crowds, Johnson was miserable. Jones, wanting to offer some words of encouragement, put his arm around his longtime friend and said, "We're going to be okay. You know how I know that? 'Cause I have the best football coach in the world."

FRIENDS TO REMEMBER

Looking back over the first 50 years of the Dallas Cowboys, the two names that immediately come to mind are Tom Landry and Jerry Jones. I have been extremely fortunate to have a relationship, a friendship really, with each of them.

In 1958 I was traded from the Chicago Cardinals to the New York Giants for what would be my sixth full season in the NFL. Tom was both my defensive coordinator and kicking coach. Many people forget he was also a punter and even led the NFL in punting yards three years (1949, 1952, 1955).

I first experienced Tom at defensive meetings where all of us were amazed with how thorough he was, down to the most minute details: how long your first step should be, how your stance should be left-handed or right-handed—very specific stuff for back then. So much detail that it was difficult to imagine having had a coach before Tom, because I hadn't been exposed to anyone who had that kind of knowledge of the techniques and details of the defense.

As a kicking coach, well, the numbers speak for themselves. In my seven seasons as a kicker without Tom Landry, I made 68 of 160 field goals, which is 42.5 percent. In my two seasons with Tom, 1958–1959, I went 32 of 52, 61.5 percent. And in 1959, I finished four points behind Hall of Famer Paul Hornung for the NFL scoring title while leading the league with 20 field goals.

> **FOR THE LIFE OF ME, AT THAT MOMENT, I COULDN'T REMEMBER HIS NAME, JUST ONE OF THOSE TIMES IN BROADCASTING, AND HE REALIZED THAT I WAS HAVING A PROBLEM— THIS IS ALL LIVE TELEVISION, NO DOING IT OVER—AND HE SAYS TO ME, "I'M TOM LANDRY, COACH OF THE COWBOYS."**

When Tom found out he was going to be hired as the Cowboys coach, we lived in the same hotel in the Bronx, the Concourse Plaza, and he called me into his apartment and said, "If you miss to the right, here's what you're doing, if you miss to the left, here's what you're doing."

He also told me, and I'll never forget this, "You might beat me someday, and you probably will, but I want you to know these things."

Tom Landry turned me from a very average kicker into a pretty accurate one.

After I became a broadcaster in 1962, there were many coaches' meetings the day before games, and not once did Tom ever criticize a player. If he wasn't happy with, say, Harvey Martin, he'd simply say, "Harvey is working, he's working." I remember one time we asked him about Bob Lilly before a game, maybe a Super Bowl, and he said, "There's only one Bob Lilly."

There was this one time at the Cotton Bowl, St. Louis Cardinals and the Cowboys, and someone at CBS had the bright idea to have me down on the field to introduce the starting lineups and coaches. Well, I get through the players fine, and the Cardinals coach, who was Charley Winner at the time, no problem, and here comes Tom Landry out of the tunnel, right where I am standing.

For the life of me, at that moment, I couldn't remember his name, just one of those times in broadcasting, and he realized that I was having a problem—this is all live television, no doing it over—and he says to me, "I'm Tom Landry, coach of the Cowboys."

▲ (clockwise from top left) Tom Landry on the sideline and writing the day's schedule; Jerry Jones; (left to right) Jerry Jones, Lions general manager Russ Thomas, Giants owner Wellington Mara, and Browns owner Art Modell in 1989.

I have definitely always had a warm relationship with Jerry. When he first bought the team in 1989, we went out to dinner and talked about things he needed to do, things that were important to him and that were going to be important to him in becoming a successful NFL owner.

In 2004 I didn't want anyone to know I was having a liver transplant. Somehow, a friend of mine called Jerry's secretary, who told him, and he called my wife at the hospital in Jacksonville and insisted that he send his private plane. My wife said no, we didn't need that, but he sent it anyway. Twice he did that after I was back in Dallas on the road to recovery and needed to fly back for an evaluation. That's a side of Jerry maybe people don't get to see all the time. He's such a kind and generous human being.

I am a pretty lucky guy to have had friends like Tom Landry and Jerry Jones in my life.

Pat Summerall is an award-winning broadcaster who covered 26 Super Bowls during his illustrious career. Before moving into the press box, he played nine seasons with Chicago and New York as primarily a kicker, appearing in three NFL Championships with the Giants, including the legendary 1958 title game.

(left to right) Letting her voice be heard; Larry Brown; Jerry Jones inducting Tom Landry into the Ring of Honor; Chad Hennings; Alvin Harper scoring in the 1993 playoffs; the Triplets; Crazy Ray.

5

TEAM OF THE
DECADE

1990–1995 ★★★★★

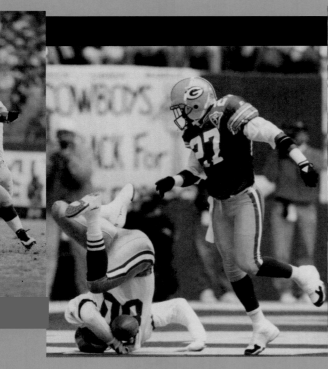

The can't-miss kid seemingly born to play quarterback for America's Team missed early and often during the infancy of his NFL career.

★★★★★

Sure, Troy Aikman arrived in Big D with Robert Redford–like looks and Roy Hobbs–like talent, but The Natural he was not. At least in terms of overnight success.

The No. 1 overall pick of the 1989 NFL Draft, which included Barry Sanders, Derrick Thomas, and Deion Sanders among the top-five selections, Aikman immediately impressed teammates, coaches, fans, and media alike. He exuded unwavering confidence in the huddle, possessed the aerial precision of a bald eagle, signed each and every autograph with the sincerest of appreciation, and respectfully responded to queries from newspaper, radio, and television folk all.

However, those first two seasons with the Cowboys wasn't the most enjoyable of experiences for Aikman, who grew up a fan long before his family relocated from Southern California to a ranch in Henryetta, Oklahoma, when Aikman was 12 years old in 1980.

"My impression of the team was pretty favorable, but I didn't have a full appreciation for the history of the franchise," Aikman said. "Roger Staubach was one of my favorite players growing up. Doug Cosbie and Ed 'Too Tall' Jones, too."

There was never a honeymoon for Aikman, as the Cowboys drafted Steve Walsh, Jimmy Johnson's quarterback at Miami, in the supplemental draft later in the spring of 1989. Prior to ever taking a preseason snap, Aikman was engrossed in a nationally publicized quarterback controversy. That first season was all-around horrific, Walsh winning the team's lone game at Washington, and Aikman missing more than a month with a fractured index finger on his left hand that required surgery. Many in the media speculated that Johnson's preferred choice behind center was Walsh, but in retrospect, this was just another psychological ploy by the head coach with a psychology degree. Then third-string quarterback Babe Laufenberg said, "I remember people were choosing sides, and I'm thinking, 'What are these people looking at?'"

The Cowboys traded Walsh to the New Orleans Saints for a trio of draft picks early in the 1990 campaign. That left Aikman solo, front and center.

▲ Emmitt Smith on draft day in 1990.

▲ Ken Norton Jr. celebrates Bill Bates's game-clinching interception in the Cowboys' 1991 NFC wild-card victory.

Through 10 games in his sophomore season, Dallas was 3-7, having scored just 125 points, second-fewest in the league. Further, the team had mustered 10 or fewer points in 10 of Aikman's first 21 NFL starts.

"When I was drafted, I thought in time, we would win, but I didn't think success would come fast," Aikman recalled. "Coming off its 3-13 finish in 1988, I don't know if I was willing to accept ownership for the struggles of the franchise my rookie season. But in 1990, I expected us to be better than we were, and offensively, we were worse.

"The first half of 1990 was the most frustrating experience of my career, much more so than 1989. I was miserable, absolutely miserable. There was a lot of soul-searching, a lot of long nights."

Personally, Aikman felt he could succeed at the highest level, as evidenced by his NFL rookie–record 379 passing yards against Phoenix a year previous. Still, through those first 21 professional starts, the UCLA product was 3-18, having thrown 14 touchdown passes against 32 interceptions.

The plight of the Dallas Cowboys changed on a Sunday afternoon in Los Angeles on November 18, 1990, the visitors defeating the host Rams, 24–21, behind 303 passing yards and 3 touchdowns from Aikman. The win would serve as the harbinger for an incomprehensible run that saw Aikman win 67 of his next 88 starts, including the playoffs.

"It's so hard to win in the NFL, and here we were 10 games into my second season with nothing to show for our efforts," Aikman said. "As a quarterback, that's depressing. The Rams game was probably the turning point for the team and definitely myself."

The Cowboys finished 7-9, with Johnson capturing NFL Coach of the Year honors. Running back Emmitt Smith was named the Offensive Rookie of the Year, rushing for 937 yards and 11 touchdowns to earn the team's lone Pro Bowl invite. The nucleus was in place; the Cowboys were primed for success.

"We just didn't know how to win," fullback Daryl "Moose" Johnston said. "Even when we finished 1-15 in 1989, in all honesty, we should've been 4-12 or 5-11. There is a process that you go through as a young team making that transition to becoming a competitive team, and one of the first things you have to do is learn how to win. That process, for us, took place in 1990."

The leap in the standings came the following season, as the Cowboys won their final five games and finished 11-5. The Triplets each made the leap as well, Smith leading the NFL with 1,563 rushing yards, Aikman finishing second with a 65.3 completion percentage, and wide receiver Michael Irvin pacing the competition with 1,523 receiving yards. Jay Novacek, signed as a free agent in 1990, added 59 receptions, and became the fifth tight end in club annals to be named to the Pro Bowl.

Earning a wild-card berth, the Cowboys traveled to Chicago and defeated the Bears, 17–13, with backup Steve Beuerlein winning his fifth straight in place of an injured Aikman. The season ended via a 38–6 loss at Detroit a week later, but the team was hardly dismayed, feeling it was primed for a legitimate Super Bowl run in 1992.

Nearly two decades removed from the resurgence, Aikman, Irvin, Smith, Johnston, and offensive linemen Nate Newton and Mark Stepnoski each reference Norv Turner when asked about the offensive turnaround that resulted in the Cowboys finishing seventh in the NFL in points in 1991, some 19 slots higher than the year before. A wide receivers coach with the San Diego Chargers for six years, Turner, then 38 years old, wasn't the first interviewed to replace David Shula as offensive coordinator, but Jerry Jones and Jimmy Johnson eventually tabbed him.

"Norv implemented a numbers system, a simple system for everybody to get on the same page," Smith said. "Once we were comfortable with our assignments, we were just reacting, no

RING OF HONOR QUARTERBACK
TROY AIKMAN

On Jimmy Johnson:
"Intense, calculated. I think he was a tremendous motivator of people and probably better at that, as far as knowing how to handle people and motivate people. More so than being a great football coach."

On Jerry Jones:
"Misunderstood and brilliant, all in one. I think he has done more for this organization and really more for the NFL than anyone I can think of. As respected as he is for all that he has done, I don't know that he'll be fully appreciated for his brilliance until he's no longer the guy in charge."

On Norv Turner: .
"A brilliant football mind, he's more of a big brother to me. The reason I had him present me [for the Pro Football Hall of Fame] was that I don't think I would have gone on and had the career that I was able to have, and I don't think our team would have gone on and done what it did, if Norv Turner had not have come to the team [as offensive coordinator] in 1991."

On the Triplets:
"Our situation was so unique because none of us ever enjoyed any NFL success without the others, so I think that's why we were able to really appreciate one another and have a pretty special bond among us that carries us even to this day."

Following pages: Emmitt Smith and Michael Irvin celebrate a touchdown against the Cardinals.

112,376	Attendance of the preseason game between the Dallas Cowboys and the Houston Oilers in Mexico City on August 15, 1994, the largest crowd to ever see an NFL game.
2,148	Yards from scrimmage for Emmitt Smith in 1995, a club record.
247	Combined points the Cowboys outscored their opponents in first quarters from 1991 to 1995.
140.7	Passer rating of Troy Aikman in earning MVP honors during Super Bowl XXVII, a 52–17 defeat of Buffalo.

▲ Russell Maryland at training camp.

Kenny Gant being congratulated by teammates, including Vinson Smith, after a touchdown return. ▼

longer thinking. That was fun. Our reactions to his system became very relevant to our style of play. As much as anyone, Norv was instrumental to our success."

As the Cowboys progressed through the 1992 preseason, expectations were lofty: an elite offense in place, one that would earn six Pro Bowl nods; an underrated defense anchored by linebacker Ken Norton Jr. and tackle Russell Maryland, the No. 1 overall pick of the 1991 NFL Draft; and a superb special teams unit led by coverage kamikazes Bill Bates and Kenny Gant.

However, they lacked a pass rush, mustering just 23 sacks the previous season, a 16-game franchise low that remained through 2009. Even including the 14-game seasons, no Cowboys defense since 1963 had tallied fewer sacks.

The phone call from San Francisco came on or around August 22 at Valley Ranch, the team's headquarters. Were the Cowboys interested in defensive end Charles Haley?

A six-year veteran, three-time Pro Bowler, and two-time Super Bowl winner, the 49ers were looking to deal Haley for reasons beyond his play on the field. Johnson and Jones weren't overly interested in his locker room issues, and happily dealt second- and third-round picks for his services on August 26. Later that night, Jones received a message from Raiders owner Al Davis, among his closest friends in the league, saying, "Congratulations. You just won the Super Bowl."

The following day, Jones himself picked Haley up at the airport.

"I was excited about the new opportunity, but also a little frightened," Haley remembered of the trade. "I knew nothing about the possibility of being traded, nor the team I was headed to or its coaching staff.

"So Jerry's at the airport, which was pretty cool. I had never been treated like that, the owner picking me up. There are cameras everywhere. On the ride to the hotel, Jerry tells me his vision for the Cowboys, explaining how I must play a vital part of this team. He really laid it down, stressing that I was now wearing the star on my helmet and that I should and would wear it with pride.

"I'll never forget this. He said, 'We will be Super Bowl champions. Not down the road; we start today. You're the final piece.'

"The guys had heard a lot of stuff about me; some were scared to even introduce themselves. The best part for me, though, was coming to a defense that was so young with so much talent. I wanted to be their leader. I wanted the opportunity to teach what I do, to teach pass rush, how to study and break down film, to have a role in their development."

Indeed, for Jones, the move was seen as the final piece of the puzzle.

DEFENSIVE END
CHARLES HALEY

On Jimmy Johnson:
"He allowed me to be me. Jimmy was a man of character and also the greatest of motivators. The best thing about Jimmy was that his word meant something. I loved Jimmy Johnson. If he showed up at my door tomorrow and told me to jump through the fire, I would. And I'm sure that Jimmy would walk through the fire after me. He was willing to go all the way, and I'll respect anyone who does so."

On the Pro Football Hall of Fame:
"Honestly, I think that moment will come in time. I would like to think I played the game the way it was meant to be played, and that I would be judged for what I accomplished on the field. I pushed a lot of guys' buttons, and sure, I have a lot of regrets, but I hope my legacy is that of a champion. I was hard on teammates. Maybe I pushed too far. But I only played because if we were keeping score, I wanted to win. And I wanted everyone to play with the same passion.

"I didn't communicate with the press that well, but [in regards to] pure football, I think my play spoke for itself."

"I remember thatride with Charles better than most of what I did yesterday," Jones recalled in the spring of 2010. "I had such an appreciation of him as a player, still do. I was aware of everything—his background, his challenges—but we did our homework and felt like he could inject such a mental strength to our team. I told him point-blank on that car ride that he had come to a team on the brink of winning a championship, and that what we didn't have was what he could bring. That being a pass rush, leadership, and mental fortitude.

"I also told him, 'Just be Charles Haley; don't try to be someone else.' I wanted him to know that we knew he was an open book. We knew exactly what we were doing, and we wanted him for him. We wanted Charles for Charles, and we were 100 percent committed to him. We wanted it all."

Behind Haley's leadership, Dave Wannstedt's unit led the NFL in total defense, a mind-boggling improvement from 1991 when the Cowboys finished 17th. Yet, somehow, someway, the Dallas defense, the modern-day Doomsday, didn't garner a single Pro Bowl selection.

Finishing the regular season at 13-3, Smith once again leading the league with 1,713 rushing yards, the Cowboys pulverized the Philadelphia Eagles, 34–10, in the division round, and in the process earned a road trip to San Francisco for the NFC Championship Game. The 49ers were favored, winners of 21 of their last 23 contests, but on the afternoon of January 17, 1993, the reclamation project of Jerry Jones and Jimmy Johnson less than four years earlier was the best football team on the planet, winning 30–20. The stars included Aikman (24 of 34 for 322 yards and two scores), Smith (173 yards from scrimmage, 2 touchdowns), and Johnston, who contributed a one-handed fumble recovery on punt coverage, rushed for a 4-yard touchdown, and caught 4 passes for 26 yards.

After the game, Johnson addressed his team in the locker room, saying in part, "Fantastic, fantastic, fantastic, every single one of you . . . you did a hell of a job. The only thing else I have to say is how 'bout them Cowboys!"

Cowboys director of public relations Rich Dalrymple recalls Johnson addressing the team less than 24 hours after the biggest win of their lives:

"Let me tell you something that I think everyone in this room already knows," began Johnson. "If we went out on our practice field with the Buffalo Bills for three hours, we would kick their ass up and down the field. I know it, and everyone in this room knows that we would do that.

"We're clearly the better team, and we all know that. But we're not going to play them on the practice field. We're going to play them in the

---

FULLBACK

DARYL "MOOSE" JOHNSTON

On blocking for Emmitt Smith:
"I had to learn what Emmitt saw. When I would watch film, I would watch his movements based on what the defense did. If the middle linebacker came through, which cut was he likely to make. If the gap was closed, would he change direction off tackle and so forth. I needed to think like Emmitt did. We were always talking about what he saw and his thought process. That was the only way for me to make the block that would help him the most. As the play developed, we were often making adjustments on the fly based on each of us knowing what the other would do."

On Jimmy Johnson:
"Thank goodness he could see what none of us could see those first few seasons. It's not like we were walking around thinking we were on the cusp of winning Super Bowls. Jimmy had a vision. He was watching practices and film and saw what we eventually became developing. Jimmy was always confident. He came in with a plan in 1989 and never wavered from that. He also knew how to motivate players based on their personalities better than anyone I have ever seen."

SUPER BOWL
XXVII

	1	2	3	4	F
Dallas Cowboys	14	14	3	21	52
Buffalo Bills	7	3	7	0	17

JANUARY 31, 1993
ROSE BOWL IN PASADENA, CALIFORNIA
ATTENDANCE: 98,374
MVP: TROY AIKMAN

▲ Troy Aikman earned MVP honors after totaling 273 yards and four touchdowns, earning a passer rating of 140.7.

▲ Jerry Jones and Jimmy Johnson in the locker room following the Lombardi Trophy presentation.

▲ Michael Jackson performs during halftime.

▲ Emmitt Smith and Michael Irvin celebrate their dominating win over the Bills.

XXVII

Leon Lett couldn't help himself.

Jimmy Johnson's halftime speech, defensive coordinator Dave Wannstedt's adjustments, hydration, uniform restructuring, those particulars all behind him, the kid from the dirt roads of Alabama, admittedly petrified of all things bright lights and big media, slipped out of the Rose Bowl locker room and migrated toward the field, stopping just outside the tunnel.

"Before that first Super Bowl, L.A. to me was Lower Alabama. That was my first time in Los Angeles," Lett says. "I remember Michael Jackson performed at halftime, and I snuck a peek; I couldn't pass that up. It was Michael Jackson, and I was just a kid from nowhere."

The kid from nowhere could have never imagined that while he watched the King of Pop, he himself was about two hours away from becoming a household name. At the moment, the Cowboys were leading the Bills 28–10 en route to one of the more dominant Super Bowl performances to date.

Dallas was favored by seven points, although many thought Buffalo held an advantage, having played in each of the previous two Super Bowls.

"I wouldn't call losing twice in the Super Bowl an advantage," Cowboys linebacker Ken Norton Jr. said. "Who were the Buffalo Bills? We beat the San Francisco 49ers."

And by game's end the Cowboys had absolutely pounded their opponent 52–17, forcing a Super Bowl–record nine turnovers while capturing the franchise's first title in 15 years. Troy Aikman was named the game's MVP, having completed 22 of 30 passes for 273 yards and four touchdowns, including a pair to Michael Irvin.

"I have never seen a quarterback throw like Troy did that afternoon," Irvin said. "Not even a second place.

"I always love when you hear athletes or coaches say the second or third championship was as sweet and meaningful as the first. They are absolutely full of it, out of their minds. There is nothing in this world like winning that first one. I can remember vividly just enjoying the final moments on the sidelines, just soaking up that emotion of winning."

Pro Bowl center Mark Stepnoski remembers thinking in the locker room at halftime that there was no way the Cowboys were losing.

▲ Leon Lett has the ball stripped by the Bills' Don Beebe just

▲ Showing off their Super Bowl trophie

➤ Jerry Jones and Troy Aikman greet fans during the championship parade.

▼ Fans gather in downtown Dallas for the parade and rally.

CENTER
MARK STEPNOSKI

On the team's turning point:
"I really don't know in hindsight if there was one moment or victory which made me think we were about to win back-to-back Super Bowls. The one thing that was huge was Norv [Turner] coming on the scene in 1991. We were better as a team in 1990; there was a ton of improvement, but not offensively. Our offense just didn't improve. But once we heard Norv talk about his plans and saw firsthand what he was doing with the offense, our optimism just took off. That first season with Norv, our offense went from 26th in scoring to 7th with basically the same players."

On playing center:
"I was drafted [out of Pittsburgh in 1989] as a guard. Most of my rookie season was learning the position. Tom Rafferty was in his 14th and final year playing center and taught me so much; I couldn't have learned from a better guy. He knew a heck of a lot about the game. For me, playing at around 265 pounds most of my career, it was about staying low and leverage more than size and strength. Technique was so crucial for me."

Super Bowl. And the Super Bowl is the biggest stage in the world. Millions of people watching in countries all over the world, everyone who has ever known you or has helped you get to where you are today, watching this one game. The biggest game you've ever played in your life.

"But our approach to this game is going to be very simple."

After a brief pause, Johnson continued, "Let me ask you this. If I took a 20-foot two-by-four piece of wood and set it down on top of two concrete blocks at the front of this meeting room, would anyone in this room have any problem with walking across that two-by-four from one end to the other?"

The response from the team was a group of NFC Champions shaking their heads in a horizontal motion with a bit of amusement.

Johnson asked, "Kenny Norton, could you walk across that two-by-four without losing your balance right here in front of me?"

"Don't think it would be a problem, Coach," said Norton.

Now all of the players in the room, who had heard so many of Johnson's Monday morning motivational talks, were leaning forward in their seats and wondering where their head coach was going with this lumberyard analogy. They had heard so many meaningful messages before but just weren't sure where their leader was headed this time.

"Okay," said Johnson, "if I took that same two-by-four and stretched it across the Twin Towers at the World Trade Center, 100 stories above New York City, would you feel as confident—or as comfortable? Would it be a different deal for any of you?"

There were uncertain looks on many of the faces in the room. Less confident body language than the confident posture that Norton offered just a minute prior.

"Well that's what this whole Super Bowl thing is all about," said Johnson. "The piece of wood is exactly the same—doesn't matter if it is stretched across two concrete blocks or across two large buildings. We're playing a football game. That's all it is. The field is a hundred yards long and the outcome will be the same if we play it on the practice field or at the Rose Bowl.

"If you know how to perform the job that is right in front of your face, and you have confidence in your ability, then the task in front of you is simple. You just do what you know how to do.

"That's what we're going to do when we play Buffalo. We're better than they are, and we have confidence in what we are doing. Doesn't matter if we play them in the parking lot here at Valley Ranch or in the middle of Times Square in New York City.

"The setting doesn't mean a thing. The field is 100 yards long. It's the same two-by-four. Regardless of the stakes, or the height of the drop, it's a football game. You know how to do it, and you're going to win."

And win the Dallas Cowboys did.

(See "Super Bowl XXVII" special insert.)

In the final seconds of Super Bowl XXVII, Johnson found veteran defensive tackle Jim Jeffcoat and asked him to walk across the field with him to shake hands with Buffalo head coach Marv Levy. A first-round draft pick back in 1983, Jeffcoat made an immediate impression on Johnson during that 1-15 campaign of 1989, the latter saying he has never seen a player work harder. And within the moment of winning the grandest title in American athletics, becoming the first to secure an NCAA national championship and a Super Bowl, Johnson wanted to share the instance with Jeffcoat, who along with Bill Bates and Mark Tuinei, was one of the longest-tenured players on the team, going back to 1983.

"That meant the world to me; I'll never forget that moment my entire life," Jeffcoat said. "I have so much respect for Jimmy, not only as a coach, but as a person. That was such a beautiful and kind gesture that he wanted me to walk to the middle of the field with him. That was the most rewarding experience of my football career."

As the reigning champions kicked off the 1993 campaign, Smith, after leading the NFL in rushing for two straight years, was looking for a new contract. He ended up missing the first two games of the regular season, the Cowboys losing both, before signing. Thereafter, Dallas rattled off seven straight wins, the streak snapped with a road setback at Atlanta. This came just four days prior to the annual Thanksgiving Day game, a holiday affair that would be anything but ordinary.

This was Don Shula and the 8-2 Miami Dolphins visiting Texas Stadium with one of the largest television audiences of the year tuned in. This was also the coldest, snowiest, and iciest Turkey Day one and all could recall in the annals of the Dallas–Fort Worth Metroplex.

Indeed, Mother Nature can serve as the cruelest of mistresses.

Thing is, there almost wasn't even a game played the afternoon of November 25, 1993.

"We had borrowed these brand-new tarps from the Cotton Bowl on Wednesday because we knew weather was coming in," Texas Stadium general manager Bruce Hardy remembered. "So we're down on the field four or five hours before kickoff, and it's only ice. Jerry and Jimmy want to keep the cover on as long as possible so about two hours before the 3:30 kickoff, we head onto the field.

"We couldn't move the tarps, there was so much ice, heavy ice. The tarp wouldn't budge. I immediately panicked. We couldn't, we wouldn't forfeit a game. Luckily, Jerry and Jimmy were more focused on the football game; they didn't realize what was going on. I was freaking out.

RING OF HONOR RUNNING BACK
EMMITT SMITH

On Daryl "Moose" Johnston:
"I have so much appreciation for Daryl, not only because we shared the same backfield together, but [also for] his analysis of the game and his ability to be . . . his humbleness. I mean you talk about a guy who was extremely humble and undersized for that position but gave his heart and his soul and also sacrificed his body for me and oftentimes did not receive the accolades that he should have received. Moose made me better, as a football player and as a person. He is such a great, great man."

On his NFL career rushing record of 18,355 yards:
"Every record that has been made thus far has to be broken by somebody. I understand that no one so far has even sniffed it, but you never know how the game itself might evolve, might evolve into an opportunity for someone to break the record. Once you reach a certain number of carries, once you get 1,600 or 1,700, those runs thereafter have more of an effect on the body."

On the dynasty:
"We had something very, very special with Jimmy Johnson as our coach. If they eliminated free agency and he remained, we might have won five or six straight Super Bowls."

Thanksgiving 1993 against Miami, the coldest regular-season home game in Cowboys history (left to right): The snow-covered field; players battle for the ball after Leon Lett's fumble; Kevin Williams returns a punt 64 yards for a touchdown.

"All we had was this little trash pickup machine, just a little thing, but we used that and shoveled what we could, we were grabbing concession workers to push snow off, whatever we could think of. Finally, we were able to get the tarp off, but it was destroyed, ripped, torn. We had to buy the Cotton Bowl some new tarps, but I had never been so happy."

By the second half, temperatures were in the mid-20s, traction simply a rumor. With 15 seconds remaining and Dallas leading 14–13, Miami kicker Pete Stoyanovich attempted a 41-yard field goal, which was blocked by defensive tackle Jimmie Jones. The game appeared over, Cowboys players screaming "Peter, Peter," the code for stay away.

Leon Lett isn't sure why he sprinted toward the football, never mind his slide-and-kick heard round the sports world that resulted in the Dolphins recovering the fumble and Stoyanovich, given a second opportunity, hitting a game-winning 19-yard field goal.

"I knew the rule. I had blocked field goals in the past," Lett recalled. "It's not like it was my first time on the field goal block team. I have been trying to think back for, what, 16 or so years now, and I don't know what happened. It was a brain freeze. I remember [safety] Thomas Everett returned a field goal earlier in the game. Maybe I thought of that, I don't know. There are no excuses.

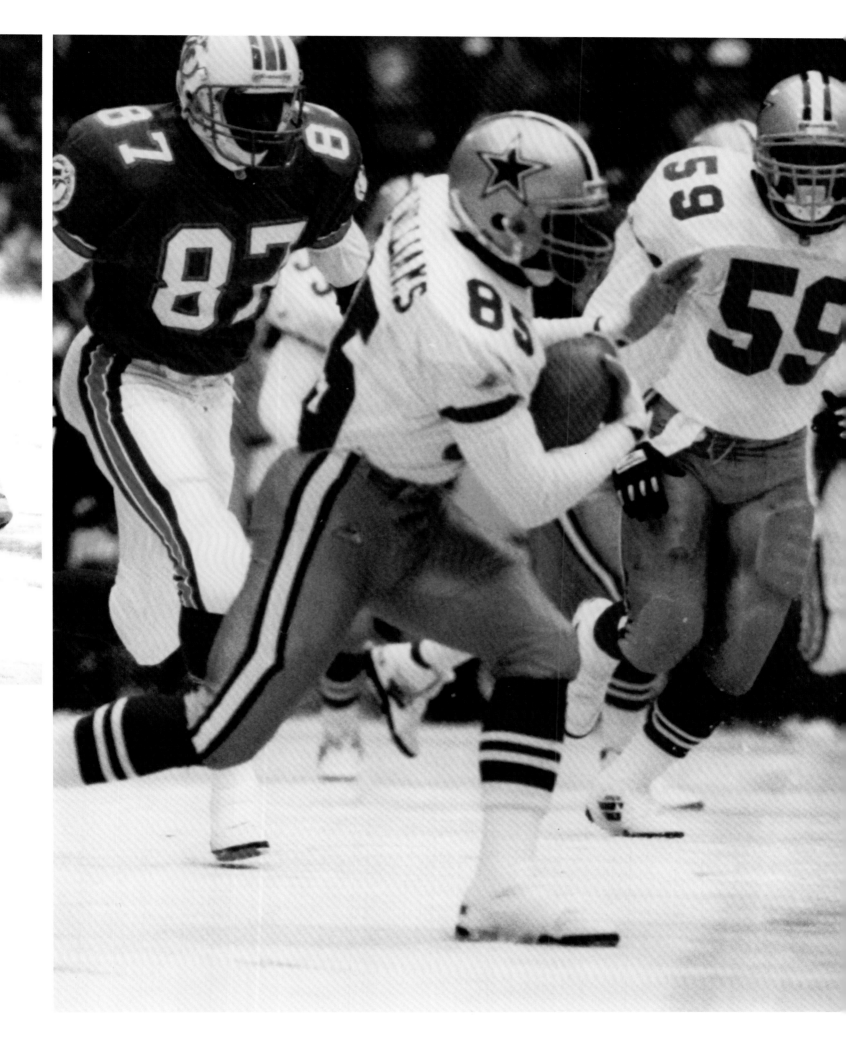

"I WAS THE FIRST ONE IN THE LOCKER ROOM. I JUST WANTED OFF THAT FIELD. I RAN RIGHT IN AND WENT TO THE TRAINERS' ROOM. I REMEMBER HEARING HELMETS FLYING, HITTING THE WALL, GUYS YELLING IN FRUSTRATION. I LOST THE GAME."

—Leon Lett

"I was the first one in the locker room. I just wanted off that field. I ran right in and went to the trainers' room. I remember hearing helmets flying, hitting the wall, guys yelling in frustration. I lost the game.

"A few guys came into the trainers' room to see me. I remember Nate coming in, Michael. Then Jimmy walked in. I didn't know what to do or say. I thought he was going to curse me out or cut me. He comes over to me, puts his hands on my shoulder, and says in a soft voice, 'Don't worry, Leon, you're my boy, and I'm sticking with you no matter what. As long as I have a job here, you have a job.' Those words meant the world to me."

Later, Johnson told the media, "Leon went to the training room and cried his eyes out. Ah, he's such a good kid. We are a team, and we made a lot of mistakes today."

Lett was a two-time Pro Bowl tackle and, if not for off-the-field issues, could've been one of the top down linemen in Cowboys history. He was vilified in the press for the miscue, especially less than a year removed from his fumble in Super Bowl XXVII.

"Leon was a tremendous talent, but because he was so quiet and introverted, people didn't understand him or know him," Johnson said. "He had the misfortune of a couple crucial errors, but he really was an outstanding player and a good person.

"Part of the mistake might have been our problem; because it snowed, we decided to put him on our field goal block team before the game. He really was not one of our main special teams players, so he hadn't gone through all the rules and regulations like somebody that was on all the special team units. We threw him into the mix because of the snow, thinking that with his size and power, he might be able to block one up the middle. It wasn't Leon's fault. We didn't have him thoroughly prepared for the situation."

While no one could've imagined so at the time, the loss would be the last for Jimmy Johnson as head coach of the Cowboys.

At 11-4, Dallas traveled to the Meadowlands to face the Giants in the regular-season finale, the winner securing the NFC East Division crown and more importantly, home-field advantage throughout the playoffs.

Following a brilliant 46-yard run with two minutes remaining in the first half, Smith was tackled, falling directly on his right shoulder. As he lay on the artificial turf in the worst pain of his life, having already rushed for 109 yards on 19 carries, the training staff assessing the damage, his

DEFENSIVE TACKLE
LEON LETT

On being drafted out of Emporia State in 1991:

"Jimmy called and said they drafted me and that I was a Dallas Cowboy. I said, 'Stop playing. You aren't Jimmy Johnson, and you aren't with the Dallas Cowboys. Who is this?' And Jimmy said, 'No, Leon, I'm serious. This is for real.' And then Jerry Jones got on the phone, and I recognized his voice and realized no one was playing a joke on me. I was numb for three or four hours."

On playing for the Cowboys:

"It was crazy, just going into restaurants and people knowing who I was. This was my rookie year. I was a backup defensive tackle. Why would anyone know who I was? After we beat San Francisco in the NFC Championship Game, we flew home and landed around 11 p.m. Here we are at some remote airstrip, and there are fans lined up, beating their cars and screaming they love you. That moment, that experience is impossible to describe. You have to be a little different to play professional football. When your body is telling you, 'No, not today; there's nothing left,' and your mind just wants to get it done. You're barely able to get out of bed. But those moments, at the airfield, that's how, and I guess why, we pushed our bodies through whatever pain we were experiencing."

best friend, Irvin, crouched nearby. At first glance, Irvin appeared to be offering moral support, but such was not the case.

"Michael did not want me to leave. He was in my ear telling me to block out the pain and keep playing football," Smith recalled. "He said the team, my family, needed me."

At halftime, the diagnosis was a grade-one shoulder separation, possibly worse, meaning no more football. However, when Smith was told no further damage could come from playing, he had the trainers wrap a harness around his shoulder with some extra padding.

"The importance of winning that game was even more so at that point, because I couldn't have turned around and played the following week if we were the wild card," Smith said. "We needed home-field advantage and the bye week so my shoulder could heal."

The Cowboys prevailed 16–13 in overtime, as Smith rushed for 168 yards on a season-high 32 carries and caught 10 passes for another 61 yards. Of his 229 yards from scrimmage, 78 came after the injury. And in the history of the franchise, no player has matched his 42 offensive touches in a single game. In overtime, he accounted for 41 of the team's 52 yards on offense.

"I went back in time," Smith said. "Went back to when I was first playing football with my cousins. They used to say to us in the park, when we got knocked down and started crying as kids because we were scared, they used to say to us all the time when we were youngsters, 'You can't play the game if you can't play with pain.'

"I kept repeating that in my mind over and over again, and for some reason it was like, it was like I had an out-of-body experience because everything else in the stadium was quiet. I couldn't hear anything but Troy Aikman calling the play and my teammates. I was just that focused on what I needed to do as far as my job goes, and I kept talking, repeating to myself that 'You can't play the game if you can't play with pain.' I kept pushing myself further and further than I thought that I could ever go. That to me, that is what football is all about."

Afterward, for the first and only time of his 30-year broadcasting career, CBS color analyst John Madden, who was calling the game, visited the locker room. He wanted to shake the hand of Emmitt Smith.

Dallas rolled through the postseason, defeating Green Bay, 27–17, and San Francisco, 38–21, with Johnson boldly guaranteeing victory in the week leading up to the showdown with the 49ers. A second Super Bowl with the Buffalo Bills beckoned.

(See "Super Bowl XXVIII" special insert.)

On March 29, 1994, Johnson resigned as head coach of the Dallas Cowboys. The relationship between Johnson and Jones had reached the point of no return, the specifics of which really aren't relevant. And while the majority was shocked, others weren't, including Jeffcoat, who remembers Johnson telling him

▲ Michael Irvin encourages an injured Emmitt Smith, who went on to help defeat the Giants in overtime despite a separated shoulder.

SUPER BOWL
XXVIII

	1	2	3	4	F
Dallas Cowboys	6	0	14	10	30
Buffalo Bills	3	10	0	0	13

JANUARY 30, 1994
GEORGIA DOME IN ATLANTA, GEORGIA
ATTENDANCE: 72,817
MVP: EMMITT SMITH

▲ Kicker Eddie Murray accounted for 12 of the Cowboys' 30 points.

"I PROMISED THEM WE WERE GOING TO WIN," JOHNSON
SAID. AND WIN THEY DID, 30–13, THE BILLS NOT SCORING
A SINGLE POINT OVER THE FINAL 30 MINUTES.

XXVIII

Somewhat forgotten from the Cowboys' dynasty that was the first half of the 1990s is that the Buffalo Bills were leading Super Bowl XXVIII at intermission and even received the second-half kickoff.

However, less than a minute in, a forced fumble by Leon Lett led to a 46-yard fumble recovery touchdown by safety James Washington, and that was more or less bedtime as far as the Bills were concerned, as Buffalo became the first and, to date, only team to fall to defeat in four straight Super Bowls.

"We weren't losing that game; we just needed a little wake-up call," Lett said. "Jimmy pushed us that entire week. We were in full pads hitting each other through Friday. Those two seasons, 1992 and '93, Sunday was usually the easiest part of the week. Our defense was going up against the best there was every day at practice—Mark Tuinei, Nate Newton, Erik Williams, Mark Stepnoski, Kevin Gogan. We just absolutely beat the crap out of each other."

Several players recall Johnson not even raising his voice at halftime, simply reassuring his team of its greatness and, well, its destiny.

"I promised them we were going to win," Johnson said.

And win they did, 30–13, the Bills not scoring a single point over the final 30 minutes.

Emmitt Smith was named MVP behind 158 yards from scrimmage and two scores, in the process becoming the first and only player in NFL history to lead the league in rushing, win league MVP honors, and take home the Super Bowl MVP trophy all in the same season. Although for the record, Washington could've just as easily earned the trip to Disney World with 11 tackles, an interception, and the fumble return for a touchdown.

For many, this was the epitome of the first 50 seasons of the Dallas Cowboys. They possessed unconditional swagger and blind confidence only attained at the apex of athletic competition when the goal is no longer winning. Victory is simply understood, a predetermined mindset, the game itself a nuisance en route to the next conquest.

Not including Smith's two-game holdout to start the 1993 regular season, the Cowboys were winners of 37 of their last 43 games including the playoffs. In capturing back-to-back Super Bowl titles, they had won each of their six postseason games by double digits.

Shockingly, less than two months after becoming the fourth head coach to win back-to-back Super Bowls—joining Vince Lombardi, Don Shula, and Chuck Noll—Jimmy Johnson and the Cowboys parted ways.

"Jimmy doesn't leave and we win five straight Super Bowls," Michael Irvin says.

To this day, no team in NFL history has won three consecutive Super Bowls.

27	Consecutive field goals converted by Chris Boniol in 1996, a team record. He also had an earlier streak of 26 made from 1995 to 1996.
4	Career blocked punts by defensive back Issiac Holt, who played for the Cowboys from 1989 to 1992. No other Cowboys player has more than 2.
3	Members of the NFL's 75th Anniversary Team, which was named in 1994, who played with the Cowboys: Lance Alworth, Mike Ditka, and Bob Lilly.
0	Number of defensive Pro Bowl selections for the Cowboys in 1992 despite allowing the fewest yards in the NFL (3,933).

OFFENSIVE LINE COACH
HUDSON HOUCK

On offensive tackle Erik Williams blocking Hall of Fame defensive end Reggie White:

"No offensive tackle played Reggie as well as Erik did, and Reggie knew that, too. We never slanted the line when we played the Eagles. We were confident and secure in Erik handling him by himself, which was a huge advantage for the rest of the offense. Erik never feared anyone. He was such a tenacious blocker, aggressive, all the physical measurements and attributes you look for, and tremendous feet, quick. And he loved playing the game, which isn't always the case with offensive linemen. Erik loved being part of the team as much as any player I've been around."

On Larry Allen:

"I still remember his first practice. Larry is opposite Charles Haley, who is talking a little trash and has no idea who this kid is. The first snap—the very first snap—Larry just manhandled Charles, which completely took him by surprise. And Charles, who wasn't a man of many words, gets up, walks over to me, and says, 'Coach, you have one hell of a player there,' and walks back to the defensive huddle."

"The two of us created an atmosphere here, an atmosphere of success that unfortunately also created an urgency that shouldn't have existed. The idea of winning was still there for both of us. Jimmy still wanted to win football games, win another Super Bowl, and I certainly did. But we just weren't able to work out our own issues."

For more than a decade, the relationship between Jones and Johnson was virtually non-existent until they reconciled in the aftermath of a Thanksgiving game at Texas Stadium. Since then, the friendship has mended enough that Johnson and his wife, Rhonda, joined Jones's family and Wade and Laurie Phillips at the George Strait concert that opened the doors of Cowboys Stadium.

"When Jerry and I are together, the two of us laugh as hard as anybody and tell stories with the best of them," Johnson said. "We both have tremendous memories of those days, and so that's a very positive time in my life. There are no regrets at all."

For the third head coach in the team's history, Jones turned to an old friend, who in fact was his second choice to run the team back in 1989 if Johnson had passed on the offer, former University of Oklahoma coach Barry Switzer.

"I came in alone, no assistant coaches, but that didn't bother me. My job was to manage the staff and players already in place," Switzer said. "I coached a different way than Jimmy had there. I never coached with fear, and I think the players responded better to that atmosphere. I didn't want to be an actor, didn't want to try to be someone I wasn't. I didn't want to create a crisis, either. I was honest and candid with the coaches, players, and media from the first day. I know the media was taking their shots at me, but I could've cared less.

"They couldn't execute me, so I'd kill them with kindness and a smile on my face."

The transition was smooth enough, the Cowboys finishing 1994 at 12-4, each loss by seven or fewer points. Smith was Smith, rushing for 1,484 yards and scoring 22 touchdowns; Irvin was Irvin, with 79 catches for 1,241 yards; Aikman was Aikman, completing 64.5 percent of his passes; and the defense was solid, led by third-year strong safety Darren Woodson, Lett, and Haley.

No regular-season win that season was anywhere in the zip code as memorable or exciting as the 42–31 Thanksgiving Day triumph over Green Bay in which third-string quarterback Jason Garrett—making his second NFL start on the 20th anniversary of Clint Longley's holiday classic—led the Cowboys to 5 touchdowns in the first 18 minutes, 40 seconds, of the second half en route to a team-record 36 second-half points. He finished the game 15 of 26 for 311 yards and 2 touchdowns.

"WE TOTALLY SELF-DESTRUCTED THAT FIRST QUARTER, BUT THE ADMIRATION I HAVE TO THIS DAY FOR HOW MY TEAM FOUGHT, THE CHARACTER THEY DISPLAYED, THAT WAS A SPECIAL GROUP OF MEN JERRY AND JIMMY ASSEMBLED."

—Barry Switzer

The following morning, the phone rang at the house of Garrett's father, Jim, a longtime Cowboys scout. Nearly 16 years later, the memory is vivid.

"Jim, this is Barry Switzer. This isn't a coach calling a scout or a coach calling a father, this is one dad calling another dad and telling him that his kid did great yesterday. What an unbelievable second half; I just wanted you to know how proud you should be of that son of yours."

As he finishes the story, Jim Garrett's voice trails off for a moment or two.

"That's him, that's Barry Switzer right there," he says. "He's one of the nicest and most humble men you'll ever meet in life. Just a class act. It has always bothered me that people don't know what a brilliant football mind he possesses.

"In my 60 years involved with football, Barry Switzer is my all-time favorite person."

Alas, for Switzer and the Cowboys, they weren't able to become the first team in the history of the league to win three straight Super Bowls, losing at San Francisco, 38–28, in the NFC Championship Game.

The Cowboys fought valiantly, though, after falling behind 21–0, with Aikman later saying he had never been prouder of his team.

"We totally self-destructed that first quarter, but the admiration I have to this day for how my team fought, the character they displayed, that was a special group of men Jerry and Jimmy assembled," Switzer said.

After starting the 1995 season 2-0, the Cowboys added one of the more electrifying athletes in sports to their secondary and special teams in one Deion Sanders, a.k.a. Prime Time, signing the free agent to a seven-year deal. The previous January, he had helped the 49ers win the Super Bowl and certainly planned on returning to the game's grandest stage.

SAFETY
BILL BATES

On playing 15 seasons with the Cowboys as an undrafted free agent:
"I always wanted to play for the Cowboys, so just that first training camp in 1983 was a dream. I never felt like I came into camp with a guaranteed roster spot, so every year was a battle for me. I never lost that edge or felt complacent. That second season was pretty special, making the Pro Bowl as a special teams guy, going from thinking you were going to be looking for a real job coming out of college to playing with the best players in the sport in Hawaii. Lot of ups and downs, obviously the 1-15 season was challenging, but then here we are in the Super Bowl a few years later."

On his connection with the fans:
"I think they could see some of themselves in me. I wasn't the biggest guy out there, oftentimes one of the smallest. I wasn't the fastest guy out there. I was the gritty, hardworking stiff who was out there living his dream, and fans appreciated that. I tell people all the time that I was able to live my dream. Not many people can say that."

SUPER BOWL

XXX

	1	2	3	4	F
Dallas Cowboys	**10**	**3**	**7**	**7**	**27**
Pittsburgh Steelers	0	7	0	10	17

JANUARY 28, 1996
SUN DEVIL STADIUM IN TEMPE, ARIZONA
ATTENDANCE: 76,347
MVP: LARRY BROWN

Bill Bates at the Cowboys championship parade.

▲ Diana Ross performs at halftime.

Emmitt Smith powered up the middle in the third quarter to give the Cowboys a 20–7 lead. ▼

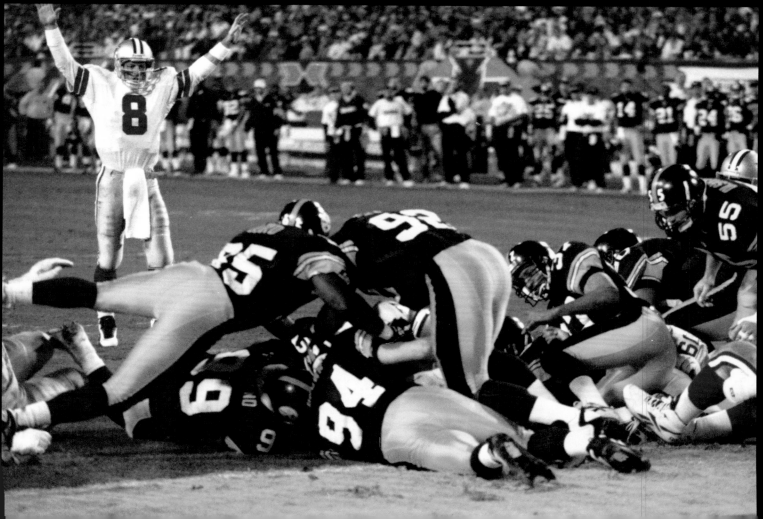

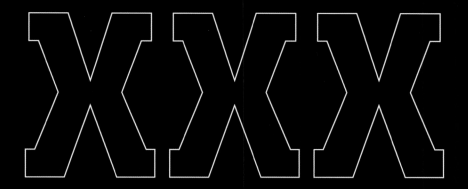

Nearly 15 years later, Barry Switzer remembers his immediate emotion as the final seconds ticked off the Sun Devil Stadium clock in Tempe, Arizona.

Sure, he was about to become the second man to ever win an NCAA national championship and a Super Bowl, following, of course, Jimmy Johnson. And, yes, there was some vindication after a brutal two-season stretch with the media, not to mention his own remarkable personal journey from a tragic childhood. But, no, none of this was at the forefront during this very moment for Switzer.

"For me, honestly, it was more of a relief," he said. "There was tremendous pressure for Jerry [Jones], not me. People always talk about how much pressure I must have been under, but that wasn't so. If we don't win that Super Bowl, they would've vilified poor Jerry. Heck, I just would've landed back on my couch in Oklahoma. There's a big difference."

For the fifth time in franchise history, the Dallas Cowboys reigned supreme on Super Bowl Sunday, defeating the Pittsburgh Steelers, 27–17, on January 28, 1996. The Lombardi Trophy was the team's third in four years, a distinction no other franchise in NFL history can claim.

Despite scoring on each of their initial three possessions to take a 13–0 lead, the Cowboys struggled offensively, with Pittsburgh outgaining Dallas in total yards over the final two quarters, 201–61. Where the Cowboys took advantage, though, was in the turnover battle, namely in the form of cornerback Larry Brown and his pair of second-half interceptions.

"I enjoyed the opportunity to make plays; I wanted folks throwing at me," Brown said of his mindset entering the game. "I honestly felt like if they came at me, they were crazy, and I'd make them pay."

As for his two picks of Pittsburgh quarterback Neil O'Donnell, Brown freely admitted that the first one, midway through the third quarter, was a floater, gift-wrapped for his Christmas-morning pleasure. However, the second, with four minutes remaining in the game, was an aggressive read, the proverbial high-risk, high-reward momentary decision that on this Sunday transformed a 12th-round draft selection into a Super Bowl hero.

"The second one wasn't O'Donnell's fault at all," Brown said. "We just made a great play. We worked all week on being aggressive, and on that

▲ Barry Switzer holds up the Lombardi Trophy after the Cowboys win their fifth Super Bowl.

▲ Deion Sanders.

"That year and beyond, I was thinking we could win at least two or three when I signed," Sanders said.

Behind an unforgettable campaign from Smith, who rushed for 1,773 yards and a then-league-record 25 touchdowns to earn NFL MVP honors, and Irvin's franchise mark of 111 catches for 1,603 receiving yards, Dallas won 12 games and secured the conference's No. 1 seed. After disposing of Philadelphia, 30–11, in the divisional round, Green Bay offered resistance but, in the end, was simply overmatched, the Cowboys winning yet another NFC Championship, 38–27, at Texas Stadium.

For the third time in the team's history, the Pittsburgh Steelers awaited in the final football game of the season.

(See "Super Bowl XXX" special insert.)

HEAD COACH
BARRY SWITZER

On coaching Jerry Jones and Jimmy Johnson as freshmen at Arkansas in 1961:
"They were both unique personalities. I recommended signing Jimmy out of Thomas Jefferson High School in Port Arthur [Texas]. He was an outstanding student and a strong player. Jerry, we knew he was wired a little differently than the rest of us pretty much the first weekend. The rest of the players, and me for that matter, were out partying, and he's out selling insurance policies. He was obviously headed in a different direction; Jerry always knew where he was going in life. On the football field, though, Jerry tried as hard as any player I ever coached; he busted his rear end every single snap."

On Jones and Johnson parting ways following the 1993 season:
"I think it was tragic what happened, and I never understood it. Only Jerry and Jimmy can explain what went wrong, but to me, it was tragic for both of them. I had absolutely nothing to do with their breakup or with the relationship in any way until Jimmy was out and Jerry called me about coaching the team. I know the fans didn't want to see Jimmy leave, but Jerry wasn't happy with the situation. My job was to keep the truck out of the ditch."

RICH DALRYMPLE
JOB OF A LIFETIME

I have been the director of public relations for the Dallas Cowboys since July of 1990. Emmitt Smith and I were rookies together. I saw Emmitt gain every single one of his 17,162 yards as a Cowboy.

At last glance, Emmitt had no hair on his head. Mine was a mixture of color but mostly gray.

I have held this job longer than any of my predecessors. I don't know if that is a testament to their wisdom or my lack thereof.

When Jerry Jones hired me, there was only one directive: "Tex Schramm was the master at publicity and creating interest. I want us to do everything he did and then do some more things that are better."

As the chief media liaison for this organization, people are always intrigued by what I do. They think this is an interesting line of work with a very unique organization. And they are right. When people ask, "What is it like?" my initial response is always the same: "It has its ups and downs, but it is never boring."

I grew up in Pittsburgh, just five miles from Three Rivers Stadium and the 1970s Steelers. My prior employment was at the University of Miami with college football's Team of the Decade in the 1980s. I've been lucky in my life to be around the very flamboyant and the very best. But nothing on my road to Texas could prepare me for the phenomenon that is the Dallas Cowboys.

There were times in the early 1990s where you felt like the road manager for the Beatles. And then there are also moments when you think that the press secretary for the White House is the only one who really understands what you're going through.

TEX AND JERRY ALSO UNDERSTOOD THAT YOU HAVE TO WIN A LOT OF FOOTBALL GAMES TO MAKE IT REALLY GOOD. AND THEY KNEW IT WAS THE GUYS IN THE LOCKER ROOM—ON THE SIDELINES AND ON THE FIELD—WHO MADE THE WINNING POSSIBLE.

The Cowboys have extreme personalities in the locker room; a nationwide fan following that carries a religious, cultlike fervor; a lightning rod for an owner who happens to have more energy and passion than anyone else in the building; and a history of past success and greatness on the field that is equal parts inspirational and suffocating for the current edition of guys who wear blue stars on their silver helmets.

Twenty years ago, in the midst of a string of three Super Bowl victories, the Cowboys were a magnet for NFL media hype involving national magazine writers, local newspaper coverage, and intense television scrutiny on both the national and local levels. Today it has evolved into a perfect storm for publicity overkill with all of the above and the accelerated development of ESPN, talk radio, websites, blogs, Twitter, and other forms of social media outlets that seem to spring up on a daily basis.

And you know what? I wouldn't want it any other way.

The Dallas Cowboys are an iconic fixture on the sporting landscape of America. When people in Asia or Africa hear "Dallas," their immediate response is usually "Dallas Cowboys." That's because this team has been blessed to be managed by only two men in its 50-year history—Tex

▲ (clockwise from top left) Rich Dalrymple with Jerry Jones; media covering a typical practice; meeting President Clinton after Super Bowl XXVII; Emmitt Smith addressing reporters.

Schramm and Jerry Jones—and both were steadfast in one fundamental premise: "If they're talking about us, then it's good."

Tex and Jerry also understood that you have to win a lot of football games to make it really good. And they knew it was the guys in the locker room—on the sidelines and on the field—who made the winning possible.

So when I finish my answer about what it's like to have this job, I always add this: "For a person in my line of work, you are measured by the number of interesting people with whom you've worked closely. My list, among others, includes Jerry, Jimmy, Michael, Troy, Emmitt, Nate, Gogan, Haley, Erik Williams, Larry Allen, Deion, Woodson, Parcells, Romo, T.O., Witten and Ware. There are so many more."

It has its ups and downs, but it's a very good job.

Rich Dalrymple has been director of public relations for the Dallas Cowboys since 1990, having served as a liaison between the team and the media for three Super Bowl championships, eight division winners, 10 Hall of Fame honorees, 38 Pro Bowlers, and six head coaches.

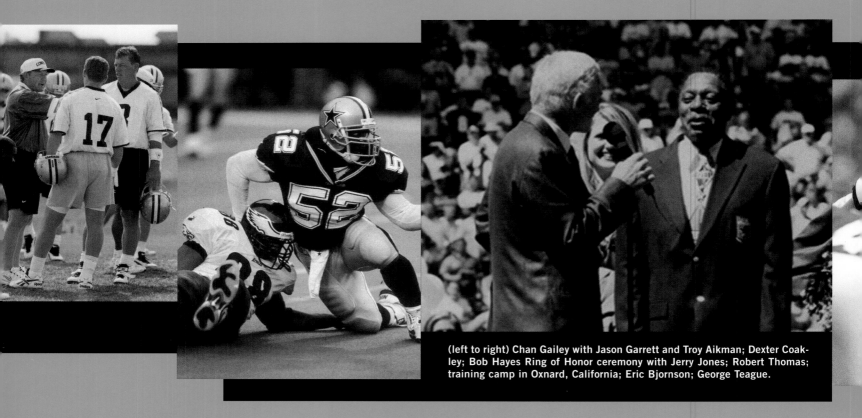

(left to right) Chan Gailey with Jason Garrett and Troy Aikman; Dexter Coakley; Bob Hayes Ring of Honor ceremony with Jerry Jones; Robert Thomas; training camp in Oxnard, California; Eric Bjornson; George Teague.

Barry Switzer has served as the head coach of 261 football games, each at the highest level of competition with the Oklahoma Sooners and Dallas Cowboys. He has lost exactly 55 times, which equates to a mind-boggling 78.2 winning percentage.

Tom Landry won barely 60 percent of his games with the Cowboys, and even if you subtract Jimmy Johnson's 1-15 campaign with Dallas in 1989, his combined collegiate and NFL record is 160-83-3, good for a 65.8 success rate. This is not in the least to diminish either Landry or Johnson, two of the definitive coaches in the sport's history. No, this is about the most complex, misunderstood, and yet simplistic of men.

In the history of professional and college football, as in forever and ever, Switzer has had the most success in terms of wins and losses among head coaches, minimum 150 games. That includes those who just coached in the NFL or at the collegiate level, never mind both. He won three national championships at Oklahoma and lost one or zero games 8 of his 16 seasons at the helm before resigning on June 19, 1989, months after the NCAA placed the Sooners on three years' probation. He said then, "I'm totally frustrated working within a set of rigid rules that does not recognize the financial needs of young athletes. I will never coach at another institution, I promise you that."

Reflecting on that sentiment some 21 years removed, Switzer said, "I never, ever paid a single cent for a recruit. Trust me, I didn't have to; they wanted to play for me. But you know, when I have a kid's father pass away and he has no means of transportation, I'll pay for his plane ticket home for the funeral every time, without hesitation."

Coaching an NFL team was never an aspiration of Switzer's. In fact, he turned down Lamar Hunt's offer to lead the Kansas City Chiefs in 1976. After stepping down at Oklahoma, he was content to be, well, Barry Switzer—dabble in business opportunities and enjoy life in Norman, Oklahoma.

Then the call came from Jerry Jones, one of his closest friends. Would he coach the Cowboys?

"After I left Oklahoma, there were other offers, but I had absolutely no interest, none," Switzer said. "But I always knew if the Dallas Cowboys job was ever open that I wouldn't be able to say no."

In the days, weeks, and even months after emerging victorious at Super Bowl XXX, vindicating his hiring in the process, Switzer thought about stepping down, feeling in some sense that he had served his purpose. After much deliberation, he decided to stick around, mostly because he didn't want to let down Jones.

▲ Dat Nguyen.

"I love Jerry so much. I enjoyed coaching the Cowboys tremendously. The Super Bowl was terrific, but honestly, the highlight for me was spending so much time with Jerry," Switzer said. "Those are the memories I have today."

Following back-to-back 12-4 regular seasons, the Cowboys—decimated by player defections through free agency—claimed a fifth straight NFC East Division title in 1996 at 10-6. After a 1-3 start, Dallas won 9 of 11 contests despite finishing the year 25th in scoring. The star power remained in tow, with nine players earning Pro Bowl honors, but this clearly wasn't the dynasty that claimed three Super Bowls in four years.

After routing Minnesota, 40–15, in the wild-card round, the reign of America's Team, the Team of the Decade—perhaps the greatest collection of talent ever assembled on an NFL roster over a five-year stretch—ended somewhat peacefully, without bells and whistles, after a 26–17 loss to a second-year expansion team in the Carolina Panthers.

More than 13 years would pass before the Cowboys would win another postseason game.

The 1997 campaign started optimistically enough for Dallas at 3-1; however, its most recent win, 27–3 over Chicago at Texas Stadium, saw the visitors outgain the home team, 243-180. This was a harbinger of defeats to come, Switzer suffering the first and only losing season of his

THERE IS NO SWITZER QUOTATION MORE OFTEN REPEATED THAN "SOME PEOPLE ARE BORN ON THIRD BASE AND GO THROUGH LIFE THINKING THEY HIT A TRIPLE."

collegiate and NFL head-coaching career at 6-10. The win against the Bears also concluded a run for the ages, the Cowboys going 79-25, including the postseason, from the latter third of the 1991 campaign through the four-game start in 1996.

At season's end, Switzer resigned. Counting the playoffs, he finished 45-26 with 14 of his first 19 regular-season defeats coming by seven or fewer points.

"It was really a no-win situation for Barry," offensive lineman Nate Newton said. "He was asked to step in as the head coach and not change a single thing. We won a Super Bowl with him; not a lot of coaches can say that. And you know what? He couldn't have been more humble or first-class. I love Barry Switzer."

Born in Arkansas, Switzer grew up without running water, electricity, or a phone. When it rained, he bathed. While he was playing college football at the University of Arkansas, his father was in the state prison for bootlegging. And when he was 23 years old, his mother shot and killed herself, Barry left to carry her body from the back porch into the house.

HEAD COACH
CHAN GAILEY

On Jerry Jones saying firing him was his singular biggest mistake as owner of the Cowboys:
"First of all, that was very nice of Jerry to say. He was very kind, and Jerry treated us very well while we were there. We just had different philosophies about how to run the football team. I wasn't surprised when I was let go because in my conversations with him I felt like we were on different planes so to speak. So, no, I wasn't surprised."

On his fondest memories of his two seasons in Dallas:
"There are two games that I remember most. The first one we played against Miami on Thanksgiving Day and beat them 20–0. We were playing against Jimmy [Johnson]. That game meant so much to Jerry. I was glad that we could win that game for Jerry. The other one was we came back from 21 [points] down against the Redskins to open the 1999 season. We won it in overtime, and that was an unbelievable feeling. That was great."

There is no Switzer quotation more often repeated than "Some people are born on third base and go through life thinking they hit a triple."

When asked of its definitive meaning many years after his original offering, Switzer said, "Those people born on third base have no idea how hard getting to first base is. They haven't the faintest clue. I do."

By the time of Switzer's departure, many of the familiar faces during the Super Bowl run were no longer wearing the silver and blue, the majority having left via the league's recent change in free agency policy. This list included Alvin Harper, Jay Novacek, Mark Stepnoski, Larry Brown, Russell Maryland, Jimmie Jones, Ken Norton Jr., Dixon Edwards, Robert Jones, and Brock Marion. The signing of Deion Sanders helped Dallas win a Super Bowl, and he was without question among the top talents in the game, but his contract limited the Cowboys in the new salary-cap era.

The Triplets were still present and accounted for, although for the first time since 1989, none of the three earned Pro Bowl honors in 1997.

The offensive line, once the most formidable in the game, was also in transition, longtime mainstay Mark Tuinei playing just six games in 1997 and retiring during the offseason, while Newton, a six-time Pro Bowler with Dallas, signed with the Carolina Panthers after 1998. Guard Larry Allen anchored the unit well into the next decade, but he was the lone mainstay.

Jerry Jones replaced Switzer with former Pittsburgh Steelers offensive coordinator Chan Gailey, who quickly impressed with an 8-3 start en route to 10-6 record and the NFC East Division crown. The season ended in shocking fashion, though, with Arizona defeating the host Cowboys, 20–7, in the first round of the playoffs. Making the loss even more painful was that the Cardinals hadn't won a postseason game in 51 years.

The following campaign, 1999, saw Dallas win its first three games, including a thrilling 41–35 overtime triumph at Washington in the opener, the teams combining for more than 1,000 yards of total offense. Aikman finished the game with 362 yards and a career-high five touchdown tosses, a 76-yarder to Raghib "Rocket" Ismail in the extra session providing the victory.

At 3-0, the Cowboys ventured to Veterans Stadium to face the Philadelphia Eagles on October 10, 1999. This would prove to be the last day Michael Irvin would compete in the game he so much adored.

The play began harmlessly enough, the slant pattern that defined his career, the ball delivered by the man he admired so profoundly. As he fought through a tackle, some eight yards from the line of scrimmage, Irvin lowered his head as Eagles safety Tim Hauck approached.

The world went black when the top of his helmet violently found the cement-like artificial turf. Moments later, team trainers were asking him whether he could cross his legs, to which Irvin replied, "I just did."

The trainers shared a quick glance, and at that instant, Irvin realized he was without feeling in his arms and legs. His thoughts turned to the previous morning, when before leaving for the airport, Irvin was playing catch with his two-year-old son, Michael.

"He was begging me to keep throwing the little ball to him, 'One more time, Daddy! One more time, please, Daddy!'" Irvin said. "So I'm laying on the carpet, thinking about him, that maybe there

SAFETY
DARREN WOODSON

On playing for the Dallas Cowboys:
"Growing up, the Cowboys were always on television, so you knew the players and the history. For me, that was always in my mind when taking the field, the idea that I was a part of something special—a tradition, a history. When you put that uniform on, it was about representing those who wore it before you, men like Randy White and Bob Lilly. Even the guys who established themselves before I was drafted—Troy, Emmitt, Michael—you wanted to honor them as football players. I wanted to give all of myself on the football field for the team and the organization."

On winning three Super Bowls during his first four years in the NFL:
"Yeah, I guess I was a little spoiled there, but that was expected. When you come in as a rookie playing for Jimmy Johnson, that was the expectation. He expected us to win, and that became our mentality. I don't think I ever lost that attitude, but we just didn't have the players and the talent to win at that level later in my career. After we won that third Super Bowl with Barry Switzer, I was thinking we could win another one, but it didn't happen."

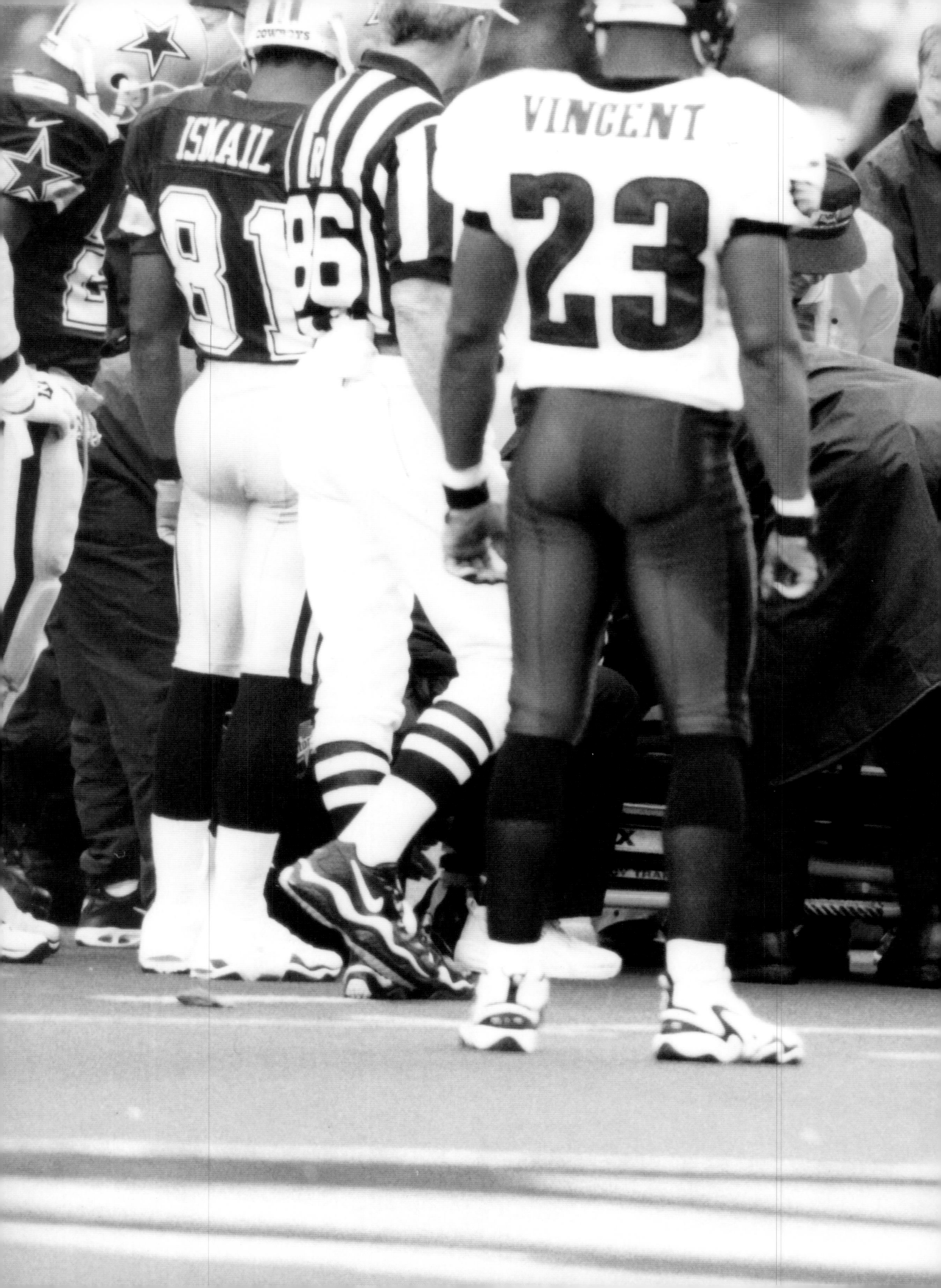
ISMAIL
81
VINCENT
23

EVEN THE EAGLES PLAYERS WERE MORTIFIED BY THE ACTIONS OF THEIR FANS, WIDE RECEIVER CHARLES JOHNSON SAYING, "THE MOST DISGUSTING THING WAS WHEN THE STRETCHER CAME OUT, AND THEY STARTED CHEERING AGAIN."

wouldn't be anymore one more times. I didn't hear the crowd or anything at that point. I was gone, making those deals with God. You know, just let me get up this last time. I'll never do anything wrong the rest of my life.

"I wake up every morning at 5 a.m., wake up my two sons about 15 minutes later, and we work out at 5:45. I can't tell you how much I appreciate those workouts and spending that time with my boys. A day doesn't pass without me thinking about laying on that carpet in Philly."

Jones rode with Irvin from the stadium to the hospital, where he eventually regained feeling within his extremities.

The Philadelphia fans, who once booed Santa Claus, cheered as Irvin lay motionless.

Even the Eagles players were mortified by the actions of their fans, wide receiver Charles Johnson saying, "The most disgusting thing was when the stretcher came out, and they started cheering again. The fans usually end up hating the good athletes, but he's a human being. He has a family and he's getting wheeled off on a stretcher; it puts everything in perspective."

Thing is, everyone was outraged by the fans' reaction except Irvin himself.

"Eagles owner Jeffrey Lurie visited me in the hospital that night; the man is a class act. He apologized, said he was embarrassed. That meant the world to me. You know what, though? I had no problem with what the fans did. I'd been killing their team for 10 years.

"We want passion, but we want to tell passion how far it can go. I'd do anything to beat you. I'd knock my own mother down if she was playing defensive back against me. And that's how Philly fans are."

The spinal cord damage suffered by Irvin was severe enough that at 33 years of age, his brilliant career was finished. The franchise's career leader in receptions and receiving yards, Irvin's impact on the Cowboys was so much more than statistics. Ask 100 players from the 1990s, assistant coaches, the guy who picks up the jockstraps after practice, and to a man they'll say Irvin was the hardest-working player on the team and the unquestioned leader. Make no mistake, the huddle was always commanded by Aikman, but in the locker room, on the sidelines, off the field, this was Irvin's team. He knew every teammate, oftentimes better than said player likely knew himself.

"Michael connected with everyone. He was vocal, obviously, but he was also a fun guy that people enjoyed being around," Newton said. "He always wanted to know every guy, wanted to know their story, their background, their fears, their hopes. There were no rookies or veterans with Michael. We were all just football players.

"He knew which guys responded from a quiet chat away from the team, knew which guys performed best with someone in their face screaming. But he was working all of us, trying to take us to his level. The man didn't sleep, though. He wasn't human."

Darren Woodson tells a story about walking by a window at Valley Ranch, the team's headquarters, and noticing Irvin running sprints on the practice field, not another soul in sight. He was wearing his usual 50-pound weight vest, the one with which he ran to and from high school back in the day, and every two or three sprints, Irvin would drop to a knee and throw up. Never mind it was the middle of July and around 105 degrees outside.

Then there's the time the Cowboys strength and conditioning coach demanded, in fact ordered, Irvin to stop working out so much during the offseason. He was leaving Valley Ranch after 10-, 11-hour days and lifting weights and running on his own at home later that night. So to make sure his orders were followed, he called Irvin's wife one night to check in on Michael, who, of course, was at the time running around his neighborhood in full pads and uniform, helmet and all, with the 50-pound weight vest.

1,196	Yards penalized for the 1999 Cowboys, a single-season team mark.
141	Receiving yards for Jackie Harris in 2001, which was third on the team. Four seasons later, Jason Witten was the Cowboys' third-leading receiver with 757 yards.
109	Degrees at kickoff of the hottest game in Cowboys franchise history, a 41–14 loss to Philadelphia at Texas Stadium on September 3, 2000.

"They all thought I was crazy, but I had that pain coming to me," Irvin said. "You cannot find greatness in this world without pain. The key is learning to control the pain when it comes. I am absolutely positive, without question, that I was damn near death many times when I was working out, but you know what? It would've been an honorable death. Who would've dishonored that death? The hurt was mine, pain is pain, and I wanted to win."

As for his leadership, Irvin lived by just one rule: never show up or disrespect the head coach or the quarterback.

"Those are the untouchables; all 22 starters, every single member of the team needs to know that those two men are in charge," Irvin said. "From a player's standpoint, a coach can't take the time to get to know all the players. You can't lead anybody unless you know what makes them tick, and the only way to know what makes them tick is getting to know them. You have to know what's inside them, and when that happens, you can get ordinary people to accomplish extraordinary things."

To this day, Irvin never wears any of his three Super Bowl rings.

"When you win a ring, you need to remind people that you won one," Irvin explains. "When you win three, people know you won three. That's the difference."

The Cowboys finished 8-8 in 1999 and lost at Minnesota in the wild-card game, leading to a quick exit for Gailey, who posted an 18-14 mark in two seasons. Looking back, considering

Dallas finished 6-10 the year before his arrival and 15-33 the three seasons thereafter, Gailey's efforts are somewhat impressive.

"A coach never feels like a team maximized its potential unless they win the Super Bowl," Gailey recalled shortly after landing his second NFL head-coaching gig with Buffalo in 2010. "And then you go back, watch the film, and find something you could have done better. There's no coach out there that thinks he's done the absolute ultimate job. We were a team in transition. We were an older team transitioning from a veteran team to a younger team.

"And what we were trying to do was win during transitioning, and we were fortunate to be able to win during that time."

The list of candidates to replace Gailey was short, consisting of just two names, both already on staff in defensive coordinator Dave Campo and special teams coach Joe Avezzano. Jones selected Campo, who came to the Cowboys with Jimmy Johnson from the University of Miami as a secondary coach in 1989.

"This is without a doubt the most exciting moment in my entire life," Campo said about his hiring on January 11, 2000.

Shortly thereafter, on February 12, Thomas Wade Landry passed away at 75 years old of leukemia.

"If Coach Landry isn't in heaven, we're all in trouble," Staubach said at the time.

There is really no way of expressing or sharing the incomprehensible impact that Tom Landry had on those who played for him, from Eddie LeBaron, Don Meredith, and Jerry Tubbs in 1960 to Herschel Walker, Michael Irvin, and Nate Newton in 1988. Almost unanimously, they speak of hearing Landry's words more and more after their playing careers. Over 100 former players attended his funeral, including Mike Ditka, who also spent nine seasons as an assistant coach under Landry before leading the Chicago Bears to Super Bowl XX.

"I loved Coach Landry very much," Ditka said. "Everything I believe in as a head coach, I learned from him. He was a great coach but a greater man."

When he addressed his team for the final time on February 27, 1989, Landry broke down in tears, telling his players they would forget about him in two weeks.

"I think of Coach Landry every day," Charlie Waters said recently. "Think about his impact. When President Kennedy was shot in Dallas in 1963, that was it. That was the legacy of the city. Dallas was where our president was assassinated in cold blood.

"Now, the Dallas Cowboys are America's Team. No one should ever underestimate Coach Landry's impact in changing the perception of Dallas."

SAFETY
GEORGE TEAGUE

On tackling Terrell Owens off the Texas Stadium Star in 2000:
"Not too many days pass without someone asking me about that, or just telling me where they were or shaking my hand and saying thank you. You know, every time brings a smile to my face, even though there are positives and negatives from that play. I have to remember that I'm a high school football coach myself now, and your players, your students like to emulate you. I certainly am not condoning the late hit, and I don't want my players running around tackling guys after a touchdown, but regrets? Nah, my only regret is that I didn't hit him harder. I've never spoken to him since. There hasn't been any makeup or anything. Since I was ejected after the hit, we didn't see each other after the game. Guess that would be interesting; couldn't say how that would turn out. We had been having words throughout the game, he wouldn't shut up, and the adrenaline was flowing, and when he went running out there the second time, I just decided enough was enough."

Greg Ellis. ➤

Following pages: George Teague hits Terrell Owens after the 49ers receiver celebrated his touchdown on the midfield star, seen here in the mixed-media art piece "Defender of the Star"; Kicker Tim Seder led the 2000 Cowboys in scoring with 108 total points, which included this touchdown on November 12 against Cincinnati.

Following the end of his tenure with the team, the city of Dallas celebrated Tom Landry Day on April 22, 1989. Informed of the occasion, Landry asked his wife, Alicia, "Do you think anybody will be there?"

More than 100,000 filled the streets.

The fifth decade of the franchise started off in disappointing fashion, the Cowboys winning just five games in 2000. If anything, the singular highlight of the season came in a 41–24 home loss to San Francisco in week 4, which, in and of itself, speaks volumes.

After catching a three-yard touchdown in the second quarter, San Francisco 49ers wide receiver Terrell Owens raced out to the Texas Stadium star at midfield and raised his arms in celebration, football still in tow. Later in the quarter, Emmitt Smith found the end zone and, furious at what he perceived as a blatant lack of respect for the franchise, ran out and slammed the ball on the star while staring at the San Francisco sideline. Come the fourth quarter, Owens caught a second score, and sure enough, headed toward midfield, chased almost immediately by Cowboys safety George Teague, who clocked him from behind and was promptly ejected. As he walked through the Cowboys' sideline, among the first players to slap him on the shoulder and offer appreciation was Smith.

"Many of my teammates knew what I was doing; there was absolutely no disrespect meant. I'll go to my grave saying that," Owens said in 2010. "I was informed beforehand that the hole in the roof at Texas Stadium was so God could watch his favorite team. So I figured this was the best opportunity for me to show my appreciation and thank him personally for my abilities.

"I was saying, 'Thank you, God,' and several players who were around me can verify that. I can't control how it looks from the outside. A number of players supported me at the time, but come Monday, it's a big deal with the networks, a Monday morning quarterback situation."

In 2006 former San Francisco 49ers receivers coach George Stewart confirmed Owens' account to the *Dallas Morning News*.

"Our team chaplain [Earl Smith] began talking about Roger Staubach and how the Cowboys were God's Team and America's Team," Stewart said. "Then he asked Terrell if he knew why there was a hole in the roof. He didn't, so the chaplain told him that it was so God could look down on the Cowboys.

"He said, 'If you score, go to the star and let God see you. Look up to the sky and praise God.' If you'll look at a replay, you'll see that he runs to the star, looks right up, praises God, and then leaves the field."

HEAD COACH
DAVE CAMPO

On coaching America's Team:
"I was invited to this 100th anniversary of the New York Yankees event shortly after I was hired as head coach. They opened the screen up and showed the history of the franchise, and that was the first time I really appreciated how big the job was. I called my wife and said, 'I'm not sure I know what we're getting into here.' In essence, for me, the history and stature of the Yankees and the Cowboys are very similar. I guess, looking back, the biggest thing for me was I went into it a little bit naïve, but at the same time, I really felt we could do some things."

On returning to the Cowboys as a secondary coach in 2008:
"I'm a Cowboy. I always will be loyal and love this organization, and Jerry has been very good to me over the years. I'm not a guy with a big ego obviously, returning as a position coach to the same team [for which] you were the head coach, not to mention defensive coordinator. But when the opportunity arose to return home, I couldn't say no. This is home."

98
Yard fumble recovery touchdown by Greg Ellis against Arizona on October 3, 1999, the longest in club history.

87
Yard interception return touchdown for Greg Ellis against Atlanta on September 20, 1999. Dallas had a bye the following week, meaning Ellis scored in back-to-back games.

5
Members of the NFL's 1990s All-Decade Team who played with the Cowboys: Larry Allen, Michael Irvin, Deion Sanders, Emmitt Smith, and Mark Stepnoski.

0
Touchdowns scored by Greg Ellis in his 160 other games with the Cowboys besides the back-to-back contests in 1999.

CHIEF OPERATING OFFICER AND DIRECTOR OF PLAYER PERSONNEL
STEPHEN JONES

On the presence of football in his life while growing up in Arkansas:
"We grew up with my dad and my grandfather taking me to the Arkansas Razorback games, which was where my love kind of grew for football. Our family really loved the Razorbacks, and we didn't miss any of the games that were in Little Rock. We also made a bunch of the games that were in Fayetteville along the way.

"Then, of course, because of the interest in it, I wanted to play youth football, peewee football. My father was the coach, and went out of his way to do it. Obviously, he enjoyed it, and I loved the fact that he enjoyed it. He was working in Oklahoma at the time even though we were in Little Rock, and he would fly back and forth just to go to practice, and then fly back to work, so it was important to him.

"But that's kind of how it got started. My love and passion for football just grew from there. When I moved over to Little Rock Catholic, which was a really big high school, and ended up starting at quarterback as a sophomore, my father moved his offices so he could watch me practice from his window."

On his father's reaction to his football scholarship to Arkansas:
"Actually, we had a little disagreement on my attending Arkansas. My father wanted me to attend Princeton, and I made pretty good grades in high school, so I was fortunate to be accepted there. The Princeton coach came to our house and definitely wanted me to come up and play for him, but he did point out that I was probably playing in front of larger crowds in high school than I would be at Princeton. And I always had wanted to play at Arkansas, but again, my dad really wanted me to attend Princeton. So we kind of made a deal that he would support me going to Arkansas if I took one of the more challenging majors there, chemical engineering. He wanted to make sure I was academically challenged as well as playing football."

On Jimmy Johnson leaving in March 1994:
"I was surprised. That was one of those times when I was trying to keep the deal together, and at the time the process was going on, Jerry was willing to let it keep rolling. But maybe it had gone too far down the road for Jimmy. I remember Jimmy telling me, 'Hey, I think we'd better back down and keep going down the path that is separate,' but I just hated to see it. I had a good relationship with Jimmy and also understood that their relationship was becoming more and more strained. Obviously, my loyalty and support stood completely with Jerry, and Jimmy understood that. But at the same time, I thought they could get through another year and try for a third straight Super Bowl, because they had some great moments together, and they respected each other immensely. There was and is a tremendous about of respect between Jerry and Jimmy. They accomplished so much for this franchise."

On bringing in Bill Parcells as head coach after the 2002 season:
"I don't want in any way to be disrespectful to Dave Campo, because Dave was our head coach, but we knew that things were tough; we were stringing together multiple tough seasons. We just knew we had to do something that was big if we couldn't get the ship right that year with Dave.

"Bill had popped up along the way. It really heated up when Jerry got the information that Bill would be interested in coming to work here, and that was the thing that really drove me nuts. We've never had a coach that wasn't interested in working with Jerry, and everybody would write that nobody wanted to work with Jerry. We were sold that we could work together; we knew we could. It was a great relationship.

"I was shocked when he stepped down; we really wanted him back, too. When he told me he wasn't going to come back, I was just floored. He really opened our eyes to his philosophies: how you build your team, some philosophies in the draft, some influence in terms of how we pick and how we run a board. He was just a huge asset to this organization. I think he would tell you from afar that he has enjoyed the way we continue to develop this team, and the types of players we pick. Obviously it goes without saying that I have respect for Bill Parcells and the things that he did to help develop me as an executive in the NFL."

> ## "SO THERE I AM WEARING A FULL-LENGTH MINK COAT, THINKING I'M MAKING A STATEMENT, AND TROY WALKS UP TO ME AFTER THE ARRAIGNMENT AND SAYS, 'I'M WITH YOU, BUT YOU'RE REALLY MAKING THIS DIFFICULT ON ME.'"
> —Michael Irvin

At the conclusion of the 2000 season, Troy Aikman's body, although just 34 years old, was battered and brutalized after a dozen NFL campaigns. Never the best of signs after suffering multiple concussions that another injury forces one's retirement, but such was the case with Aikman's back.

Still, talk with those who saw Aikman throw the ball in practice every day, and the stuff of legend flows from each and every account. Leon Lett said, "Troy would complete 20 straight passes during practices, and we're not talking screens."

His final numbers aren't overwhelming, although he finished among the league's top two in completion percentage in five of six seasons from 1991 to 1996. Aikman also won 11 of his first 12 postseason starts, and in the words of Jimmy Johnson, "Troy always played his best in the biggest games. There aren't many quarterbacks who can say that."

Aikman was also the consummate teammate, always lavishing his offensive linemen with gifts at season's end and, more importantly, showing up when it mattered most.

"We always went all-out for my son's birthday parties. We had clowns, the booths, lights, the works," Newton said. "And Troy never missed a party, not once. This is before he was married or had kids, but he always showed up. Now, I was blocking my ass off for him to begin with, I always respected Troy to the highest magnitude, but here he is showing up for my kid's birthday."

When Irvin appeared in court following an arrest in 1996, Aikman was the lone teammate on hand, telling the media, "I'm supporting a friend."

Reminded of the story some 14 years thereafter, Irvin looks away, still emotional of the gesture.

"So there I am wearing a full-length mink coat, thinking I'm making a statement, and Troy walks up to me after the arraignment and says, 'I'm with you, but you're really making this difficult on me,'" Irvin said.

"All I ever wanted was to be Troy's favorite teammate. I always felt connected with him. By our second season together, in 1990, I would leave the line of scrimmage on the snap count before the actual snap. We figured out that from where I lined up, the speed of sound was such that once I heard the word or number that preceded the actual snap count, Troy was calling the snap signal. Teams were always saying I was offside, but I wasn't. Troy and I were just that much in sync."

When told that Roger Staubach, his childhood idol and friend, said Troy would've broken all the NFL passing records if given the opportunity to throw the ball more, Aikman hesitated before offering his response. He fully appreciates that history judges the likes of Dan Fouts and Dan Marino differently than Terry Bradshaw and Bart Starr. The records are nice, but the rings define immortality, whether fair or otherwise.

"Well, first of all it's nice of Roger to say those things," Aikman said. "All we know is what has happened, but I had as much confidence in my ability to put the ball where I wanted to put it as anybody. And there's not a doubt in my mind that had I been in a different system, then the numbers would have been dramatically different. But for some reason, I almost feel as if I'm supposed to apologize for my modest numbers.

"I take exception to that to a certain extent because at the end of the day, the only thing I was paid for was for us to go out and win football games. I feel that I did that, and we did that as well as anybody. I hear often if this particular quarterback had had a defense or if this particular quarterback had a running game then they would have been able to win championships, and maybe they wouldn't have been who they were.

"So I'm who I am because we won championships, and with that it meant that I didn't have to necessarily put up huge numbers, and I don't apologize for that. But I think if given different

RING OF HONOR WIDE RECEIVER
MICHAEL IRVIN

On the impact of football during his childhood:

"I was one of 17 children. We grew up in this little three-bedroom house in Florida. I didn't go to preschool because we had no money. In kindergarten, some of the kids are spelling their names and counting, and I didn't know anything about it. How did they know all these things? So I had tutors those first few years. Then I get to third grade, and my tutor brings a football one day, and we play catch after school. I was catching everything he threw; no matter how hard he threw the football. For the first time in my life, I felt equal or superior, although back then, I had no idea what it was that I was feeling. Football was such an amazing equalizer in my life. I felt inferior during school hours, in the classroom, but not playing ball. I said right then and there, 'This is what I'm going to do for a living,' and that was that. People think that it's about the money. It has absolutely nothing to do with the money. This goes back to the mindset of a little kid, intimidated by the world, playing catch in the third grade."

circumstances and had I been asked to do things differently, then there's no doubt in my mind that I would have been able to do whatever was required."

Four quarterbacks started at least two games for the Cowboys in 2001, none of whom were able to muster a passer rating higher than 63.0. The quartet included Quincy Carter, Anthony Wright, Ryan Leaf, and Clint Stoerner.

For the second of three consecutive seasons, Dallas finished 5-11, with only linebacker Dexter Coakley and Larry Allen earning Pro Bowl nods.

Emmitt Smith broke the most sacred of NFL career marks in style, rushing for 109 yards in a 17–14 loss to Seattle on October 27, 2002. His history-making run—the play was called 15-Lead—was essential Smith: 11 yards behind left guard inclusive of a broken tackle in the fourth quarter. Walter Payton's previous mark—thought unreachable to many considering only Jim Brown had held the title previously, dating back to the 1960s—was 16,726 yards. By the time he was finished, after two seasons with the Arizona Cardinals, Smith's otherworldly rushing total was 18,355 yards. Yet, he has always been underappreciated among the lexicon of the transcendent legends.

"I don't know how many negative plays he's had in his career," New England Patriots head coach Bill Belichick said upon Smith breaking the record. "My guess is it's not too many. He doesn't have bad plays."

Following the season, Campo was fired. Engaging, dedicated, committed, and truly one of the good guys of the NFL, Campo had little hope for success. When reminded of his four starting quarterbacks in 2001, he laughed and said, "Probably a bad sign when Quincy Carter is far and away your best option."

Campo returned to the organization in 2008 as the secondary coach.

"When I had the opportunity to become the head coach, in my mind, I felt that we could overcome whatever situation it was. But yes, I knew we were in a little bit of trouble; there was no question in my mind," Campo recalled. "Although the first year, in 2000, I felt okay going in because we had Troy Aikman, so we still had enough offensive firepower. But then Joey Galloway went down right away, and it didn't work out.

"I was a company man. I still am today. Sure, it was tough because we didn't have any draft picks, we didn't have any money or salary-cap maneuverability, and Jerry would say the same exact thing. You also can't win without a quarterback. From that standpoint, it was tough, but at the same time, I consider myself very fortunate. There are not a lot of people that can say they were the head coach of the Dallas Cowboys, win or lose."

BRAD SHAM
CERTAINLY MEMORABLE

Even for a franchise with a 50-year history of achieving excellence and avoiding the dull, the period from 1997 to 2002 was noteworthy for the Dallas Cowboys.

It wasn't always very good. But it was remarkable.

Start with this: From their founding in 1960 through 1997, the Cowboys had three head coaches.

They matched that in the next five years.

A franchise with a record of overall success unmatched in the football business began a playoff dry spell of club-record proportions in 1997.

The Triplets' reign came to an end.

And the sexiest record in professional football was broken and claimed by a Cowboys' future Hall of Famer.

When the '97 season began, the Cowboys were just a year and a half removed from their third Super Bowl title of the decade and were coming off a game (and a loss) in the divisional playoff. Who knew it would be the last year of Barry Switzer's four-year coaching tenure?

The year 1998 brought Chan Gailey, and 1999 saw him out. Longtime assistant Dave Campo was a popular choice to take the reins in 2000. By the end of '02, after three salary-cap hampered 5-11 seasons, Campo may have been relieved to hand them back.

As much as anything, those of us fortunate enough to be associated with the Cowboys of the '90s will always remember what seems now (not then) as the rapid ascent of the Triplets. We knew they weren't indestructible, but they sure looked it.

That dream was shattered in '99, on October 10 in Philadelphia, when Michael Irvin was carried off the turf, to a chorus of hollow cheers from craven Eagles fans who had tired of seeing the future Hall of Fame receiver beat their team. The list of stomach-turning sights these eyes have seen in 31 seasons in the Cowboys' broadcast booth is pretty small, considering the violent nature of the game. That moment was at the top of the list.

> **THE COMBINATION OF KNOWING IRVIN'S IMPORTANCE TO THE FRANCHISE, THE OBVIOUS SEVERITY OF HIS INJURY, AND THE REACTION OF THE PHILADELPHIA FANS MADE IT A MEMORABLE DAY. NOT GOOD, BUT CERTAINLY MEMORABLE.**

The combination of knowing Irvin's importance to the franchise, the obvious severity of his injury, and the reaction of the Philadelphia fans made it a memorable day. Not good, but certainly memorable.

The end of Troy Aikman's career was the same, only different.

The Hall of Fame quarterback, the captain of the championship ship, started taking a beating in '97. The two-year Gailey administration was hard on Aikman and Irvin, because the head coach brought an offensive approach those two players were convinced wouldn't work. Things got tense (and we're not even talking about the Everett McIver–Michael Irvin training camp haircut mishap in Gailey's first camp in '98).

By 2000 Aikman was done. The all-star fullback, Daryl Johnston, had retired with Irvin because of injuries after '99. The receiving corps was depleted, and the injuries mounted.

Aikman's final game was not spent in uniform, and it's hard to forget. The last game of a dismal 2000 season was on Christmas night in Nashville. Aikman, injured, spent the first half

▲ (clockwise from top left) Brad Sham and Babe Laufenberg in the Cowboys' radio booth; Dave Campo; Daryl Johnston; 1992 NFC Championship pep rally at Texas Stadium.

in our radio booth, watching his toothless team get shut out. I can't recall many times when I've seen someone look more miserable. It was a memorable night. Not good, but certainly memorable.

But life gives us downs so we appreciate the ups. When Emmitt Smith broke the NFL's all-time rushing record at Texas Stadium against Seattle on October 27, 2002, it gave everyone who saw it and knew him goose bumps.

Some of my favorite memories over the years have involved moments not on the field, like the open pep rally at Texas Stadium before the '92 Championship Game. The post-game celebration for Emmitt was one of those.

The now-retired Johnston, working for Fox as a game analyst, was at the stadium to hug his backfield mate on a podium after the game. Seeing the tears stream down Emmitt's face when he saw the all-time rushing leader banner unfurled made a person understand why so much work goes into the game.

That was a memorable day. And a good one.

Brad Sham has broadcast Cowboys games for over three decades, having won eight Katie Awards from the Press Club of Dallas as well as earning Texas Sportscaster of the Year honors 10 times. He was an inaugural inductee into the Texas Radio Hall of Fame in 2002.

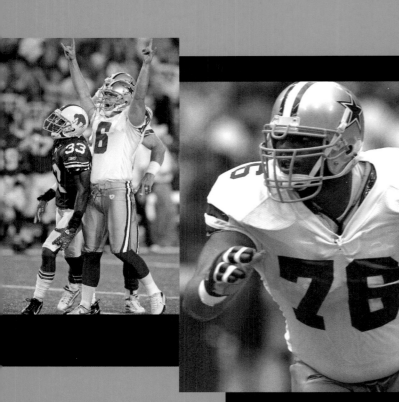

(left to right) Nick Folk; Flozell Adams; Jerry Jones signing Terence Newman; La'Roi Glover; Andre Gurode; Miles Austin; Rob Petitti, Jason Witten, Jose Cortez, and Tony Romo celebrate.

7

THE 'BOYS
ARE BACK

2003–2009 ★★★★★★★

Duane Charles Parcells was finished with coaching. Absolutely, positively, cross-his-heart-and-hope-to-die done. Three years removed from his last days on the sidelines with the New York Jets, there was no reason to doubt him, except that, well, this was Bill Parcells,

and football was his life going back some forty years, except for his family and horses, maybe the occasional baseball game sprinkled in.

There were phone calls from several NFL teams with openings, Parcells saying thanks, but no thanks, I really am retired, although he briefly—as in less than 24 hours—signed on with Tampa Bay in 2002 before having a change of heart. The Pro Football Hall of Fame committee debated electing him in both 2001 and 2002, his merits obviously worthy, but decided against enshrinement as they, too, thought a return was possible. Parcells, long nicknamed the Tuna, admitted his disappointment on both occasions and reiterated that his coaching status was past tense, as in no more.

At least until Elvis and Jerry Jones joined forces at the Teterboro Airport in New Jersey.

"Jerry and I met in his private plane out there at the airport and we're talking about this possibly working," Parcells recalled in 2010. "He asked why now and why the Cowboys, and I told Jerry the story about when Elvis Presley was making his comeback after 10 years in the movies. He decided to do a concert, which was going to be his first one in 10 years, but rather than go around and go to some smaller cities to work his way back into performing, the only thing he did in preparation was a little warm-up with family and friends in Nashville, maybe 100 people or less.

"After that, the next day he went right to the Las Vegas Hilton and he worked what I would call the Big World room. You know how there are lounge acts in Vegas? That's not where Elvis played. So that's what the Dallas Cowboys were to me. It was an opportunity to work in the Big World, and I wanted to play with Elvis."

Nearly 20 years previous, when Parcells was struggling through his first season as an NFL head coach with the New York Giants, he received a pep talk from a man he would one day join as a two-time Super Bowl winner.

"Tom Landry was someone that I looked up to personally and certainly aspired to be like," Parcells said. "He was very good to me on a personal basis when I was starting out

---

LINEBACKER
DAT NGUYEN

On becoming the first player of Vietnamese descent to play in the NFL:
"I really never thought I'd play college football, never mind at Texas A&M. When you factor in my size and background, the odds of me becoming a starting linebacker in the NFL were astronomical. It was definitely a humbling honor to have had the opportunity to be a sort of trendsetter."

On playing for Bill Parcells:
"When he came in, everything changed. Bill just commands a room. I wanted to impress him so much, so I could play in his defense. When he said that I could have played for any of his teams, that meant the world to me."

On being forced to retire at 30 years of age in 2005:
"I just couldn't compete at that level any longer. My body had nothing left after years of beating myself up. There comes a point where you have to step back and say, 'The time has come to step away.' My neck and knees didn't have another football season in them."

with the Giants. When we won three games my first season in 1983, he gave me some much-needed words of encouragement that meant so much. Coaching against him was always a very special experience for me."

On January 2, 2003, in a move that absolutely stunned the majority of those in football, if not every human being who had ever met either Jones or Parcells, the latter became the sixth head coach in franchise history.

"It's understandable to have some down times, but it's inexcusable to let them continue for any length," Jones said.

At the press conference introducing Parcells to the media, Jones added, "I've made a lot of mistakes. You know I have. I'm not going to be careless with this relationship. Frankly, I think the fact that Bill is sitting here says a lot about this organization and what we're willing to do to win. This is a partnership. I want to emphasize that. We're going to make this work."

And make it work Jerry and the Tuna did, the Cowboys winning 10 games that first season and earning a wild-card berth. Not counting the strike-shortened year of 1982, the five-win improvement is the second highest in franchise history, behind the six-game leap Jones and Jimmy Johnson orchestrated after hitting rock bottom in 1989 at 1-15.

After losing the opener to Atlanta, the Cowboys quickly became the talk of the league, winners of five straight behind a superb defense—led by tackle La'Roi Glover, linebackers Dat Nguyen and Dexter Coakley, and hard-hitting safety Roy Williams—strong special teams play, and all the smoke and mirrors the offensive staff, inclusive of future NFL head coaches Sean Payton and Tony Sparano, could muster.

"I can't tell you that I knew coming in what the team's potential was that first season. I knew that there was an unsettled quarterback situation with Quincy Carter and Chad Hutchinson," Parcells said. "I wasn't sure about the situation, but I just tried to go about it the best I could and make the best of what we had. We tried to change the culture as best we could and get going. We caught a few breaks and things kind of went our way in a couple games and we wound up making it through into the tournament."

Carter wasn't bad, throwing for 3,302 yards and running for another 257, but the 21 interceptions didn't exactly endear him to Parcells. The team's success was definitely anchored by the defense, which allowed the fewest yards and first downs in the NFL.

Not even a 29–10 loss at Carolina in the playoffs dampened the rejuvenation of the franchise.

DEFENSIVE TACKLE
LA'ROI GLOVER

On the change in culture in 2003:
"Bill Parcells comes in and there's going to be a lot of accountability, player-coach- and player-player-wise. We immediately felt we had an opportunity to win and challenge for a playoff berth, which seems strange after finishing 5-11 in 2002, but that's what Bill brings. Everyone on the team was pulling in the same direction. Also, there's no question the talent increased as well. We brought in Terry Glenn at wide receiver, and he brought so much to the team, on and off the field, and Terence Newman was able to start as a rookie."

On his four straight Pro Bowl nods:
"For me, the biggest thing was always technique. I was always one of the smallest tackles in the league, so I had to become a student of the game, study all my opposing linemen, know which direction they were pulling on runs as opposed to passes. I would study film so much I would recognize formations and know the guard was pulling, meaning the play would come through a certain gap. To achieve the level of success I strived for, at my size, my technique and game preparation had to be almost perfect."

WIDE RECEIVER
TERRELL OWENS

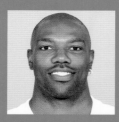

On signing with the Cowboys:

"That was exciting for me. Obviously the fans hated me when I was performing for San Francisco and Philadelphia and had beat their team in a number of situations, but I think for the most part, they were buzzed about me coming to play for the Cowboys, America's Team. I know the team was looking for an explosive player in its offense, and I felt I could bring that."

On Bill Parcells:

"Bill always calling me 'the player' didn't bother me. That was more of a big issue for the media. I knew his makeup. I knew he used tactics with his players, tried to get under their skin, but I didn't have a problem with it. I also had no problem with him. I went into the relationship open-minded. Jerry did pull me aside after we signed the contract and said Bill wasn't thrilled with me being there. But the first time I spoke with Bill, in his office, he said that while we had both heard things about each other, he was looking forward to working together. I'm not sure if he was being untruthful, but I left his office excited to play for him."

Asked recently if training camps under Parcells were as brutal as players often recalled, Glover laughed and said, "As tough as people say, yeah, and then some. And then some more. There were no excuses. They didn't exist. But there were many sides to Bill. He had a great sense of humor, was always making us laugh, and he really tried to relate to each player. He also had all these sayings, expressions, and stories. Now that I'm retired, many of them are starting to make sense. I find myself thinking of stuff he said all the time. It was an honor playing for him."

For a bevy of reasons, the Cowboys released Carter early in the 2004 preseason with Parcells turning to his former signal caller with the Jets, 41-year-old Vinny Testaverde. In a campaign with few highlights, showing perhaps just how remarkable the previous season was, Dallas finished just 6-10. Among the lone bright spots was the emergence of second-year tight end Jason Witten, who earned Pro Bowl honors behind a team-high 87 receptions, which also represented a franchise record for the position at the time.

A third-round pick out of Tennessee in 2003, Witten is equal parts pass catcher and blocker in an era where the majority of tight ends are basically an extension of the wide receivers. Parcells took an immediate liking to him, but rather than praise him in any way, shape, or form, he challenged him.

"Coming into a franchise like the Cowboys that had had a lot of success with tight ends, it was such a neat opportunity to take that platform built by Billy Joe DuPree, Doug Cosbie, and Jay Novacek and try and take it to another level," Witten said. "Those guys set such a high standard here that the fans are knowledgeable about the position and expect their tight ends to block and catch. Coach Parcells does, too.

"He tried to break me for four months—literally, for four months he tried to break my will—and what happened is that he realized I was a tough guy and that I was his guy. At that time, I also realized that, hey, this legendary coach believes in me. That's why he's pushing me to places I didn't know existed.

"I have to give Bill so much credit. He coached some of the best, guys like Mark Bavaro and Ben Coates, and he really challenged me to become a better blocker. I think his mentality is 'if this guy has talent physically, then I can develop him and see how tough he is, whether or not he's going to give me everything that he has. When he realizes the answer is yes, we're fine.'

"When that moment happened, it was like, man, this guy believes in me now, and when I had that, every day when I came to work I just wanted to soak up everything that he knew about this game, about playing tight end. To have reached that point with Bill was really special."

Among the plethora of problems in 2004 was the absence of team leader Darren Woodson, who was diagnosed with a herniated disk before the first kickoff of the preseason. One of the most respected players in team history, and the last man standing from each of the three Super Bowl wins of the 1990s, Woodson retired that December. His final tally included a franchise-record 1,350 tackles.

"Darren is the greatest team player I've coached at any level," Dave Campo said. "As good of a human being as I have ever been around, and just an outstanding football player. He should be in the Ring of Honor and the Pro Football Hall of Fame, without question. I can't put enough superlatives on Darren Woodson."

The Cowboys appeared headed for another postseason, or as Parcells calls it, "the tournament," in 2005, winning 7 of 10 behind quarterback Drew Bledsoe, the backfield duo of Julius Jones and rookie Marion Barber, veteran receivers Terry Glenn and Keyshawn Johnson and Witten at the skill positions, Larry Allen still anchoring the line and a balanced defense. However, an overtime loss to Denver on Thanksgiving proved the first of four defeats down the stretch, leading to a disappointing 9-7 record and a third-place finish in the NFC East.

Following pages (left to right): Keyshawn Johnson, Terry Glenn, and Jason Witten.

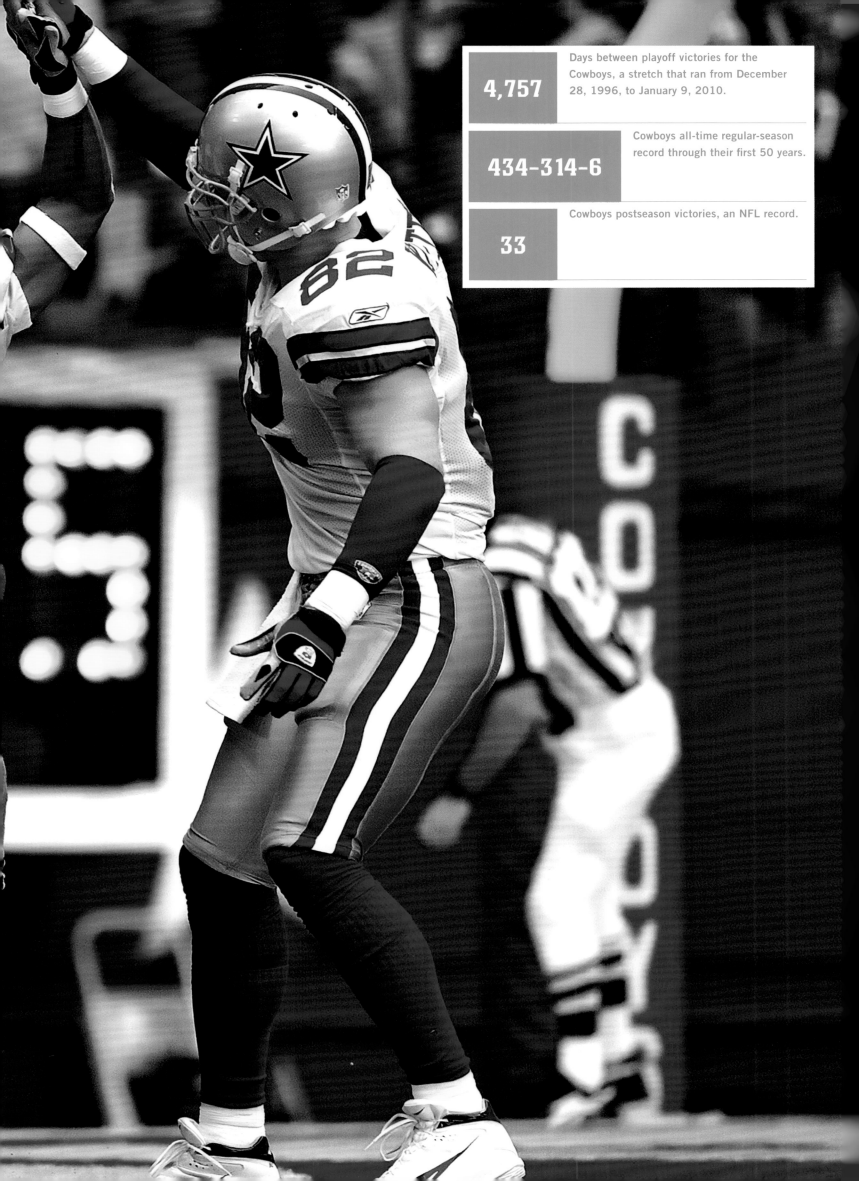

4,757 Days between playoff victories for the Cowboys, a stretch that ran from December 28, 1996, to January 9, 2010.

434–314–6 Cowboys all-time regular-season record through their first 50 years.

33 Cowboys postseason victories, an NFL record.

AT THE TIME, FOR THE MOST PART, ROMO WAS SIMPLY AN ATHLETE PLAYING THE QUARTERBACK POSITION. HE WAS ACTUALLY A BETTER BASKETBALL PLAYER AND GOLFER IN HIGH SCHOOL.

Bledsoe was at the helm once again in 2006, at least for the first six games. While few realized it at the time, since the preseason Parcells had been talking himself into handing the reins to an undrafted free agent from Eastern Illinois, and at halftime of a home game against the New York Giants, on *Monday Night Football* no less, the keys were handed to Tony Romo.

He was equal parts reckless and brilliant, throwing for 227 yards, two touchdowns, and three interceptions in two quarters of the 36–22 loss. But the energy at Texas Stadium was feverish as Romo raced around the pocket with an abandon not seen since, well, unfair or not, Roger Staubach.

"You just recognize that it's time to do something; that things aren't going to get better the way they are, and that was the time without question," Parcells said.

In his first NFL start six days later, Romo threw for 270 yards in an easy 35–14 road win at Carolina. Recalling that game in the spring of 2010, Romo said, "I think you always hope and you always believe, but you always have differing doubts that say, 'Am I good enough to do this?' You think you are, you think you have the ability, but you never really know until you go there and prove it. Not just to yourself, but to your teammates and coaches."

The ensuing six weeks were the stuff of fairy tales. This kid from nowhere, who started on the practice squad and was barely seen or heard in his three previous seasons with the Cowboys, became a household name overnight, and not only among the fandom. Romo was the talk of the NFL with Dallas winning five of his first six starts. As the country watched on Thanksgiving, Romo threw for 306 yards and five touchdowns in a dominant 38–10 defeat of Tampa Bay.

"I think any time a young player goes in, you have to be a little bit surprised. But he had spent quite a bit of time getting ready for that opportunity," Parcells said. "It wasn't like he was a first-year player. Yeah, I think I was surprised a little bit, but it was a pleasant surprise, and I wasn't astounded by it. I think things went kind of according to plan."

When he was finishing his NFL playing days as a backup with the New York Giants, Jason Garrett remembers his offensive coordinator, Sean Payton, telling him about this quarterback from Eastern Illinois, his alma mater.

"I had known about Tony for a while. Sean was always talking about him, about how he was a scratch golfer and possessed all these interesting traits, and he thought Tony could be a player," Garrett said.

At the time, for the most part, Romo was simply an athlete playing the quarterback position. He was actually a better basketball player and golfer in high school. When he went undrafted in 2003, Payton, now with the Cowboys, recommended signing him.

QUARTERBACK
TONY ROMO

On becoming the starting quarterback in 2006:
"I owe Bill Parcells a lot because that's a very hard decision to make, especially with a guy as talented as Drew [Bledsoe] was. Drew had a great NFL career, and people sometimes forget a little bit, but he's been all the way at the top. So I think for someone in Bill's position, who had coached him—he had gone to a Super Bowl with this guy—that's not an easy decision to make. Let's be honest, that call took a lot of balls. To do it that early in the year, it was a situation where not everybody would have done it, so I owe Bill a lot for what I've accomplished. And in a lot of other ways, too, I wouldn't be where I am today without Bill Parcells."

On dealing with criticism:
"Bill talked about it with me before he left. He told me I had to have a turtle shell, let stuff just bounce off and move on, because if you let it affect you day in and day out, you're destined for a life of solitude. You can use it as motivation, but you can't think that other people know more about what's going on with this team than you do."

Outside of his holding responsibilities and running the scout team, those first few seasons were spent invisibly, although Romo made noticeable progress under the tutelage of Payton and Parcells.

"Bill understands different people's mentality. He knew I was competitive, and he knew that when I go out to practice, I treat it like a game in my approach," Romo said. "He also knew that there was a whole other side that I never really learned, as far as the mental side of the game that's outside the realm of competing. It's the things you have to do to be at your best to compete. I think with Bill, he tapped into that a little bit with the sense of allowing you to know that the game isn't just won or lost because you necessarily care a lot. It's all the preparation and time you have to put in.

"I needed to think what the defenses and what different people were thinking out on the field instead of just my own game. There's so much that goes into it. I needed to understand which of my teammates do things well. Some of them do different things better than others, and I had to start thinking, 'Okay, this guy is different from that guy.' I had to start understanding that I had to help everyone else around me and it's not just about me. I was always under the impression that if I just keep improving and keep getting better myself, everything takes care of itself. But to take that next step, a quarterback needs to help everybody else around him.

"Bill possessed a great understanding of that and allowed me to start to think just outside of the small little bubble of my own thought process each day. I needed to think about the group."

Despite starting just the final 10 games of the season, Romo was selected to the Pro Bowl in 2006. Alas, he also suffered the most painful of defeats, as he dropped the snap on a potential game-winning field goal at Seattle in the playoff opener. The Cowboys lost, 21–20.

"I stood on the podium after the Seattle game and told everybody it was my fault because it was," Romo said. "That loss was on me. It's one of those things where there are a lot of plays and blah, blah, blah, but the percentage goes way up that we would have won that football game if I had held on to the football. I felt bad for our team, I felt bad for Coach Parcells, I felt bad for a lot of people who worked hard to be in that position and deserved to win."

For Parcells, the loss would be the last for him as head coach of the Dallas Cowboys, saying at the time, "Physically, I could still do it. But mentally, this is a 12-month-a-year job and I've been doing it since 1964. It was time to stop. I just have to let go."

While his ultimate goal of becoming the first coach to lead three franchises to the Super Bowl fell short, Parcells was instrumental in returning the Cowboys to the forefront of the NFL. In the three seasons before his arrival, Dallas was 15-33, scoring 14 or fewer points 25 times. Since then, through 2009, the club was 67-45, having won

QUARTERBACK AND OFFENSIVE COORDINATOR
JASON GARRETT

On Troy Aikman:

"I never learned more from a quarterback or coach than I did from Troy. I was always watching and listening to him. Here was a first-ballot Hall of Famer, and I knew that when I was playing with him, and I was able to watch him in the meetings, on the practice field, during games. He had such a great approach to playing the position. He kept everything really simple, which allowed him to be decisive. He always did the most important things well. This was an education like no other for not only an aspiring quarterback, but also a future coach. Much of what I teach our quarterbacks now can be traced back to Troy."

On Tony Romo:

"He is a very natural competitor. He is not afraid of the moment, he enjoys playing, he enjoys the challenge that comes with it. He enjoys all of that and you see that when he plays. I think that this is really important for all players but really important for great quarterbacks. I think that all great quarterbacks have that trait. What follows from that is the desire to be great. "

at least nine games in six of seven seasons. He also left behind a collection of young players who crafted their talents under his watch, the likes of Romo, Witten, and linebacker DeMarcus Ware, the team's first-round pick in 2005.

"I knew of his past and what type of coach he was," Ware said. "It was a constant mind game with Coach Parcells. He needed to know you were listening to him. You needed to know the answer to any question he could ask you. Coach worked with me individually as a pass rusher all the time, always telling me about Lawrence Taylor and their relationship. He talked about how great of a pass rusher he was, the best to ever play. He wanted me to have the goal of reaching what Lawrence Taylor was on the football field from the first day we met.

"I appreciate him now, and even when he was here I did. Yes, he was hard on me, but he came to me, told me about football, about the past, about how things should be done, about the right way of doing things, and as a young guy, I needed that. I needed that guidance from my coach; I wanted it. I wanted to learn, soak, absorb as much as I could from him."

Among the most accomplished defensive coaches of his generation, Wade Phillips was the hire to replace Parcells. He produced immediate success, too, the Cowboys tying a franchise record with 13 wins in 2007 behind Romo (4,211 yards, 36 touchdown passes), Witten (96 catches), and wide receiver Terrell Owens, who racked up 1,355 receiving yards. A record 13 players were named to the Pro Bowl, including left tackle Flozell Adams, center Andre Gurode, and defensive end Greg Ellis. Yet again, though, postseason success eluded Dallas, a shocking 21–17 home defeat to the New York Giants the team's sixth straight playoff loss.

The final season of Texas Stadium brought another disappointing finish, the Cowboys losing three of their last four including a brutal 44–6 setback at Philadelphia in Week 17 that cost Dallas a playoff berth. After the game, Romo told the media, "If this is the worst thing that ever happens to me, then I'll have lived a pretty good life."

First off, while some in the media and among the fans were bothered by Romo's comments, honestly, if losing a football game is the worst moment of anyone's life, that's not a bad run. Still, the words weren't an indication of Romo's competitive spirit, not in the least.

"The reality of it is the game was over when the fourth quarter started, so I sat down on the sidelines and thought about everything," Romo said. "You're dealing with your emotions throughout the game, and I have to figure out a way to somehow make this okay in my brain. You end up talking yourself into it a little bit; that's where the quote came from in terms of my thought process.

HEAD COACH
BILL PARCELLS

On his decision to step down after losing at Seattle in the playoffs:
"Well, that last game was a very, very, very disappointing loss for me and the Cowboys, and sometimes the resignation of 'well, it's another offseason or a regular season'—just all the things that are in front of you, just to get to that opportunity again—they kind of weigh on you a little bit. I would say my energy level at that time was a little bit diminished, and after thinking about it for a little while, I thought it might just be a good time. Retrospectively, I think I did the right thing. They won a lot of games the next year and, quite frankly, I was glad to see that because at least you know some of the work that you did kind of helped them a little bit. Not that I'm taking any credit for that next year because I'm not, but I just feel like some of the work we did helped."

On Jason Witten:
"I'd put him right there with the best I've coached: Mark Bavaro and Ben Coates. Jason came in with better knowledge of the passing game than either of them, and he's gone on to do a tremendous job."

Following pages: Wade Phillips signs his contract as Stephen Jones, Jerry Jones, and Wade's father, legendary coach Bum Phillips, look on.

HEAD COACH
WADE PHILLIPS

On his father, Bum:

"My dad was a high school football coach when I was growing up. To see my dad, I had to go to the field house where he worked after school because he didn't come home until real late and he left real early. I played for my father in high school—quarterback and linebacker. He said, 'Not only do I have to know you're better but all the players on the team and all the coaches have to know you're better for you to be able to play.' Our coach-player relationship was different than our father-son relationship, and that's the way I expected it. My dad treated me like a player when he was coaching me and like a son away from the field."

On coaching with Buddy Ryan:

"He's actually a likeable guy. I met him just here and there being in the NFL 10 years with my father in Houston and New Orleans, and when he got the head-coaching job with the Eagles, he called and asked me to be his defensive coordinator. The 46 was a different defense than what everybody was playing, so it gave me an opportunity to get in on the ground floor. We use aspects of the 46 in our defense in Dallas."

"The next two weeks, I couldn't sleep, I couldn't do anything, I just sat there and replayed every play, trying to figure out why I wasn't as good as I thought I could possibly be one day and what was keeping me from taking that next step.

"And then one day, you wake up and say 'BAM!' Now's the time to start, now is another moment, and I'm going to take this opportunity to decide I'm going to do this better. I'm going to go out and work on this extra so that it will never happen again, and it doesn't mean you're never going to lose again, but what happens is you find yourself a better player the next time you're in that situation."

The conclusion of the 2008 campaign also represented the third and final season of Owens in Dallas. He caught 38 touchdown passes over that stretch and was responsible for nearly as many off-the-field headlines, but that was T.O. When asked in the spring of 2010 of his release by the Cowboys, Owens said he was shocked.

"I didn't believe it. I knew for a fact they would not release me," Owens said. "Are you kidding me? The decision certainly wasn't performance based, that's for sure.

"I missed my friends, missed the direction the team was headed, missed the opening of the new stadium. I felt like we were close, especially to making a push in the playoffs. I was preparing for a deep run with Dallas in 2009. I'm not going to lie. I couldn't help but look at the scoreboard during games last year, see how they were doing. I'm sure some of them were keeping an eye on me, too.

"I still really don't have any thoughts on what happened. I know people think I was released because of Tony and a couple of other people. I guess people change, things change, but I was always for Tony, 100 percent. When I cried while defending him after the playoff loss to the Giants, I mean, I don't cry for other dudes. Those emotions don't come for no reason. I felt like a big brother to Tony; that's where those emotions came from. I truly loved him as a person and as a quarterback."

By all accounts, the decision to release Owens was among the more difficult of the last 21 years for Jones, in part because the two had developed a strong bond away from the football field.

"We covered a lot of ground; I really felt like we shared a great friendship," Owens said. "I would sit on the couch in his office and we'd talk for hours about business, football, and our personal lives. He told me about how he grew up and how he came to buy the Cowboys. Jerry got to see a personal side of me not too many people in this world know. I have nothing but respect and love for Jerry Jones. He's a beautiful man."

The 50th season of America's Team coincided with the debut of Cowboys Stadium, a spectacular structure that drew rave reviews from one and all. On the field, Dallas appeared headed for another disappointing finish after a 20–17 home loss to San Diego in Week 14 dropped the club to 8-5 with a road date at undefeated New Orleans looming. However, thoughts were elsewhere early in the fourth quarter when Ware, after a violent collision with a Chargers lineman, was immobilized on a stretcher and carted off the field with a neck injury. The haunting image reminded many of Michael Irvin's final game at Veterans Stadium just 10 years earlier.

"Lying on the turf, I'm thinking I'm a big, strong guy with all this ability, but I couldn't get up. I wasn't able to feel anything, I wasn't able to move; that's when you start getting scared," Ware recalled. "What's going to happen to me? Am I ever going to play again? Then they started taking my facemask off, and I thought it was going to be the last time I was going to play football. There were tears in my eyes.

"On any given play, you can be lying there and it's done. Your career is finished. People fail to realize that that's the reason we play the way we do. When they say to play as if it is your last play every play, you could be playing one week or playing for 20 years. You don't know what your destiny is."

Ware, who was walking later that night having suffered just tissue damage and swelling, received a phone call the next morning from Irvin.

"I already knew about his situation, and we talked about the emotions of lying on the field and the emotions of that moment. It was some heavy stuff," Ware said. "I told him I was fine to play the next day, but that I was scared to hit somebody. I didn't want to hurt myself. I didn't want to hurt someone else, either. I have a family, I have a daughter, I have all those things. Now what do I do? Michael really helped me deal with some of those emotions."

The season on the line, Ware played that Saturday night and was spectacular, recording two sacks and two forced fumbles as the Cowboys stunned the previously undefeated Saints, 24–17. They finished the regular season with back-to-back shutouts of Washington and Philadelphia and won the NFC East crown, their second in three years under Phillips.

A 34–14 trouncing of the Eagles in the opening round of the playoffs followed, the first postseason victory for the Cowboys since 1996.

The late-season success helped take some of the unwarranted criticism off Phillips and Romo. Phillips guided a defense that allowed the second-fewest points in the NFL, while his record in his first three years with Dallas was 33-15. Overall, his career mark of 81-54 through 2009 equated to a 60.0 winning percentage, which makes him

LINEBACKER
DeMARCUS WARE

On playing at Troy University:
"I didn't even play football my sophomore year of high school because I wasn't good enough. I played baseball and basketball and ran track. I played as a junior, played a little bit of quarterback, then I moved to wide receiver and played linebacker on defense. I was never a big guy. I graduated high school at six foot one, about 190 pounds. Troy was the only school to offer me a scholarship and that was only because a few of my friends were there and convinced the coach I was a good enough athlete. I never received a single recruiting letter from anyone. There weren't any phone calls, nothing. I mean, Division I-AA, Division II, Division whatever, Troy was the only college who ever talked to me about playing college football. When I got there, they tried me at defensive end and that wasn't good, so we tried linebacker. Each year I got better, I got a little bigger, especially with the freshman 15, but I still wasn't that fast. That came later. Then suddenly, here I am running a 4.5 my senior year at 240 pounds. By the Scouting Combine, I was 255 and running a 4.4."

COWBOYS STADIUM
2009

Make no mistake, Cowboys Stadium is indeed the vision of owner Jerry Jones. In a process that was over 15 years in the making, he was involved from the early architectural drawings to the final decorative additions seen in the suites. Start to finish, top to bottom, inside and out, Jones was there.

And, while items like the world's largest video board and the priceless works of art hanging throughout help make a trip to Cowboys Stadium an unforgettable experience, its true signature landmarks, and perhaps Jones' greatest decision, are the massive arches that serve as the foundation for the entire structure.

"The contour of the roof that Jerry wanted to have, and to not lose the 35 years of tradition that the Cowboys had with the hole in the roof, dictated that the roof needed to have a curve to it," said John Dixon, executive vice president of special projects for Manhattan Construction. "Jerry liked the full arch, so from the very beginning it became an engineering feat to figure out what kind of foundation to put under a quarter-mile span."

Although an arch is actually one of the strongest elements that can be used, the question became, could one be created that big? Each arch would weigh over 6.5 million pounds and would hold nearly 20 million pounds of thrust, figures that were literally unheard of in a building of this type.

Dixon recalled with a laugh a meeting that took place at the stadium site early in the development with a group that included head engineer Dave Platten. Upon looking out and seeing the abutments that would hold the arches on either end, Platten said, "Oh my God, look at that span. I sure hope this works."

"We said, 'Dave you're the guy that designed it. Don't even think like that,'" said Dixon. "I think even he was apprehensive for a little bit."

The process began at a mill in Luxembourg of all places, the only plant in the world that could produce the strength of steel needed for such a project. The raw steel was shipped to New Orleans, then loaded on a train bound for Oklahoma City, a company there cleaning, cutting, fabricating, and finally painting the massive pieces. Eventually, each section was trucked down to the job site in Arlington, where only then could they finally be connected. In all, the process took 10 months to complete.

"A foot of each beam weighs 782 pounds," said Dixon. "They cut off slivers, had them chrome-plated, and gave one to Jerry. Just that quarter-inch sliver was a 50- to 60-pound weight."

Even before the arches could be erected, though, the four abutments had to be created to hold the structures and withstand the gigantic thrust. While fans can see over 500 cubic yards

> # "THE CHALLENGE IS MEETING AND EXCEEDING THE EXPECTATIONS OF OUR FAN BASE, WHICH ARE HIGH, AS THEY SHOULD BE."
>
> —Jerry Jones Jr.

EXECUTIVE VICE PRESIDENT AND CHIEF SALES AND MARKETING OFFICER
JERRY JONES JR.

On his earliest football memories:
"There was this picture of my parents at my grandparents' house. My father was in his Arkansas Razorbacks uniform. I remember him telling me the story. It was right before a home game, and he had run out of the locker room before the game to sell his player tickets. He ran over to see my mother, who he was dating at the time, and they took that picture. I just remember asking him about that picture when I was really young, before I even understood anything about football.

"Razorbacks games were a huge family event for us growing up, for both sides of the family—cousins, grandparents, everyone went. Football itself was highly emphasized for me at an early age."

On first hearing the news, when he was a freshman at Georgetown, that his father bought the Dallas Cowboys:
"I was studying in the library for a philosophy exam. I have no idea why I remember that, maybe from just telling the story before. So I get back to my dorm room—and this is back in the day when you had to rewind the answering machine before hitting the play button—and it was my dad on the phone. He says, 'I wanted to call you and let you be the first one to know that I just bought the Dallas Cowboys.' And you can hear my mother screaming in the background, 'Don't tell him on the answering machine, Jerry.' It was pretty funny. I figured he'd be staying up late, so I called him back, and he was still up. But yeah, the first time I heard was on the answering machine."

On being 1,500 miles away at Georgetown during the first three seasons his father owned the Cowboys:
"I was so removed from the criticism my father was dealing with. I mean, most people around campus, even some of my friends, had no idea my family owned the Cowboys. There was definitely no heckling about it. I do remember one guy saying, 'I had no idea your family was worth $14 million to even buy the Cowboys,' and I just smiled rather than saying add another zero onto that. My freshman year, we could never get tickets for Redskins games. A few of us tried almost every home game to find even two, but it was impossible. Then my sophomore year, my father's team is playing at RFK. That was surreal."

On selling suites and seats in the middle of the worst economic recession since the Great Depression:
"We were fortunate to have started the process early enough, in part because we knew of the magnitude and importance of the sales aspect of it, so that when the stock market crashed, and we realized we were in the midst of one of the most difficult economic times in our country's history, we were pretty far down the road. We were a long way with our sponsorship sales, the majority of the suite sales were finished, and while ticket sales had barely just begun, we were optimistic on that front. We really never wavered from our original plan marketing-wise, although we were definitely sensitive to the change in our economic culture."

On the future of merchandising and marketing for the Dallas Cowboys:
"Obviously, as far as our brand, the Dallas Cowboys, we're fortunate. The challenge is meeting and exceeding the expectations of our fan base, which are high, as they should be. Take the new stadium. We wanted the highest level of technology available. We want to be cutting edge, not necessarily saddles and cowboy hats. We're an entertainment business at the end of the day.

"As far as merchandising, we now have our own warehouse headquarters. The night of the 2010 NFL Draft, we drafted Dez Bryant around 10 p.m., and by 11:30 we had 1,000 or so of his jerseys ready to ship. There were people walking around that next day with Dez Bryant rookie jerseys with his name and number on the back."

one of 15 head coaches (minimum 10 seasons) since 1960 to have won at least 60 percent of his games. The only others active on that list entering the 2010 season were Bill Belichick and Andy Reid.

"I know those things and I also know people don't want to hear about it," Phillips said. "It's always tough to follow a legend. Tony has gone through it as well with Staubach and Aikman, and I'm coming in behind Tom Landry, Jimmy Johnson, and Bill Parcells.

"We all heard it every day; how we hadn't won a playoff game in 13 years. Well, I haven't been here 13 years. I'm proud of what we've done here and think we are on the verge of something pretty special."

As for Romo, he was 38-17 as a starter and headed into the 2010 season with the third-highest quarterback rating (minimum 50 starts) in the history of the National Football League behind only Steve Young and Philip Rivers.

"It's one of those things where you're never going to live up to the expectations of the position of Dallas Cowboys starting quarterback until you win the Super Bowl," Romo said. "And it's kind of a good problem to have in the sense that you get way too much credit when you're the quarterback here if you're winning and winning championships, but you also probably get the other side of the coin when you're losing.

"The thing about it is if you win, you probably don't want to win anywhere else but here. It's a great challenge; it's a great motivational factor. And we're close, too. I really feel [in 2009] we made the leap, won that first playoff game. I think we're ready."

Ready to start creating those indelible memories that endure for generations, the kind celebrated within these very pages. And while there's always hope among the Dallas Cowboys' faithful that the next half century will be as satisfying and successful as the last 50 years, it will not be easy to top the utterly implausible, that of a winless expansion team captivating the imagination and hearts of a nation and earning the moniker of America's Team.

TIGHT END
JASON WITTEN

On Tony Romo, his friend:

"We were on the same shuttle bus from the airport to the hotel for the rookie weekend minicamp, the very first one after the draft. Just me, him, and the driver, the only ones on the shuttle bus. So I asked him if he wanted to grab a pizza and he said, 'Yeah, let's go.' Right then, it had nothing to do with football. Honestly, I had no clue who he was, and I'm pretty sure he had no clue who I was, and then from there it just clicked. From there, it was just a couple of football players saying we were going to do this together because it was tough being the young guys, the guinea pigs. We have kind of the same personalities and we enjoy a lot of the same hobbies, so it's been good to see that grow."

On Tony Romo, the quarterback:

"Even when he was on the practice squad, he always had this rare ability to make things happen, when it just seemed like everything else broke down around him. I don't know if I ever realized he would be this good, especially how quickly he reached that elite level, but there is something in Tony that not many others have, an inner strength, where you knew success would happen for him."

PAUL TAGLIABUE

THE COWBOYS' VISIONARY LEADER

For 50 years, extraordinary owners and chief executives have led the Dallas Cowboys. Clint Murchison, Tex Schramm, and, of course, Jerry Jones and his family, who over the past two decades have been the leaders of the Cowboys, taking a unique enterprise—and making it better.

It was my privilege to collaborate with these exceptional people for almost four decades. From 1989, when Jerry acquired the Cowboys and I became NFL commissioner, until 2006 when I left the position, we worked together closely.

Jerry excels in all he does, both leading the Cowboys and contributing to the success of the NFL. In doing so, he has continued on a path initially cut by prior Cowboys owners.

During my time as commissioner, Jerry played a critical leadership role in increasing the revenue pie throughout the 1990s, which created conditions for labor peace with the NFL's players. He helped the league expand its presence internationally and assisted with the financing and building of stadiums in the late 1990s and the current decade.

A thinker, challenger, and innovator, Jerry understands foremost how rapidly technology, demographics, and other underlying forces constantly change the business of sports. He also knows that even the most successful operations have to aggressively pursue transformative innovations and change. The new Cowboys Stadium is an example of this vision as both a regional development project and a revolutionary stadium design.

> **A THINKER, CHALLENGER, AND INNOVATOR, JERRY UNDERSTANDS FOREMOST HOW RAPIDLY TECHNOLOGY, DEMOGRAPHICS, AND OTHER UNDERLYING FORCES CONSTANTLY CHANGE THE BUSINESS OF SPORTS. HE ALSO KNOWS THAT EVEN THE MOST SUCCESSFUL OPERATIONS HAVE TO AGGRESSIVELY PURSUE TRANSFORMATIVE INNOVATIONS AND CHANGE.**

In 2004 I traveled to Texas to meet with Jerry and support his innovative plan. His concept was that the new stadium would be between Dallas and Fort Worth in Arlington near the Texas Rangers' ballpark and would create an extraordinary sports complex and regional entertainment hub.

When I arrived on that Saturday, the Cowboys took me to a youth football rally in support of the new stadium, where I met with hundreds of parents and kids supporting Cowboys Youth Football programs.

I then attended the game on Sunday and spoke on the Dallas Cowboys' radio network in strong support of the extraordinarily cutting-edge stadium and the sharing of the cost between the Cowboys and the public authorities in a very strong public-private partnership.

The trip continued on Monday, when I was the keynote speaker at a civic luncheon in Fort Worth. A large crowd of several thousand people turned out, all wildly enthusiastic in support of the new stadium and its location between Dallas and Fort Worth.

Today, the stadium in Arlington is not only home to football but is one of the world's premier sports and entertainment venues. It is a magnificent state-of-the-art facility with the world's largest high-definition video board as the centerpiece, giving fans the ultimate in-stadium experience.

▲ (clockwise from top left) Banner for the "Vote Yes" election effort; Arlington Mayor Robert Cluck, Stephen Jones, and Jerry Jones making the project official; Mayor Cluck and Jerry Jones at the grand opening of Cowboys Stadium; President George W. Bush with the coin toss at the first regular-season game played at Cowboys Stadium.

In just its first season, Cowboys Stadium set an NFL regular-season attendance record (105,121) and hosted marquee events including the NBA All-Star Game, the AT&T Cotton Bowl Classic, soccer tournaments, boxing matches, and concerts. In addition, Super Bowl XLV will be played at Cowboys Stadium—North Texas' first ever Super Bowl—as will the 2014 NCAA Men's Final Four.

This was Jerry's vision. He wanted his venue to transcend football and provide a technologically advanced stadium for sports and entertainment. This stunning achievement is just part of Jerry's legacy and another symbol of the rich tradition of the Dallas Cowboys.

Paul Tagliabue served as commissioner of the National Football League from 1989 to 2006. During his tenure, the league experienced unprecedented growth, expanding to 32 teams, with 17 of those, including the Cowboys, building new stadiums.

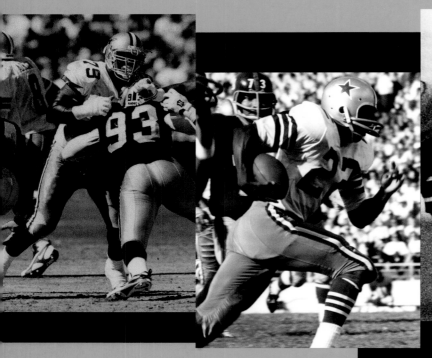

(left to right) Erik Williams; Bob Hayes; Lee Roy Jordan; Ed "Too Tall" Jones; Mel Renfro; Michael Irvin and Deion Sanders; Jason Witten.

8

THE GOLDEN ANNIVERSARY
TEAM

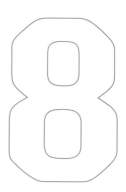

After spending nearly 90 minutes answering various questions about his playing days, Roger Staubach had just one question of his own.

★ ★ ★ ★ ★ ★ ★ ★

"There's not going to be a 50th anniversary team, right?"

Well, actually, Roger, yes, there is a Golden Anniversary Team.

"That's not going to be easy."

Yes, we know.

The process started innocently enough back in January 2009. The majority of selections were no-brainers based on accomplishments and level of performance. But, a franchise five decades deep in tradition has a plethora of options at just about every position, so deciphering the criteria was instrumental.

Without hesitation, the idea of sustained success in favor of isolated brilliance became the standard, for this was the Dallas Cowboys Golden Anniversary Team, not that of the NFL. Three seasons of excellence by Player A shouldn't trump 10 solid campaigns of commitment by Player B when ranking the contributions to America's Team.

Again, this point should be stressed: each position's selection was based solely on the player's contributions to the Cowboys franchise.

The team was selected in the exact manner of an All-Pro ballot: a quarterback, two running backs, a fullback, two wide receivers, a tight end, two tackles, two guards, and a center on offense. Two ends, two tackles, three linebackers, two cornerbacks, a strong safety, and a free safety were chosen on defense as well as a kicker, punter, kick returner, punt returner, and a special teams player. Oh, also a head coach, although obviously that wasn't the most difficult of decisions.

We only wavered from this format once, on the issue of quarterback, where including both Troy Aikman and Roger Staubach—who combined to win each of the franchise's five Super Bowls—seemed logical. Asked if we were taking the easy way out not selecting only one, Staubach said, "Not at all. Not when it's the right thing to do. If they let him throw the football, Troy Aikman would've broken every passing record that exists. The Dallas Cowboys have won five Super Bowls, and he won three of them. He also never lost a Super Bowl. Troy should be on that team."

And so should Staubach.

Disagreement can inspire the most healthy and educational of debates, and hopefully the representatives of the Golden Anniversary Team inspire just that. Much consideration and research went into the process, and there were changes made along the way. That said, we are confident in each of the 29 selections that make up the best of the best in the last 50 years of Dallas Cowboys football.

12 | ROGER STAUBACH

QUARTERBACK

There was a time when Roger Staubach was just a guy playing football. A place where Captain America wasn't running around throwing Hail Mary passes and winning Super Bowls. When his name wasn't referenced in the same sentence with words like "icon," "legend," and "American hero."

As of October 1, 1971, some four months shy of his 30th birthday, Staubach's career NFL numbers included 986 passing yards, 11 interceptions, three touchdown passes, and an anemic 49.3 passer rating.

By comparison, at the same age, Dan Marino had already thrown for 31,000 yards and 241 touchdowns.

Not that Staubach was riding the pine waiting for his chance. Instead, the 1963 Heisman Trophy winner from the Naval Academy and 10th-round selection in the 1964 NFL Draft was sidetracked by a four-year military commitment that involved a year as a supply officer during the height of the Vietnam War.

Still, he was becoming increasingly impatient with head coach Tom Landry's quarterback shuffling, to the point that Staubach was on the verge of demanding a trade. Finally inserted as the starter in favor of Craig Morton on November 7, 1971, Staubach led the

> "THERE WAS ALWAYS A CHANCE IN ANY GAME WITH ROGER OUT THERE. WE ALWAYS BELIEVED THAT IF ANY GAME WAS TIGHT AT THE END AND THE DEFENSE COULD HOLD, THAT ROGER WOULD GET THE POINTS WE NEEDED TO WIN. AND HE ALWAYS DID."
>
> —Hall of Fame defensive tackle Randy White

Cowboys to 10 straight victories, culminating in the franchise's first Super Bowl win, a 24–3 defeat of Miami in New Orleans. Staubach was named the game's MVP.

When he retired following the 1979 campaign, Staubach's 83.4 career passer rating was the best in NFL history, as was his 74.6 winning percentage (minimum 100 starts). In fact, some 30 years after his final pass attempt, Staubach's 85-29 regular-season record still ranks second in league annals.

Staubach, a six-time Pro Bowler who led the NFL in passer rating four times, was inducted into the Ring of Honor in 1983 and the Pro Football Hall of Fame two years thereafter.

8 | TROY AIKMAN

QUARTERBACK

His former coach, Jimmy Johnson, calls Troy Aikman the greatest team player with whom he was ever associated, while Roger Staubach says, "He's the most accurate passer of the football I have ever seen."

There is no exact science to measuring a quarterback's greatness or where he ranks among the icons of the sport. One guy throws for thousands of yards and doesn't win a Super Bowl, while another owns multiple rings with lesser numbers. Which was the more accomplished signal caller?

In the case of Aikman, such debate isn't needed. The No. 1 overall pick of the 1989 NFL Draft retired after 12 seasons with a 61.5 completion percentage, the fourth highest in league lore at the time, and, of course, three Super Bowl rings. Also, his 32,942 career passing yards are easily a franchise mark and were 23rd in league history entering the 2010 campaign.

The enduring legacy of this man seemingly born to take snaps is universal among those who played with him. His presence and leadership in the huddle was unwavering. Make no mistake, when Aikman was on the field, this was his football team. The Cowboys were confident—some would say cocky, even arrogant—in their collective belief that in the most important of games, there would be no greater quarterback. And almost without fail, he delivered.

In the Cowboys' nine playoff wins during their three Super Bowl runs of the 1990s, Aikman posted a quarterback rating of at least 101.6 eight times, highlighted by his near-perfect Super Bowl XXVII MVP performance (22 of 30, 273 yards, four touchdown passes, 140.7 rating).

A six-time Pro Bowler, Aikman was a first-ballot selection to the Pro Football Hall of Fame in 2006, one year following his induction into the Ring of Honor.

> **"TROY WAS CONSISTENTLY THE MOST ACCURATE PASSER I'VE EVER SEEN. IN AN ERA OF SUPER EGOS, HE NEVER LET HIS GET IN THE WAY OF WINNING. SUPER BOWLS WERE MORE IMPORTANT THAN STATISTICS. IF I HAD TO COACH ONE GAME, TROY WOULD BE MY QUARTERBACK."**
>
> —*Former Cowboys assistant and current San Diego head coach Norv Turner*

22 | EMMITT SMITH

RUNNING BACK

★ ★ ★ ★ ★ ★ ★ ★ ★ ★ ★ ★ ★ ★ ★ ★ ★ ★

Often lost amidst the fog of his consistent brilliance was the football player.

Unblocked linebacker blitzes outside left, textbook diving block, eliminating the pursuit at the legs before crashing facemask to turf, instantly rolling 180 degrees and simultaneously exploding vertically while drifting ever so slightly downfield. As the protection collapses, the screen pass is floated . . . broken tackle . . . first down.

Then there was the regular-season finale against the New York Giants at the Meadowlands on January 2, 1994, where a grade-one shoulder separation late in the first half wasn't enough with the division title at stake. En route to a one-night hospital stay, Smith, with 42 touches for 229 yards from scrimmage, was instrumental in securing an overtime win.

And that, more than the records and the accolades, is the enduring legacy of Emmitt Smith.

Some five seasons after his retirement, Smith's NFL-record 18,355 career rushing yards hasn't been remotely sniffed, and considering Walter Payton remains second on the list 23 years after his final carry with 16,726 yards, the mark seems as secure as any in football. An eight-time Pro Bowler and

> **"I LOVED SWEETNESS [WALTER PAYTON], BUT EMMITT IS JUST A BETTER OVERALL PLAYER. I LIKE TO WATCH EMMITT WHEN HE DOESN'T HAVE THE BALL. I GUARANTEE YOU, HE CAN BLOCK. AND HE WILL BLOCK. JIM BROWN WOULDN'T BLOCK."**
>
> —*Former NFL head coach Bum Phillips*

four-time All-Pro selection, Smith also caught 486 passes in his 13 campaigns with the Cowboys. Keep in mind only Michael Irvin and Jason Witten cracked 500 in the first 50 seasons of the franchise, with Drew Pearson finishing with 489 receptions.

The Cowboys traded up in the 1990 NFL Draft to select Smith with the No. 17 overall pick, and after claiming NFL Offensive Rookie of the Year honors, he led the league in rushing four of the next five seasons. Along the way, he won 1993 NFL MVP and Super Bowl XXVIII MVP honors and broke the league's single-season record with 25 rushing touchdowns in 1995.

Inducted into the Ring of Honor in 2005, Smith was enshrined into the Pro Football Hall of Fame in 2010.

33 | TONY DORSETT

RUNNING BACK

★★★★★★★★★★★★★★★★★

For 28 years, former Cowboys director of player personnel Gil Brandt ran the numbers through the team's computer, be it speed, endurance, quickness, intellect, how quickly they tied their cleats—if the data was available, Brandt used it. And of the more than 15,000 collegiate players inputted into the system over nearly three decades, only one rated a perfect score.

"The one and only can't-miss prospect the computer ever gave us was Tony Dorsett," Brandt said.

> "IN MY 40 YEARS IN THE NFL AS A PLAYER, ASSISTANT COACH, AND HEAD COACH, I NEVER SAW A RUNNING BACK WITH THE SPEED OF TONY DORSETT. I'VE ALSO NEVER SEEN A PLAYER THAT WAS A THREAT TO GO THE DISTANCE EVERY TIME HE TOUCHED THE FOOTBALL LIKE TONY WAS. WHEN TONY TOOK THE BALL, OPPOSING TEAMS, EVEN THE GUYS ON THE FIELD, WOULD HOLD THEIR BREATH."
>
> —Former Cowboys player and NFL head coach Dan Reeves

The Cowboys traded up in the 1977 NFL Draft and took the reigning Heisman Trophy winner with the No. 2 overall pick. Tom Landry attempted to bring him along slowly, in part because Dorsett didn't always follow his blocking schemes, once telling his coach, "I run to daylight."

This became apparent soon enough as Dorsett reversed field into a strong-side front, which was against the rules of offensive coordinator Dan Reeves. When the rookie back later asked Reeves about the play, the latter replied, "Forget it, go ahead and break all the rules."

Dorsett earned NFL Offensive Rookie of the Year honors behind a still-standing club first-year mark of 1,007 yards, his 13 total touchdowns helping the Cowboys to their second Super Bowl title.

For the next eight seasons, there was no better running back in the league, with Dorsett rushing for at least 1,100 yards in each campaign outside of the strike-shortened 1982 schedule. A four-time Pro Bowler, he retired in 1988 with 12,739 yards, which ranked second in NFL history behind only the great Walter Payton. Some 22 years later, Dorsett was still seventh in career rushing yards entering the 2010 season.

Of course, there's also his record-that-wasn't-made-to-be-broken 99-yard run at Minnesota on *Monday Night Football* in the 1982 regular-season finale.

Dorsett was inducted into both the Ring of Honor and Pro Football Hall of Fame in 1994.

43 | DON PERKINS

RING OF HONOR

FULLBACK

★★★★★★★★★★★★★★★★★★

No position in football has evolved more over the last 50 years than fullback. These days, many teams don't even have one on their roster, never mind on the field, for each and every offensive snap. Even as recently as the 1990s, one of the elite fullbacks in Cowboys franchise history, Daryl "Moose" Johnston, earned two Pro Bowl nods behind nearly 3,000 career yards from scrimmage and ferocious blocking in front of Emmitt Smith.

Dallas has featured other elite fullbacks, including Robert Newhouse and Walt Garrison, who was named to the Pro Bowl in 1972. But even Garrison acknowledges the obvious: "Don Perkins is the best fullback who ever played for the Dallas Cowboys."

When Perkins played in the 1960s, the fullback routinely saw as many carries as the tailback and was often featured. However, Perkins was also the primary blocking back, and oh, could the five-foot-ten-inch 204-pounder open holes with fury. Tom Landry himself said after his days on the sidelines were done that Perkins was the most accomplished backfield blocker he ever coached.

However, there's also this: When Perkins retired in July of 1969, he was fifth in NFL history with 6,217 rushing yards, behind only

> **"IN ALL MY YEARS OF PLAYING AND WATCHING FOOTBALL, I HAVE NEVER SEEN A RUNNING BACK HIT A HOLE QUICKER THAN DON PERKINS. IF WE RAN A TRAP FOR DON, I LITERALLY HAD TO BE AWARE OF TURNING AROUND AS QUICKLY AS POSSIBLE AND HANDING THE BALL OFF IN THE FEAR THAT HE'D RUN RIGHT PAST ME."**
>
> —Cowboys quarterback Eddie LeBaron

Jim Brown, Jim Taylor, Joe Perry, and John Henry Johnson, each of whom are members of the Pro Football Hall of Fame.

That's all the more impressive considering Perkins never took a snap past the age of 30 and missed his rookie season with a broken foot. His last year was arguably his best with 836 rushing yards at 4.4 yards per carry.

A six-time Pro Bowl selection and an All-Pro in 1962, Perkins was fittingly inducted into the Ring of Honor with Don Meredith in 1976.

88 | MICHAEL IRVIN

WIDE RECEIVER

★★★★★★★★★★★★★★★★★★

He was the trash-talking, flamboyant, mink coat–wearing, talk-the-talk, walk-the-walk wide receiver who dominated the headlines.

But even the Playmaker couldn't overshadow Michael Irvin the football player, the one who, in the words of longtime Cowboys radio announcer Brad Sham, "was the hardest worker on the team from the day he was drafted until the day he retired."

Irvin landed in Dallas from the University of Miami, where he won a national championship with Jimmy Johnson, as the No. 11 overall pick of the 1988 NFL Draft. After three mediocre, injury-riddled campaigns, Irvin exploded in 1991 with 93 catches for 1,523 yards and eight touchdowns. He also helped the Cowboys win their first Super Bowl since 1977 that season, beginning a run of three titles in a span of just four years.

During that dynasty, Irvin was considered the emotional leader, his incomparable work ethic forcing teammates to elevate theirs. The stories are legend, those of Irvin running gassers until he puked, only to run 10 or 15 more. Thing is, this wasn't at afternoon practice; this was Irvin on the field by himself at 6 a.m.

When Irvin retired because of a spine injury in 1999, only Jerry Rice and Steve Largent

> "I HAVE NEVER COACHED A PLAYER WITH MORE PASSION THAN MICHAEL IRVIN. HE'S EVERYTHING YOU WANTED IN A FOOTBALL PLAYER: A TREMENDOUS WORKER, AN OUTSTANDING LEADER, AND THE GUY WHO ALWAYS CAME THROUGH WITH THE KEY PLAY IN CRUNCH TIME. HIS WORK ETHIC INSPIRED US."
>
> —Former Cowboys head coach Jimmy Johnson

had more 1,000-yard seasons than his seven, while his eleven 100-yard receiving games in 1995 remains an NFL best. His final numbers that season included 111 receptions for 1,603 yards, both of which are still team records.

And no one was better in big games, as Irvin ranks second in NFL postseason history in receptions (87), receiving yards (1,315), and 100-yard games (six).

A five-time Pro Bowler, Irvin was inducted into the Ring of Honor in 2005 and the Pro Football Hall of Fame in 2007. His 750 career catches and 11,904 yards are easily all-time Cowboys marks with no other player having reached 8,000 receiving yards through the first 50 seasons.

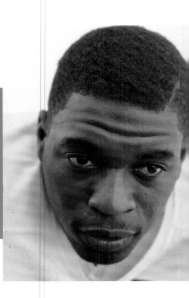

22 | BOB HAYES

WIDE RECEIVER

★★★★★★★★★★★★★★★★★★

"BOB REVOLUTIONIZED THE PASSING GAME AND FORCED THEM TO COME UP WITH THE ZONE DEFENSE, JUST LIKE WILT CHAMBERLAIN FORCED THEM TO CHANGE CERTAIN RULES IN BASKETBALL. HE SHOULD'VE BEEN A FIRST-BALLOT HALL OF FAMER."

—*Hall of Fame defensive back Herb Adderley*

Statistics are nice: receptions, yards, touchdowns, whatever. Bob Hayes caught a lot of passes and found the end zone more than most. Know what, though? His numbers are as inconsequential as any football player's since the laces were first interwoven.

Hayes changed the sport, changed how defenses played, changed how quarterbacks threw the ball. Heck, the NFL changed its rules all because of the Cowboys' seventh-round draft pick out of Florida A&M in 1964.

In terms of coolest monikers, World's Fastest Human ranks up there, if not at the top, and at the conclusion of the 1964 Summer Olympics in Tokyo, the title was undisputed as Hayes won two gold medals, broke the world

record in the 100 meters, and ran arguably the greatest anchor leg of the 4x100 relay in Olympic history.

A backup running back in both high school and college, the Cowboys immediately moved Hayes to wide receiver. Sure enough, after four offensive touches in the NFL, Bullet Bob had scored three touchdowns. As a rookie in 1965, he finished fourth in the league with 1,598 all-purpose yards, while his 1,003 receiving yards easily remain a Cowboys rookie record.

Various zone defenses were introduced in an attempt to slow Hayes, as obviously single coverage wasn't going to work. Even more impressive is that in the era when Hayes played, defensive backs could hit receivers all the way downfield. A three-time Pro Bowler, he was also among the elite punt returners of his era.

The only man to ever win an Olympic gold medal and a Super Bowl, he was inducted to the Ring of Honor in 2001, a year before his death at 59 years of age due to kidney failure. Hayes, who scored 72 touchdowns in his first 91 games with the Cowboys, was finally elected into the Pro Football Hall of Fame in 2009.

82 | JASON WITTEN

TIGHT END

The lone offensive inclusion on the Golden Anniversary Team who played in the team's 50th NFL campaign, Jason Witten finished 2009 as the second-leading receiver in franchise history with 523 career receptions. And if Witten remains healthy, Michael Irvin's 750 catches appear more than reachable, because despite his already significant accomplishments, Witten played in his seventh regular season at only 27 years of age.

Perhaps no NFL team has utilized the tight end position with as much success as the Cowboys the last four decades or so. Through 2009, four of the 10 leading receivers in franchise history were tight ends, earning 17 combined Pro Bowl nods: Witten (6),

Jay Novacek (5), Billy Joe DuPree (3), and Doug Cosbie (3).

To many, Witten was the Cowboys' Player of the Decade for the 2000s, if not for his impressive statistics, then perhaps for the one play that signified his determination and passion for the game. In Philadelphia on November 4, 2007, Witten hauled in a pass over the middle, only to immediately be hit by two defenders. Despite losing his helmet, he broke the tackle and rumbled downfield for a 53-yard reception. His effort helped Dallas to a 38–17 defeat of its NFC East rivals and secured his place in Cowboys lore.

Also, in an era where many tight ends are more wide receivers, simply lining up with their hands on the ground, Witten ranks among the top blockers at his position. Of course, his numbers in the passing game are there, too, as the Cowboys' third-round selection out of Tennessee in 2003 is one of three tight ends in league history with more than 60 receptions in six consecutive seasons. Tony Gonzalez and Shannon Sharpe are the others.

A few more years at his current pace, and Witten should one day reside in the Ring of Honor and the Pro Football Hall of Fame.

> "JASON'S A RARITY IN THE NFL THESE DAYS. OUR OFFENSE REQUIRES THE TIGHT END TO BE A PHYSICAL BLOCKER AND A THREAT IN THE PASSING GAME, AND HE RANKS AMONG THE LEAGUE'S ELITE AT BOTH. HE WANTS TO BE SO GREAT, HE MAKES US BETTER COACHES, FORCES US TO HIS LEVEL. THERE IS NO TIGHT END IN FOOTBALL I WOULD WANT OVER JASON WITTEN. AND HIS TRAITS AS A HUMAN BEING ARE EVEN MORE SPECIAL AND RARE. I LOVE THE GUY SO MUCH."
>
> —*Cowboys offensive coordinator Jason Garrett*

70 | RAYFIELD WRIGHT

OFFENSIVE TACKLE

★★★★★★★★★★★★★★★★★★

Among the more improbable success stories in league history, Rayfield Wright grew up in Griffin, Georgia, in the 1950s, his childhood home without heat or electricity. He landed what he thought was a basketball scholarship to Fort Valley State only to find out it was an athletic scholarship, which meant playing football as well. No problem, Wright thought, except that, well, he had never played the sport in his life.

Having barely made the Cowboys' roster as a seventh-round pick in 1967, Wright spent his first two seasons bouncing around from tight end to defensive end to offensive tackle, while earning his keep on special teams. His weight up to 255 by 1969, he earned his first NFL start opposite Deacon Jones, the future Hall of Fame defensive end. Told Jones was big, mean, and strong before the game, Wright famously replied, "Well, so am I."

His efforts that afternoon earned him a game ball and the enduring confidence of Tom Landry.

Entrenched as the starting right tackle in 1970, Wright was named to six straight Pro Bowls (1971–1976) and earned three All-Pro nods en route to All-Decade honors. He also earned the respect of the elite defensive ends

> **"ANYBODY THAT RAYFIELD WRIGHT WAS BLOCKING NEVER TOUCHED ME. IN PASS PROTECTION, HE DIDN'T MAKE MISTAKES. HE WAS SUCH AN ATHLETE. HE HAD THE GREAT FEET TO HANDLE THE SPEED GUYS AND THE SIZE TO HANDLE THE POWER GUYS."**
>
> —*Hall of Fame quarterback Roger Staubach*

of his era, with the likes of Jack Youngblood, Carl Eller, and L.C. Greenwood saying he was among the best they ever faced.

When Wright was finally inducted into the Pro Football Hall of Fame in 2006, legendary Pittsburgh Steelers defensive tackle Mean Joe Greene said, "He just had so much size and quickness. This guy had great range and punch. Rayfield Wright should have been in the Hall of Fame long ago."

The Cowboys played in five Super Bowls, winning two, with the Big Cat anchoring the offensive line. He was named to the Ring of Honor in 2004.

79 | ERIK WILLIAMS

OFFENSIVE TACKLE

For offensive coordinators around the NFL, lining up against Hall of Fame defensive end Reggie White meant late nights of developing double- and triple-team blocking schemes. Except, that is, the Cowboys who simply sent Erik Williams on to the field and played as if it were any other week. At his best, Williams was *that* good, capable of containing the most dangerous end of the last 30 years by his lonesome.

When the Cowboys were winning three Super Bowls as the Team of the 1990s, there was often debate among media and fans about who the most important player was among the Triplets. However, within the inner circles of the players and coaching staff, many would've injected Williams into that conversation, with Michael Irvin himself once saying "Erik is the best player in football. Not the best offensive lineman, the best player."

Selected by the Cowboys in the third round of the 1991 NFL Draft out of Central State (Ohio), Williams cracked the starting lineup the following season at right tackle, a position he would anchor throughout eight of nine campaigns. The lone exception came in 1994 when Williams missed the final nine games of the season following a broken leg suffered in a car accident.

A four-time Pro Bowler and two-time All-Pro, Williams is also the lone Cowboys' offensive lineman to have won NFC Player of the Week honors, chosen for his superhuman performance in a 20–10 defeat of Philadelphia on November 1, 1992. Since the award began in 1985, only two other individual offensive linemen have won the honor. At the time, Dallas head coach Jimmy Johnson said, "Erik has played spectacular."

"A BEAST. WHAT HE BROUGHT AT THE TIME HE BROUGHT IT, ERIK WILLIAMS WAS THE BEGINNING OF THE END FOR REGGIE WHITE. AND AT THAT TIME, THAT INTIMIDATING FORCE THAT REGGIE WHITE WAS, REGGIE WHITE SET TEAMS ON FIRE UNTIL ERIK WILLIAMS SAID, 'NO MORE, RIGHT HERE NO MORE.' AND HE DIDN'T JUST SAY, 'REGGIE, I'M NOT GOING TO LET YOU TOUCH MY BOY BACK THERE.' HE SAID, 'I'M GOING TO BEAT YOUR ASS.'"

—Hall of Fame wide receiver Michael Irvin

73 | LARRY ALLEN

GUARD

★ ★ ★ ★ ★ ★ ★ ★ ★ ★ ★ ★ ★ ★ ★ ★ ★ ★

The list of truly dominant guards in NFL history reads something like this: Gene Upshaw, John Hannah, Bruce Matthews, Randall McDaniel, and Larry Allen. And come 2013, the 11-time Pro Bowl selection should take his rightful place in Canton along with the other four.

To say Allen was strong is akin to saying Tom Landry preferred fedoras. Considered the strongest man to ever grace a football field, Allen routinely bench-pressed 650-plus pounds and once squatted 900 pounds.

He arrived in Dallas as a second-round selection in 1994, the first player ever drafted out of Sonoma State University, a Division II school in Northern California. After earning All-Rookie honors, he helped the Cowboys win their third Super Bowl in four years and was named to his first Pro Bowl. The following season, though, Allen started his reign of sheer dominance with six straight first-team All-Pro selections, meaning one and all considered him among the top two guards in the NFL.

But Allen wasn't just blocking defensive linemen; he was physically abusing them behind the strength of Hercules and deceiving quickness for a 335-pound man.

In the first 50 years of the franchise, the three fewest sacks allowed by a Cowboys team

> **"THIS GUY IS ONE OF THE BEST FOOTBALL PLAYERS I'VE BEEN AROUND IN MY 27 YEARS IN THE NFL. LARRY WAS ALWAYS STAYING AFTER PRACTICE TO WORK, HE ALWAYS WANTED TO BE THE BEST, AND HE WAS ALWAYS ASKING QUESTIONS ON HOW TO IMPROVE. HE WORKED AT HIS CRAFT AS MUCH AS ANY PLAYER I'VE COACHED."**
>
> —*Offensive line coach Hudson Houck*

came in 1995 (18), 1996 (19), and 1998 (19), which coincide with Allen's prime. That's not a coincidence.

Allen's 10 Pro Bowl nods with the Cowboys are tied for second most with Mel Renfro, behind only Bob Lilly's 11. He also joined Willie Roaf and Warren Sapp among the lone three players selected to the All-Decade Team for both the 1990s and the 2000s.

After 12 seasons with Dallas, Allen spent two with San Francisco before signing a one-day contract to retire as a member of the Cowboys on August 29, 2008.

76 | JOHN NILAND

1966–1974

GUARD

★★★★★★★★★★★★★★★★

Talk about a prodigy, John Niland was named to his first Pro Bowl in 1968 at six years old.

Well, at least officially speaking, as the first All-Pro guard in franchise history was born on February 29, 1944—a leap year.

For those who have never seen film of Niland with the Cowboys, appreciating his quickness, especially on running plays as the pulling guard, is impossible. There were instances when the former All-American at Iowa would execute the lead block on snaps where he was lined up opposite the direction of the run. His footwork and lateral speed made believing that the six-foot-four-inch, 247-pound NFL guard was an All-State fullback in high school all the easier.

The No. 5 overall pick of the 1966 draft, Niland became a full-time starter the following year and missed just one start over the next eight seasons. In 1968 the Cowboys led the NFL in points scored (431), total offense (5,117), first downs (297), passing yards (3,026), and rushing touchdowns (24), with Niland the lone Cowboy offensive lineman named to the Pro Bowl. Most considered him the premier guard in the NFL at the time.

The Cowboys won their first Super Bowl following the 1971 campaign, outscoring their three postseason opponents 58–18. The team's overpowering offensive line featured Blaine Nye, Dave Manders, Rayfield Wright, and Niland, who many teammates said played his best game, especially run blocking, in the 24–3 defeat of Miami in Super Bowl VI.

When his run with the Cowboys concluded in 1974, Niland was a six-time Pro Bowler and two-time All-Pro. Dallas was also 91-33-2 in the regular season and qualified for the playoffs eight times in his nine campaigns.

> "WHEN YOU PUT NILAND AGAINST SOME OF THE PEOPLE THAT PLAYED HIS POSITION OR WERE OFFENSIVE LINEMEN, I THINK HE DESERVES TO BE IN THE PRO FOOTBALL HALL OF FAME AS MUCH OR MORE THAN A LOT OF THOSE PEOPLE THAT ARE THERE."
>
> —Former player personnel director Gil Brandt

221

1989–1994, 1999–2001

53 | MARK STEPNOSKI

CENTER

★★★★★★★★★★★★★★★★★★

"MARK WAS A TECHNICIAN. WATCH HIM ON FILM. THERE WAS NO WASTED MOVEMENT, AND HIS QUICKNESS WAS ON ANOTHER LEVEL THAN EVERY OTHER OFFENSIVE LINE-MAN. AFTER HE'D BLOCK ONE GUY, HE WAS RUNNING DOWNFIELD AND HITTING SOME-ONE ELSE."

—*Guard Nate Newton*

The first three draft picks of the Jerry Jones–Jimmy Johnson era were Troy Aikman, Daryl "Moose" Johnston, and Mark Stepnoski. The trio combined for 13 Pro Bowl nods, with the latter earning five while being named the second-team center on the NFL's 1990s All-Decade squad by the Pro Football Hall of Fame.

Considered undersized at six feet two inches and 265 pounds, Stepnoski started 121 games with the Cowboys over a 13-year career that included a four-year stint with the Houston Oilers/Tennessee Titans from 1995 to 1998.

While there were bigger—in fact, much bigger—and stronger linemen blocking in front of Emmitt Smith and Troy Aikman, none were more technically precise than Stepnoski, who perfected the art of staying low after the snap, thus allowing him more leverage as he pushed upward from his stance. His quickness also allowed many a split-second hole up the gut, which proved invaluable for a runner like Smith, who relied on his field vision as much as predetermined directional gaps. More times than not, if Smith saw a hole on either side of Stepnoski, he was running through.

The Cowboys scored the second most points in the league three consecutive years, from 1992 to 1994, a streak that included 37 regular-season wins and two Super Bowls. There was no debate at the time that Dallas possessed the best and meanest offensive line in football, anchored by Nate Newton, Mark Tuinei, Erik Williams, and Stepnoski.

"The defensive linemen honestly looked at Sundays as a day off compared to going up against that offensive line at practice; it was brutal," former Cowboys defensive tackle Leon Lett said in 2009.

Stepnoski was also named second-team All-Pro in 1992 and 1994.

Tony Dorsett takes off on his record-breaking 99-yard touchdown run at Minnesota on January 3, 1983. ▶

◄ Bob Lilly takes his turn behind the camera during photo day, snapping a shot of George Andrie.

79 | HARVEY MARTIN

DEFENSIVE END

The Hollywood script wrote itself.

Following Duane Thomas' selection three years previous, Harvey Martin was the second Dallas native drafted by the Cowboys, taken in the third round out of East Texas State in 1973. He became the premier pass rusher in football, winning 1977 NFL Defensive Player of the Year and Super Bowl XII co-MVP honors. A fan favorite of the highest magnitude, the kid from nearby South Oak Cliff High School even landed a weekday morning radio gig, *The Beautiful Harvey Martin Show*.

Surprisingly, he almost didn't make it out of his first training camp, as then defensive coordinator Ernie Stautner thought Martin was too nice and threatened to cut him. Almost instantly, Martin's on-field attitude was transformed; rather than helping up opponents, he was stepping on them and hitting anyone who moved before, during, and after the play. That nastiness—he was dubbed "Too Mean" when Ed "Too Tall" Jones arrived in 1974—combined with prototypical size (six feet five inches, 250 pounds) and an explosive first step made Martin the most dangerous pass rusher in the NFL for the majority of his 11-year career.

In fact, his name should reside in the record books, as his 23 sacks in 1977—in 14 games no less—remains the NFL's single-season best. However, the league didn't start recognizing sacks until 1982, so Michael Strahan's 22.5 in 2001 is the official mark. Martin did lead the Cowboys in sacks seven times and is the franchise's unofficial career sack leader with 114.

A four-time Pro Bowler, Martin died on Christmas Eve 2001 after a lengthy battle with pancreatic cancer. "I find myself thinking of Harvey a lot these days," Jones said in 2008. "He was one of my best friends. I miss him. Harvey really was a beautiful man."

> **"THE TWO FASTEST DEFENSIVE ENDS I EVER SAW PLAY WERE DEACON JONES AND HARVEY. WHEN WE DID WIND SPRINTS AS A TEAM, HARVEY WOULD BEAT SOME OF THE DEFENSIVE BACKS. THERE IS NO QUESTION THAT HARVEY BELONGS IN THE PRO FOOTBALL HALL OF FAME. AS A MEMBER, I ATTEND THE INDUCTIONS EVERY YEAR, AND I SEE THESE PEOPLE GOING IN THAT COULDN'T TIE HARVEY'S SHOES."**
>
> —*Hall of Fame defensive back Mel Renfro*

72 | ED "TOO TALL" JONES

DEFENSIVE END

The Cowboys drafted Bob Lilly in 1961, Troy Aikman 28 years thereafter, yet Ed "Too Tall" Jones was a teammate of each. Now that's longevity.

Sure enough, through the first 50 seasons of the Dallas Cowboys, Jones is the franchise leader with 224 games, a mind-boggling feat for a defensive lineman. Over his 15 seasons, which is tied with Mark Tuinei and Bill Bates for most in team history, Jones missed exactly one game. Several teammates and coaches have said they can't recall Jones ever missing a practice.

> **"WHEN TOO TALL COMES AT ME, I THINK OF A GIANT PREHISTORIC BIRD SAILING THROUGH THE AIR."**
>
> —*Washington Redskins quarterback Joe Theismann*

The No. 1 overall pick out of Tennessee State in 1974, Jones never intended on playing professional football. He didn't even know the rules as a senior in high school, having only played basketball and baseball. Then again, his real passion, even throughout his extensive NFL career, was boxing, a sport for which he actually left the Cowboys in 1979, winning each of his six bouts.

At six feet nine inches and 271 pounds, Jones was a superior athlete who forced an array of double teams, which often freed up teammates for one-on-one pursuit.

"He didn't have a quantity of statistics," said Drew Pearson. "But he sure opened a lot of holes for Randy White and Harvey Martin. Ed was a spectacular force. If there was anyone who could play the run better, I would like to see him."

A three-time Pro Bowler, Jones was an All-Pro in 1982. He finished his career with more than 1,000 combined tackles, 127 batted passes, 106 sacks, and a franchise-record 19 fumble recoveries. Only Martin and White have more career sacks with the Cowboys.

Among his 20 playoff games were six NFC Championship Games and three Super Bowls.

74 | BOB LILLY

DEFENSIVE TACKLE

★ ★ ★ ★ ★ ★ ★ ★ ★ ★ ★ ★ ★ ★ ★ ★ ★

Of the 99 uniform numbers that were issued by the Dallas Cowboys through the first 50 seasons of the franchise, only one, fittingly, has been worn by a single player.

Bob Lilly, No. 74.

Born in Olney, Texas, raised in nearby Throckmorton, an All-American at Texas Christian University—where, one end at a time, he lifted Volkswagen Beetles onto campus sidewalks—Lilly was the first-ever draft selection of the Cowboys, 13th overall, in 1961. Some 14 years thereafter, he was the charter inductee to the Ring of Honor. And in 1980, Mr. Cowboy was the team's first to gain enshrinement in the Pro Football Hall of Fame.

Most importantly, though, he also helped lead the Cowboys to their first championship with a 29-yard sack in a 24–3 defeat of Miami in Super Bowl VI.

After an impressive rookie campaign in 1961, Lilly, at six feet five inches and 255 pounds, tallied a team-high 10.0 sacks the following season to earn his first Pro Bowl nod. But after a 1-6 start in 1963, head coach Tom Landry decided Lilly's rare combination of brute strength and burst of quickness was more suited for tackle. From that moment until his retirement, the Cowboys were 106-52-3 in the regular season.

> **"A MAN LIKE (HIM) COMES ALONG ONCE IN A LIFETIME. HE IS SOMETHING A LITTLE BIT MORE THAN GREAT. NOBODY IS BETTER THAN BOB LILLY."**
>
> —Hall of Fame head coach Tom Landry

The cause and effect were not accidental as Lilly became the most disruptive defensive force in football.

"Bob Lilly is the greatest defensive lineman I ever saw," Pro Football Hall of Fame offensive lineman Dan Dierdorf said.

There are no numbers to measure the greatness of Lilly. Sure, he was credited with 94.0 sacks, even scored four touchdowns, but his influence was so much more. Offenses planned around him. "They triple-teamed Bob and still couldn't block him," teammate Dan Reeves said.

An 11-time Pro Bowler and seven-time All-Pro, Lilly never missed a regular-season game, playing in 196 straight, a Cowboys' record. He was also named to the NFL All-Decade Team for the 1960s and the 1970s and was selected to the NFL 75th Anniversary Team in 1994.

54 | RANDY WHITE

DEFENSIVE TACKLE

★★★★★★★★★★★★★★★★★★

"HE'S THE MOST INTENSE PLAYER I HAVE SEEN IN MY 42 YEARS AS A PLAYER AND COACH IN THE NFL. RANDY WAS A THROW-BACK TO THE OLD TIMERS. NOTHING INTER-FERED WITH HIS DESIRE TO WIN. HE ALSO PLAYED WITH INJURIES THAT WOULD KEEP MOST PLAYERS OUT OF THE GAME."

—*Former Cowboys defensive coordinator Ernie Stautner*

The Cowboys brass had narrowed down its potential selections with the No. 2 overall pick of the 1975 NFL Draft to a consensus All-American defensive end from Maryland and a running back from Jackson State.

And in retrospect, there is no regret taking Randy White in favor of Walter Payton, for the Manster and Sweetness each rank in the highest of tiers when speaking of football's immortals.

"Randy White might be the finest defensive player I ever coached against," Super Bowl–winning head coach Dick Vermeil said. "He created a war on every snap."

After two disappointing seasons at middle linebacker, White was moved to tackle by Tom Landry before the 1977 campaign. Over the next two years, he tallied 241 tackles, 29 sacks, and helped the Cowboys to back-to-back Super Bowl appearances, sharing co-MVP honors with Harvey Martin in a 27–10 defeat of Denver in Super Bowl XII.

At six feet four inches, 257 pounds, White could run with just about any offensive player in the league, as evidenced by his memorable tackle of Philadelphia wide receiver Scott Fitzkee 49 yards after the catch on December 21, 1980. And no, White hadn't dropped back in coverage on the play; he simply reversed direction and sprinted with every ounce of his being.

"His performances range anywhere from spectacular to spectacular," Tom Landry said.

Cited by teammates as the most tireless and intense on the practice field, White missed just two games over a 14-year career. He's also the lone player in franchise history with at least 700 solo tackles and 100 sacks.

A nine-time Pro Bowler and seven-time All-Pro, White was inducted into the Ring of Honor and the Pro Football Hall of Fame in 1994.

54 | CHUCK HOWLEY

1961–1973

RING OF HONOR

LINEBACKER

★★★★★★★★★★★★★★★★★★

While the Dallas Cowboys were playing their inaugural season of 1960—and finishing 0-11-1—Chuck Howley was home in Wheeling, West Virginia, pumping gas. He was 24 years old, a former first-round pick of the Chicago Bears just two years previous, but a knee injury had forced an early retirement.

The Cowboys inquired about Howley possibly returning, and after testing his knee at a West Virginia alumni game, he agreed. Dallas sent a few draft picks to Chicago for compensation, as the Bears still retained his rights. The trade was an afterthought to most, with Howley considered damaged goods.

Yeah, not so much.

When he retired 13 seasons later, in 1973, Howley was simply one of the most accomplished linebackers in NFL history. "I don't know that I've seen anybody better at linebacker than Howley," Tom Landry said.

As far as the injuries, Howley missed exactly four games his first 12 seasons with Dallas. He was a fixture on the weak side, which in Landry's Flex defense meant an abundance of pass coverage, especially on the running back. To this day, Howley remains the only Cowboys player with 20 sacks and 20 interceptions, finishing with 26 and 24, respectively.

His 16 fumble recoveries are also tied for second most in franchise history.

Perhaps Howley is best remembered as a "big game" player, especially in The Game. He remains the lone Super Bowl MVP from a losing team, with two interceptions and a fumble recovery in the devastating 16–13 loss to the Baltimore Colts in Super Bowl V. A six-time Pro Bowler, Howley could've easily been named MVP of Super Bowl VI as well, having recorded an interception and a fumble recovery in Dallas' 24–3 defeat of Miami.

A five-sport letterman at West Virginia, Howley was inducted into the Ring of Honor in 1977.

"CHUCK ALWAYS POSSESSED SUPERIOR ABILITY, BUT WOW, WHEN HE WAS REALLY MOTIVATED, HE PLAYED AT THAT HIGHEST OF LEVELS WHERE FEW LINEBACKERS HAVE REACHED BEFORE OR SINCE. HE WAS SUCH A GREAT ATHLETE: FAST, QUICK, STRONG, AND SO AGILE. WHEN WE WERE WINNING ALL THOSE GAMES, PLAYING IN THE SUPER BOWLS, CHUCK HOWLEY WAS ONE OF THE TWO OR THREE BEST ATHLETES ON THE TEAM, AND THAT'S INCLUDING THE WIDE RECEIVERS, DEFENSIVE BACKS, WHOMEVER."

—*Former Cowboys linebacker and assistant coach Jerry Tubbs*

55 | LEE ROY JORDAN

LINEBACKER

★★★★★★★★★★★★★★★★★★

Throughout his collegiate and NFL career, Lee Roy Jordan knew just two head coaches: Paul "Bear" Bryant and Tom Landry. Talk about a football education.

In 1962 Jordan finished fourth in the Heisman Trophy balloting and earned Orange Bowl MVP honors behind 31 tackles. Yes, 31. Considered somewhat undersized at six feet one inch, 215 pounds, he slipped to the Cowboys with the sixth overall pick.

After three injury-plagued seasons at weakside linebacker, Landry tabbed Jordan his starter in the middle in 1966, replacing veteran Jerry Tubbs. Almost instantly, Jordan became the leader of the defense, a role in which he thrived for the next 11 seasons, not missing a single start along the way.

"His leadership was sincere," Landry said. "And it was effective. He had the respect of the team, and you can't have success on a team without leadership on the team level."

He also called Landry's plays in the huddle, and in many ways became an extension of the coach himself. No one outside of Landry watched more game film, to the point where Jordan would position teammates before the snap based on formations or movement.

> "I NEVER HAD ANOTHER ONE LIKE LEE ROY JORDAN. HE WAS THE BEST LINEBACKER IN COLLEGE FOOTBALL, BAR NONE. HE WOULD HAVE MADE EVERY TACKLE ON EVERY PLAY IF THEY HAD STAYED IN BOUNDS. I CAN REMEMBER NOTHING BAD ABOUT LEE ROY."
>
> —Former Alabama head coach Paul "Bear" Bryant

The first two words usually associated with Jordan are "winner" and "tough." In his 17 combined seasons at Alabama and Dallas as a starting middle linebacker, his teams were 141-42-4.

"No player in Cowboys history meant more to the Cowboys' overall team than Lee Roy Jordan," Roger Staubach said.

The anchor of the Doomsday Defense, Jordan was a five-time Pro Bowler. An All-Pro selection in 1969, he played in seven conference championship games and three Super Bowls. His 1,236 combined tackles and 743 solo stops each rank second in franchise history, while his 32 interceptions are seventh behind six defensive backs.

Jordan was inducted into the Ring of Honor in 1989.

94 | DeMARCUS WARE

LINEBACKER

The only offensive and defensive selections with fewer than eight seasons of service for the Cowboys are Jason Witten (seven) and DeMarcus Ware, who completed his fifth campaign in 2009. Make no mistake, though, both have earned their place based on past accomplishments rather than future projections.

Ware, the 2005 first-round pick from Troy, was already the franchise leader among linebackers with 64.5 career sacks entering the 2010 season. Also, Ware has been an All-Pro selection three seasons running, a feat matched among Dallas Cowboys linebackers by only Chuck Howley. Yes, Bob Breunig was superb in the middle for 10 seasons, starting 125 games to Ware's 79 through 2009, and earning Pro Bowl accolades on three occasions, but Breunig was never the focus of opposing defenses, nor was he an All-Pro.

As for Ware, he finished second in the NFL Defensive Player of the Year voting in 2008 behind 20.0 sacks—tied for sixth most in league history—and six forced fumbles. He also showed considerable improvement against the run and in pass protection, becoming more of a complete player than a pass-rushing specialist.

That evolution continued in 2009 as Ware registered 11.0 sacks and six forced fumbles despite a steady dose of double teams. Still, in retrospect, his fifth season in the pros wasn't defined by numbers as much as an inspirational performance in a 24–17 defeat of host New Orleans in week 15. Carted off the field with a frightening neck injury just six days previous, Ware anchored a stunning defensive effort against the Saints with two sacks and two forced fumbles. New Orleans had entered the game 13-0 and went on to eventually win the Super Bowl.

A four-time Pro Bowler, only injury can prevent Ware from becoming one of the elite defensive players to ever wear the Cowboys uniform.

> **"I'VE BEEN LUCKY TO BE AROUND A LOT OF THE GOOD ONES. I'VE COACHED REGGIE WHITE, BRUCE SMITH. DeMARCUS IS AT THE TOP OF THE CLASS, AND IT DOESN'T TAKE LONG TO CALL THE ROLL."**
>
> —*Head coach Wade Phillips*

20 | MEL RENFRO

CORNERBACK/KICK RETURNER

★★★★★★★★★★★★★★★★★★

The lone multiple honoree to the Golden Anniversary Team, Mel Renfro was the easiest of selections at both cornerback and kick returner.

A second-round pick in the 1964 NFL Draft, Renfro ranks atop a multitude of franchise career lists including interceptions (52), interception return yards (626), kickoff return average (26.4), and kickoff return touchdowns (2), while his 10 Pro Bowl selections are bested only by Bob Lilly's 11.

An All-American running back at Oregon, where he also played free safety, Renfro's rookie campaign is among the most accomplished in the history of the NFL. He led the league in punt (418) and kick return (1,017) yardage and finished fifth in all-purpose yards (1,435) despite not taking an offensive snap. His defensive numbers included seven interceptions, with one returned for a touchdown, and two fumble recoveries.

After six seasons and 31 interceptions at safety, Tom Landry moved Renfro to cornerback before the 1970 campaign, later saying, "The reason was simple. Mel could cover any receiver in the league. If you have someone out there on the corner who can handle that man-to-man coverage, it frees the rest of your defense up to attack. It's an incredible advantage."

> "HIS MOST AMAZING GIFT WAS MENTAL. HE ALWAYS SEEMED TO KNOW WHAT THE OTHER TEAM WAS GOING TO DO BEFORE THEY SNAPPED THE BALL. MEL WAS ONE OF THOSE PLAYERS THAT YOU ALWAYS KNEW WOULD BE IN THE HALL OF FAME SOMEDAY."
>
> —*Hall of Fame defensive tackle Bob Lilly*

Almost immediately, quarterbacks simply stopped throwing in Renfro's direction. During one 10-game stretch, opponents tossed 36 passes his way. Six were completed. The majority considered him the best shutdown corner in the game.

Then there was the 1971 Pro Bowl where he returned two punts for touchdowns, shut out future Hall of Fame receiver Paul Warfield and earned MVP honors. With the elite athletes of the sport, he stood alone.

An All-Pro in 1969, Renfro helped Dallas win nine division titles and two Super Bowls. He was inducted into the Ring of Honor into 1981 and the Pro Football Hall of Fame in 1996.

24 | EVERSON WALLS

CORNERBACK

★★★★★★★★★★★★★★★★★

The second cornerback selection was the most difficult decision in the Golden Anniversary Team process, with Cornell Green more than deserving of the honor. Working against the five-time Pro Bowler is that he split his career at corner and strong safety, while our pick was a pure shutdown corner.

After playing for the legendary Eddie Robinson at Grambling State, Everson Walls had the incredible fortune of playing for Tom Landry, Jimmy Johnson, Bill Parcells, and Bill Belichick in the NFL.

Born in Dallas and raised two miles from where the Cowboys practiced before moving to Valley Ranch, Walls didn't play football until his final year of high school. He went on to become a Division I-AA All-American at Grambling as he led the nation with 11 interceptions his senior season in 1980. However, a slow 40-yard dash hurt his draft status and,

amazingly, he was bypassed for 12 rounds and 333 selections. The Cowboys quickly signed him as a free agent, and following a stellar preseason, which included three interceptions and a touchdown off his own blocked punt, he made the team.

Showing that natural instinct for the football, Walls started 12 games as a rookie and set the still-standing single-season team record with 11 interceptions. In the process, he became the first rookie to lead the NFL in picks since Detroit's Lem Barney in 1967. Walls added two more interceptions in the NFC Championship Game against San Francisco and another two in the Pro Bowl, concluding one of the more improbable debut campaigns in league history.

A ball hawk of the highest order, Walls also paced the competition with seven interceptions in 1982 and nine picks in 1985. His 44 total interceptions with the Cowboys rank second in franchise history behind only Mel Renfro, while his 57 career picks were tied for 11th most in league annals entering the 2010 season.

A four-time Pro Bowl selection with the Cowboys, Walls was also an All-Pro in 1983.

> **"ONE OF THOSE GREAT STORIES IN THE NFL OF A GUY THAT SLIPPED THROUGH THE DRAFT. EVERSON WALLS MIGHT HAVE HAD THE BEST BALL RECOGNITION SKILLS OF ANY CORNERBACK I'VE EVER SEEN."**
>
> —*Cowboys radio broadcaster Brad Sham*

43 | CLIFF HARRIS

RING OF HONOR

FREE SAFETY

★★★★★★★★★★★★★★★★★★★

Coming out of Ouachita Baptist University in Arkansas in 1970, Cliff Harris was not among the 442 players, including more than 70 defensive backs, selected in the NFL Draft. The Cowboys had told him beforehand they would take him, so when they called about a free agent deal, Harris wasn't thrilled. Nonetheless, he signed and joined 120 other rookies at training camp. Yes, 120, including 23 defensive backs.

For Harris, the mentality was simplistic enough: run around and hit people as hard as possible. Sure enough, he made the team and even started five games at free safety.

Thereafter, Harris was a fixture, not missing a single game his final nine seasons. A fan favorite for obvious reasons, Captain Crash was a menacing physical presence in the defensive backfield with many wide receivers hearing his footsteps, especially on crossing patterns. When Harris delivered a hit, well, let's just say the vibrations were felt, which was all the more amazing considering he was barely six feet and 188 pounds.

Early in his career, Harris also returned punts and kicks for the Cowboys, finishing among the league's top 10 in combined return yards in both 1971 and 1972, but after his

first Pro Bowl selection at free safety in 1974, his return duties ended.

Harris joined Rayfield Wright and Roger Staubach in retiring after the 1979 campaign. His final numbers included 29 career interceptions and 16 fumble recoveries, which ties for second most in franchise history. A six-time Pro Bowler and three-time All-Pro, Harris was also named to the NFL All-Decade team of the 1970s.

The undrafted free agent from Ouachita was inducted into the Ring of Honor in 2004.

"CLIFF COULD DICTATE WHAT AN OFFENSE WOULD DO. MUCH LIKE BOB HAYES WAS RESPONSIBLE FOR THE ZONE DEFENSE AND CHANGING THE GAME, CLIFF WAS RESPONSIBLE FOR CHANGING THE SAFETY POSITION WITH HIS PHYSICAL STYLE. HE IS INCREDIBLY DESERVING OF THE PRO FOOTBALL HALL OF FAME. IT'S A TRAGEDY HE'S NOT IN THERE."

—Safety Charlie Waters

1992–2003

28 | DARREN WOODSON

STRONG SAFETY

> "HE'S CERTAINLY EARNED MY RESPECT. HE HAD IT BEFORE I CAME HERE FROM WATCHING HIM PLAY, BUT NOW THAT I'VE GOTTEN TO KNOW HIM, I THINK HE'S ONE OF THOSE PEOPLE THAT YOU REALLY THINK A LOT OF. HE'S THE KIND OF GUY THAT MAKES THIS PROFESSION SOMETHING THAT YOU LIKE TO ENGAGE IN. DARREN IS THE EPITOME OF A PROFESSIONAL."
>
> —Former Cowboys head coach Bill Parcells

The 1992 Cowboys were on the cusp of greatness. They had won their first playoff game in a decade a season previous and appeared ready to challenge for a Super Bowl. Their draft that April proved a successful haul, with soon-to-be starters Kevin Smith and Robert Jones taken in the first round and a linebacker from Arizona State selected shortly thereafter courtesy of the 37th overall pick.

Darren Woodson, who was immediately moved to strong safety, won three Super Bowls in his first four seasons with the Cowboys and was the last member of that 1992 class still standing with the team, retiring in December of 2004 because of a herniated disk in his back. He was there for the rings, the back-to-back-to-back 5-11 campaigns, and, in the end, a final return to the postseason under Bill Parcells in 2003.

Over his 12 seasons, Woodson ranked among the most beloved and respected of Cowboys by fans, teammates, and coaches alike. He played the game with honor and class.

"For 13 years, he was everything you could ask for—unselfish, reliable, dependable, a team player first, and a team leader always," Cowboys owner Jerry Jones said. "He's a living, breathing example of the saying that character does matter."

After starring on special teams, especially kickoff coverage as a rookie, Woodson cracked the starting lineup in 1993 and finished with 155 tackles, which remains the single-season team record among defensive backs. The following campaign saw him earn Pro Bowl and All-Pro honors behind a career-high five interceptions, one of which he returned 94 yards for a touchdown.

In the end, Woodson registered more tackles than any player in franchise history, 1,350 to be exact, including 787 of the solo variety, also a team mark. He also registered 23 interceptions and 16 forced fumbles.

Likely destined for the Ring of Honor, Woodson was a five-time Pro Bowler and three-time All-Pro.

Eleven of the 17 members of the Cowboys Ring of Honor: (front row, left to right) Michael Irvin, Emmitt Smith, Cliff Harris, Tony Dorsett, Don Perkins, and Mel Renfro; (back row, left to right) Troy Aikman, Bob Lilly, Randy White, Rayfield Wright, and Roger Staubach.

1 | RAFAEL SEPTIEN

KICKER

> **"RAFAEL WAS A GREAT KICKER FOR 10 YEARS. IT'S NOT EASY TO FIND A RELIABLE KICKER. THAT'S WHY KICKERS MOVE AROUND SO MUCH."**
>
> —*Hall of Fame head coach Tom Landry*

Among the easiest selections on the Golden Anniversary Team, Jose Rafael Septien is literally the only placekicker listed in the Cowboys media guide under all-time leaders/field goals. His 162 field goals are twice as many as any other kicker in franchise history. In fact, while Septien led the team in scoring nine times, only one other player has even done so on four occasions, kicker Mike Clark from 1968 to 1971.

Born in Mexico City, Septien played three seasons of professional soccer before deciding to give football a chance. He landed at the University of Louisiana, Lafayette, where he honed his placekicking enough to earn a shot at the NFL. A 10th-round pick of the New Orleans Saints in 1977, Septien ended up plying his trade for the Rams in his rookie campaign before landing with the Cowboys the following year.

Over his nine seasons in Dallas, Septien converted nearly 72 percent of his field goals and finished among the league's top-five scorers four times. His best season came in 1981 as he drilled 27 of 35 field goals en route to Pro Bowl and All-Pro honors. Two years thereafter, he was 22 of 25 on kicks of fewer than 50 yards.

And in terms of leg strength, he had few peers, with eight boots of at least 50 yards in his career.

Perhaps there is no greater indication of a kicker's success than how he performs in the clutch, and when the stakes were at their highest, Septien was almost automatic. In 13 postseason contests with the Cowboys, Septien converted 18 of 20 field goals, including 15 straight. His 94 points in the playoffs are second most in team history, behind only Emmitt Smith's 126.

Septien's 874 regular-season points are also second in franchise history, again trailing only Smith's 986.

1 | MAT McBRIAR

PUNTER

Entering the 2009 campaign, this was the closest of competitions, with Toby Gowin, Mike Saxon, and Danny White each deserving of consideration. However, after another other-worldly performance by Mat McBriar, the decision was obvious.

Of the four highest single-season punting averages in team history, the fourth Australian to play in the NFL is the owner of three, and that doesn't include his 49.0 mark through six games in 2008 before a foot injury ended his year.

> "NOT ONLY IS HE THE BEST I'VE SEEN PUNT FOR THE COWBOYS, McBRIAR IS ONE OF THE BEST IN THE HISTORY OF THE SPORT. HE'S THE FULL PACKAGE, TOO: HANG TIME, DISTANCE, ANGLING, AND JUST AN INCREDIBLE LEG."
>
> —*Quarterback and punter Danny White*

Never mind the Cowboys, though; among those with 350 career punts in the history of the NFL, McBriar's 45.0 average ranked third entering the 2010 season. And when *Sports Illustrated* derived a formula based on the quarterback rating to determine the league's top punter in 2009, few were remotely sur-

prised to see McBriar's name entrenched in the No. 1 position.

By season's end, McBriar was the lone launcher in the NFL who forced opponents to start inside their 20-yard line more than half the time. He did so on 38 of his 72 punts and, perhaps more amazingly, with just three touchbacks.

And while numbers aren't the end-all of determining the best punter—it's more about field position—McBriar is the total package. Through the first half century of the Cowboys, McBriar's 45.0 average is more than three yards better than second-place Gowin (41.7), while his 37.9 net average also easily outdistances the competition, with Gowin at 35.5.

The only career Cowboys punting statistic that McBriar doesn't own is punts themselves, with White holding the team mark with 612 total.

A Pro Bowl selection in 2006, behind a ridiculous 48.2 yards per boot, McBriar also finished his sixth season having had just one punt blocked in 371 kicks.

21 | DEION SANDERS

PUNT RETURNER

★★★★★★★★★★★★★★★★

Yes, Prime Time was considered at cornerback, but remember, this is about accomplishments with the Dallas Cowboys, and in the end, Deion Sanders started only 61 games with America's Team . . . or less than four full seasons.

Still, Sanders was worth every cent Jerry Jones paid him, with 14 interceptions, four Pro Bowl invites, and three All-Pro nods over five campaigns with the Cowboys. He also scored eight touchdowns with Dallas, half of which came via electrifying punt returns, making him a no-brainer pick here. His 13.3 punt return average is easily tops in franchise history.

Thing is, over his first two seasons in Dallas, in 1995–96, Sanders returned just two punts, albeit one for 54 yards. The following three campaigns, he changed many a game with "Did you see that?" returns and led the NFL with 15.6 yards per punt return in 1998. To this day, no one is entirely, or even remotely, sure why opposing teams ever punted a ball anywhere near Sanders. But luckily for highlight reels, they did.

The only man to play in a Super Bowl and a World Series, Sanders further showcased

"DEION POSSESSED MORE FOOTBALL SPEED THAN ANYONE I'VE EVER SEEN. AND WHEN HE HAD THE FOOTBALL IN HIS HANDS, THAT WAS SOMETHING TO WATCH. IN TERMS OF A SHUTDOWN CORNER, THERE WAS DEION AND EVERYONE ELSE."

—Former head coach and current secondary coach Dave Campo

his versatility with the Cowboys in 1996 by becoming the first NFL player to start both ways in 34 years. As a wide receiver that season, the Florida State product caught 36 passes for 475 yards and a touchdown. He did it all that year, returning a defensive fumble for a touchdown and somehow intercepting two passes despite a general lack of opportunity. By this time, opposing offenses more or less devised game plans based on which side of the field Sanders was positioned.

In his first season with the Cowboys in 1995, Sanders helped secure the franchise's fifth Super Bowl triumph.

40 | BILL BATES

SPECIAL TEAMS

Some 335 players were selected in the 1983 NFL Draft. Bill Bates was not among them.

Yet, through 50 seasons of the Dallas Cowboys, only Ed "Too Tall" Jones has appeared in more games than Bates, and no one has played in more seasons. Not a bad final tally for an undrafted free agent: 15 seasons, 217 games, three Super Bowl rings, and the eternal appreciation of teammates and coaches.

He was primarily a special teams player, although few safeties in franchise history can match his combination of career tackles (701), sacks (17), and interceptions (14). A Pro Bowler for his coverage efforts in 1984, Bates was an immediate fan favorite, in part because he was the everyman: six feet one inch, 204 pounds, not quite fast or quick enough, but determined to give every ounce of himself. Even in his last season in 1997, Bates finished second on the team with 21 special teams tackles.

"If we had 11 players on the field who played as hard as Bill Bates does and did their homework like he does, we'd be almost impossible to beat," Tom Landry once said.

A product of Tennessee, Bates was the lone Cowboys player to have donned the pads in the postseason for Landry, Jimmy Johnson, and Barry Switzer. He also stands alone as having been teammates of both Harvey Martin and Deion Sanders, an example of just how long Bates represented America's Team.

Bates broke in when the Cowboys were still among the league's elite, finishing 12-4 in 1983. He was there when they finished 1-15 six years later and, fittingly, when Dallas returned to glory. In fact, serving as one of the team captains, Bates was the one chosen to call the coin flip before Super Bowl XXVII.

"BILL BATES WAS ONE OF THOSE SPECIAL PEOPLE THAT MADE ALL HE HAS POSSIBLE BECAUSE OF HIS HEART. HE DIDN'T HAVE SPECTACULAR ATHLETIC ABILITY. HE JUST PLAYED BECAUSE HE HAD RAW DETERMINATION, WILL TO GET THE JOB DONE."

—Cowboys Hall of Fame president Tex Schramm

TOM LANDRY

HEAD COACH

★ ★ ★ ★ ★ ★ ★ ★ ★ ★ ★ ★ ★ ★ ★ ★ ★ ★

The résumé of one Thomas Wade Landry is nearly unparalleled in the annals of professional football. Still, there could be no greater disservice than recognizing his accomplishments rather than the man.

While his sideline demeanor was indeed stoic, the idea that he was robotic is a gross misinterpretation. Landry, who for the majority of his career called the offensive and defensive plays himself, once said, "The way I trained myself to concentrate, I blanked everything else out. You can't show emotion."

Landry could be funny, saying of the 0-11-1 inaugural 1960 season, "Our quarterback [Eddie LeBaron] used to raise his hand for a fair catch before taking the snap."

He could be emotional, breaking down when reading the last rookie cuts in 1975 and again when addressing his team for the final time on February 27, 1989.

He could be engaging, often challenging his punters and kickers to contests after practice, and even flying with a former player who earned his pilot's license.

Said Don Meredith, "He's the finest man I have ever known. I loved him."

Entering the 2010 season, no coach in NFL history has won more postseason games

> "COACH LANDRY WAS THE MOST WONDERFUL MAN. HE TAUGHT ME HOW TO BE A BETTER MAN, NEVER MIND FOOTBALL. HIS INFLUENCE ON MY LIFE HAS BEEN SO MUCH GREATER THAN HIS INFLUENCE ON MY FOOTBALL, WHICH IS SAYING SOMETHING, SINCE HE'S THE GREATEST FOOTBALL COACH THE SPORT HAS KNOWN."
>
> —Hall of Fame running back Tony Dorsett

than Landry's 20, while his 250 regular-season career victories rank third behind just Don Shula and George Halas. However, perhaps Landry's most impressive on-field coaching accomplishment was guiding the Cowboys to a still-standing NFL-record 20 consecutive winning seasons from 1966 to 1985. He also won 13 divisional titles, five NFC crowns, and two Super Bowls.

A fighter pilot who flew more than 30 missions in World War II, Landry was an All-Pro cornerback with the New York Giants in 1954 before eventually entering the coaching ranks. He was inducted into the Pro Football Hall of Fame in 1990 and the Ring of Honor in 1993.

"THE DIFFERENCE BETWEEN THEM IS THAT VINCE LOMBARDI RAN THE SAME BASIC PLAYS HUNDREDS OF TIMES IN PRACTICE, AND BASICALLY SAID TO OPPOSING TEAMS, 'HERE IT IS, STOP US.' LANDRY, THOUGH, WAS VERY INTERESTED IN HIS OFFENSE. HE STUDIED THE FILMS UNTIL HE FELT HE HAD MASTERED THEM TO THEIR FULL EXTENT. THEN HE WOULD CREATE HIS GAME PLAN ON THE BASIS OF, 'IF THEY DO THIS, WE'LL DO THIS. IF THEY LINE UP LIKE THIS, HERE'S THE PLAY WE'LL RUN.' LANDRY BASICALLY MADE FOOT-BALL INTO A GAME OF CHESS, AND NO ONE WAS EVER BETTER."

—*Quarterback Eddie LeBaron*

"I THINK EVERY ONE OF US FORTUNATE ENOUGH TO HAVE PLAYED FOR COACH LAN-DRY FALL BACK ON SOMETHING HE TOLD OR TAUGHT US ALMOST EVERY DAY OF OUR LIVES. I LOVED HIM VERY MUCH."

—*Hall of Fame defensive tackle Randy White*

"COACH LANDRY WAS A STRONG AND GREAT MAN, ONE WHO SIGNIFICANTLY INFLUENCED MANY PLAYERS IN THEIR LIVES AFTER FOOTBALL. I BECAME A CHRISTIAN BECAUSE OF HIS BELIEF. THE WAY HE SPOKE AND THE WAY HE COACHED WAS STRAIGHT FROM THE SCRIPTURES IN THE BIBLE. SO MANY OF HIS PLAYERS BECAME BETTER MEN BECAUSE OF HIM, AND REALLY, THAT IS THE MOST SIGNIFICANT OF LEGACIES."

—*Hall of Fame cornerback Mel Renfro*

"THE CLASSIEST MEN I HAVE EVER MET ARE THOSE OLD-TIME COW-BOYS PLAYERS. THEY'D COME AROUND WHEN WE WERE PLAYING HERE AND THERE, AND I'VE GOTTEN TO KNOW THEM THROUGH FUNCTIONS AND WHATNOT. I HAVE ALWAYS BEEN AMAZED BY HOW HUMBLE AND KIND THEY ARE, OF THE HIGHEST OF MORAL CHARACTER. THEY ARE AN EXTENSION OF COACH LANDRY."

—*Offensive guard Nate Newton*

(left to right) Performing a trick-rope routine; signing autographs; the 1969 squad; taking the field; 2009 tryouts; poster from the 1980s; visiting a military base.

AMERICA'S
SWEETHEARTS

★★★★★★★★★★

DALLAS COWBOYS
Cheerleaders
AMERICA'S SWEETHEARTS

9

Barely fourteen years removed from a long weekend at Woodstock, Suzanne Mitchell found herself in another place and time, one where peace was the most distant of memories.

★ ★ ★ ★ ★ ★ ★ ★ ★ ★

As the director and mother hen of the Dallas Cowboys Cheerleaders, Mitchell and eight of her girls danced and entertained at the United States Marine base in Beirut, Lebanon, in the spring of 1983. Beyond the admiring gazes of the servicemen front and center, gunfire and illuminating warfare exploded in the background. Less than a month previous, in the midst of the Lebanese Civil War, a suicide bombing at the nearby U.S. Embassy resulted in 63 deaths, and later that year, on October 23, 1983, the Beirut barracks bombing killed 299 American and French troops.

This was the final performance of the two-week tour, with previous stops in Turkey and the Sinai Desert. After the last of their eight costume changes in a nearby guntub covered by a tarp, the cheerleaders headed out shortly before midnight. Mitchell was in the first of the marine jeeps headed for the beach where a helicopter would take them to the nearby USS *New Jersey*.

"We stopped at an Israeli checkpoint, and the marine who was driving suddenly grabbed the back of my neck and slammed it into the dash," Mitchell said. "There was blood everywhere, coming out of my forehead. It took me a few seconds to realize . . . he saved my life. The bullet would've hit me between the eyes."

There is much glitz and glamour being one of America's Sweethearts—the photo shoots on exotic islands, the adoration of women and men alike, the idolization by young girls, the national television and media exposure—but since their first USO tour in 1979, make no mistake, many of these women have also served as American heroes. And not for their pom-poms and leg kicks, although those are nice, too.

The call came in December 1979 from four-star army general John A. Wickham Jr., who as commander of the United States forces in Korea was trying to keep peace following the assassination earlier that year of South Korean president Park Chung Hee. Wickham asked Cowboys president Tex Schramm if he'd be willing to send some of the cheerleaders over for a USO Christmas tour in Korea.

▲ Sharing the USO stage with Wayne Newton and Paul Rodriguez in June of 2003.

At first, Schramm was hesitant, concerned about having fewer cheerleaders for a home playoff game. But after Mitchell gave her immediate approval, Schramm called Wickham and said, "We have your back, General; the girls will be there."

Some thirty years later, the Cowboys Cheerleaders returned to Korea over the holidays for their 69th USO tour, a record that eclipses even the efforts of Bob Hope himself. They added No. 70 in January 2010 with a trip to Europe. Their tours have also taken them to Germany, Turkey, Greece, Iceland, Greenland, Cuba, Spain, Italy, Israel, Bosnia, Kuwait, Iraq, and Afghanistan, just to name a few.

More than 200 Cowboys cheerleaders have experienced at least one USO mission, each having returned with life-altering memories.

"My first trip was in 1981, my second year as a cheerleader. We went to Korea, the Philippines, Diego Garcia, and also performed on a navy ship in the Indian Ocean," said current choreographer Judy Trammell, a cheerleader from 1980 to 1984. "We were gone 21 days over Christmas and New Year's. It was without question the best experience of my career, the most fulfilling and rewarding three weeks imaginable. There really isn't any way to explain it in words. You see these young men and women who are the same age as you and what they are dealing with, risking their lives. It really opens your eyes to the bigger world.

"I was on that Beirut trip where Suzanne was almost killed. That was a different experience. We were so honored to be there. Our soldiers were constantly on guard; they had about an hour of personal time a day. We weren't there long, but we tried to touch each of them, just to let them know how much we appreciated what they were doing."

In 1991 the Cheerleaders received the USO's prestigious 50th Anniversary Award, and six years thereafter they were the first honorees of the USO Spirit of Hope award, named, of course, for the legendary entertainer.

Before stepping down as director in 1989 after 15 years, Mitchell collected an abundance of military unit crests, medals, pins, and insignias, personally presented by soldiers on her 18 USO tours. At one point, she started pinning them on a leather Dallas Cowboys jacket, which is now proudly displayed at the door of the Cheerleaders' practice facility at Valley Ranch. The jacket weighs approximately 14 pounds.

"They would literally pin them on me. I remember this one time in Turkey, I was wearing the jacket, and this solider came running at me. He was all excited, yelling, 'There's my pin, there's my pin!'" Mitchell said. "I remembered him from three years earlier at Camp Casey in Korea. He gave me another pin, bless his heart."

FORMER DIRECTOR
SUZANNE MITCHELL

On Tex Schramm:

"I first came to the Cowboys in 1975 as Tex's secretary. During the job interview, Tex asked me where I envisioned myself in ten years if he hired me, and I said, 'Your chair looks pretty good.' He slammed his fist down on the desk laughing and said, 'You're hired.'

"He was the P. T. Barnum of football in every way, shape, and form. Tex loved people with ideas. He liked you to fight with him, and sometimes he'd pick a fight with you to try to get the best from you. He was also funny; Tex loved to laugh.

"Tex believed strongly in the concept of professional cheerleaders. Without him, there would be no America's Sweethearts.

"Tex was amazing at hiring good people and then leaving them alone. He always stood behind me and believed in me. Just a fabulous man.

"I almost didn't work for him. He told me that his whole life was the Cowboys, which made me think his secretary would be working a lot of hours. But his passion was contagious; I couldn't say no."

There was a popular *Sports Illustrated* cover in July 2001 entitled "Where Are They Now?" which featured five of the original Dallas Cowboys Cheerleaders from 1972. They looked phenomenal in their uniforms some 29 years later, and the issue was a huge hit.

However, one minor detail was overlooked: the Cowboys have always had cheerleaders, dating back to their first game at the Cotton Bowl in 1960. Under the direction of Dee Brock, mother of three sons, college professor, and part-time model, the initial squads were a collection of the top high school cheerleaders in the Dallas–Fort Worth area. After a few years, Schramm allowed Brock to include local high school boys, creating the CowBelles & Beaux.

"We were popular from the beginning; the local press wrote stories about us all the time. I knew we would become more popular, too," Brock said. "We only performed at home games, but we went to Super Bowl V and VI, the latter being in New Orleans. I came back from that game and told Mr. Schramm that we have to rethink the cheerleaders. They have to be at least 18 years old."

The week in New Orleans with high school students was adventurous to say the least. Also, Brock wanted to change the very essence of the squad from cheerleaders to dancers. She approached Schramm with the idea, and he quickly approved. Brock then brought in one of the premier dancers in the country, Texie Waterman, as choreographer.

Following pages: The 1992 squad performing at the Super Bowl.

43 Foreign countries where the Dallas Cowboys Cheerleaders have performed, not inclusive of ships at sea in the Indian Ocean, Mediterranean Sea, and Persian Gulf.

38 Age of Linda Badami as a second-year Cheerleader in 1997. She remains the oldest member in the history of the squad. When Badami made the team in 1996, her four sons ranged in age from 3 to 13 years old.

29 Cheerleaders who have been on the squad at least five years.

4 Directors of the Dallas Cowboys Cheerleaders since 1976. Suzanne Mitchell held the position until 1989, and was followed by Debbie Bond, Leslie Haynes, and current director Kelli McGonagill Finglass, who began in 1991.

"When they told me they wanted dancing cheerleaders, I told them they were crazy," Waterman said in 1984.

Next up were new uniforms, which Brock sketched on a yellow legal pad before handing the task off to Paula Van Waggoner, a designer with the Lester Melnick store in Dallas.

"I will say that my original costume might have had a few more inches of material," Brock joked in 2010. "But the uniform represented the glamour, the showbiz, the Dallas Cowboys theme. We wanted the new cheerleaders to be a little spicier. The short hot pants were the rage then, so the shorts seemed like a natural fit."

The "new" Cheerleaders were no doubt well received, and over the ensuing four years they were widely popular with Cowboys fans. However, the local sensation became an international phenomenon following "The Wink Heard Round the World."

More than 75 million viewers were watching Super Bowl X between Dallas and the Pittsburgh Steelers when the cameraman found Cowboys Cheerleader Gwenda Swearingen. She smiled and winked.

Less than three months later, his desk flooded with requests for the Cheerleaders and with Brock having left a year earlier, Schramm needed help. He asked Mitchell, his recently hired secretary, to manage the squad knowing Waterman was overworked already with coaching and choreographing responsibilities. By the ensuing football season, the Cheerleaders preceded the season opener of *Monday Night Football* with a one-hour special, "The 36 Most Beautiful Girls in Texas."

The 33 years since have been a magical carpet ride for not only those millions entertained by America's Sweethearts but also for those fortunate enough to have performed with them.

Among those is Kelli McGonagill Finglass. A drum majorette in high school, she had just completed her freshman year at TCU in May of 1984 when a mention of tryouts on a morning radio show piqued her interest. She spent five years on the Cowboys' cheerleading squad while earning a bachelor's degree in international marketing from North Texas. For the last 19 years, Finglass has served as the director of the Cheerleaders, a position that is more or less 24/7.

COWBELLES & BEAUX MANAGER
DEE BROCK

On forming the original Cowboys cheerleaders in 1960:
"I was a high school teacher in Dallas when someone recommended me to Mr. Schramm. I met with him, he was a delightful man, and his plan was to have models as the cheerleaders. I asked how much he would pay them and he was surprised and said he figured they would do it for free, just for the exposure. I told him that was unlikely, but also that models as a rule weren't athletic. I suggested a countywide tryout of high school cheerleaders. They already knew the basic cheers. It was simpler than starting from scratch. We had 100 tryouts from the Dallas–Fort Worth area. Before the season we had five or six practices, and then during the year we would practice once a week."

On leaving the Cowboys in 1975:
"Mr. Schramm offered to make the position full-time, but I was teaching college by then and was also part of a group that developed the Instructional Television Center. I thought about his offer, but I didn't want to give up that side of my career. I ended up becoming the senior vice-president of education for PBS."

DIRECTOR
KELLI McGONAGILL FINGLASS

On the strenuous tryout process:
"We are hard on the girls; we recognize that and accept that. We've got 36 positions that, individually, go out and represent the Dallas Cowboys in so many different situations—from the White House to the burn unit at Parkland Hospital. So to that I say, yes, we go through an incredible amount of thorough evaluation to pick the right girls. But the good side of it is, 99 percent of the emails that we receive are from people impressed with how hard the girls work, how selective our process is."

On a typical practice session:
"All the cheerleaders have jobs or go to college, so their day is very compressed with classes or work, probably skipping lunch hours, and getting here around 5:00 a.m. or 6:00 a.m. We start at 7:00 a.m., but they practice before and after on their own. We practice physical conditioning, including a heavy cardio boot camp, which is designed by an army master sergeant—push-ups, sit-ups, suicide runs. We also throw in yoga and technique dance classes. That's just to condition their bodies and flexibility."

▲ (clockwise from above) Dancing in 1980; autographing a poster for fans; USO visit to South Korea.

CHOREOGRAPHER
JUDY TRAMMELL

On making the team in 1980:
"I was on the drill team in high school and took dance lessons in my spare time. My sister-in-law wanted to try out but didn't want to go alone, so I went with her. I actually filled out an application in 1979 but was scared to go. The process was very intimidating; there were 2,000 girls trying out over four days. I remember expecting much more after making the team. I was walking home and literally knew nothing. When I walked in the door and told my husband I made it, he said, 'What happens now?'"

On how the Cheerleaders have changed over the last 30 years:
"There is more of a time commitment now, without question. Also, when I was cheering, we were good for the time, but we weren't the best dancers. We were less athletic and competitive for that matter. The feeling then was if you looked pretty good in the uniform, you could pick up the dancing. Now we're looking for quality talent. We want to pick the perfect ladies."

▲ (top) The 1975 Dallas Cowboys Cheerleaders.
(bottom) Texie Waterman and Suzanne Mitchell.

▲ Cassie Trammell (center) and Meredith Oden (right), two of three Cheerleaders in club history whose mothers were also Dallas Cowboys Cheerleaders.

Performing on a U.S. Navy ship. ▶

Her responsibilities are widespread and never-ending, especially in this era of media when any anecdote involving the squad equates to instant headlines.

Finglass and Trammell readily admit that the background check on each applicant is exhaustive for this very reason, as the Cowboys Cheerleaders have long served as role models to young girls around the world. And that's not about to change.

"We don't worry about overexposure, but I'd say we turn down as many opportunities as we accept," Finglass said. "The girls are so exposed to the fans and media, but I'm proud of the way they have always handled themselves. I think it also reflects well on those who built that reputation— Dee Brock, Suzanne Mitchell, and Texie Waterman."

For Trammell, the team's choreographer since 1991, her actions speak louder than words, as her daughter, Cassie, joined the squad in 2008.

"I was proud when she was hanging a poster of the Cheerleaders on her wall in kindergarten," Trammell said. "That hasn't changed. We were fortunate to follow the right people and have tried to keep the traditions established by Suzanne and others. We like to think everyone would be proud to put the Dallas Cowboys Cheerleaders on their wall."

50,000	Fans who showed up for an appearance by two Cheerleaders at a Toronto mall in 1980. The local media called it a "riot."
4,000	Approximate number of candidates at the 1978 tryouts.
60	Share of the national television audience who tuned in for the TV movie *Dallas Cowboys Cheerleaders*, which aired on January 14, 1979. It remains the second-highest-rated made-for-TV movie in history.
3	Mother-daughter legacies in the history of the organization: Billie Gosdin and daughter Amber Gosdin; Kim Oden and daughter Meredith Oden; and Judy Trammell and daughter Cassie Trammell.

BRAINS AND BEAUTY

One of the key components to becoming a Dallas Cowboys Cheerleader is passing the audition test, which in 2009 was comprised of 83 questions covering various topics such as the Cowboys, their history, the NFL, current events, nutrition, and dance terminology. The test was first given almost 20 years ago by current director Kelli McGonagill Finglass.

"The girls are vulnerable to the media and fans when they are out doing a charity event or even in their everyday lives," Finglass said. "We want them to be articulate and understand the sport and team they are representing."

Here's a sampling of questions from the 2009 exam:

List two 2009 Cowboys draft picks: Name, Position, and School

How many Super Bowls have the Dallas Cowboys won?

List the NFL seasons in which the Cowboys won the Super Bowl.

List 3 members of the Dallas Cowboys Ring of Honor:_____ _____ _____

In their most recent Super Bowl appearance, the Dallas Cowboys defeated:

      Pittsburgh Steelers   Philadelphia Eagles

      Buffalo Bills   Miami Dolphins

Name the original choreographer who transformed the Cheerleaders' performances with her Broadway-style choreography.

How many stars are there on the Cheerleaders uniform?

How many yards are in an NFL end zone?

      (A) 10   (B) 20   (C) 30   (D) 50

What industry first felt the effects of the recession?

What movie won best picture at the 2009 Academy Awards?

How many servings of fruits and/or vegetables should you have per day?

      2   5   3   4

When executing a proper right outside turn, the right foot should be in _____ .

After executing a grand jeté, would you land one foot or two?

FORMER COWBOYS CHEERLEADER
CHACHIS ORTIZ HECHT ★

On making the team in 1984:
"I had never been a cheerleader but decided to try out at the spur of the moment. I was 24 years old and had just moved to Dallas alone; I didn't have any family. Most of them were still in Mexico where I grew up. I didn't make the team, but two days after final cuts, Suzanne Mitchell called me and said she would give me another week to prove myself. She said if my feet would follow my talent, I would be okay. I have never worked that hard in my life, before or since. Even during that first season, I was working at a bank in Dallas but would stay up until 3:00 a.m. some nights practicing."

On her family's reaction:
"I think I was the first DCC born in Mexico. There were a lot of stories written in the newspapers back home. My family was so proud. The Cowboys are so huge in Mexico; it's almost hard to explain. The joy and happiness of so many people because I made the team just made me work harder. I didn't want to let anyone down. My family flew up to watch me at Texas Stadium. That was the proudest moment of my life."

◀ Posing with a young fan.

FORMER COWBOYS CHEERLEADER
MISTY DUNCAN

On representing the Cheerleaders for five years (2003–2007):
"From the first time walking into the studio at Valley Ranch, to the first time out of the tunnel at Texas Stadium, the history, legacy, and impact of our uniform precedes each one of us, but we all hope to continue the tradition of excellence. The memories we create are immeasurable and certainly we are all bonded through our challenges as well as achievements in sort of an unnamed sisterhood. The impact we have on our community might be grand, but the impact the organization has on each of us is far greater, and we take that with us and carry it for the rest of our lives."

On her rookie season:
"First-year team members are under more of a watchful eye, so you want to get there early and stay late. I had just graduated from Texas A&M and was working a full-time job, too. All the cheerleaders have to either be attending college or working full-time. I'd get to Valley Ranch around 5:30 p.m., stretch, work on a few routines, and then practice was from 7:00 p.m. to about 10:30 p.m. or 11:00 p.m. The rookies would usually stay another 30 minutes or so after, too. There were a lot of late nights."

▲ Practicing during training camp.

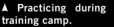

Finishing their famous kick-line routine. ▶

GENERAL TOMMY FRANKS
AN ENDURING IMPACT

Make no mistake, every soldier knows the Dallas Cowboys Cheerleaders. They have been entertaining troops around the world for over three decades, bringing a taste of home to those brave men and women stationed overseas.

But while I, too, knew of the Cheerleaders throughout my military career, not until 2001 did I come to truly understand both their impact and dedication.

In October of that year we executed the order to begin Operation Enduring Freedom to liberate Afghanistan. By December the main resistance had been shattered and the ceremonies to install the United Nations–sanctioned interim government were being arranged. The troops had done an outstanding job, and they deserved a little Christmas cheer.

So, I got in touch with Wayne Newton and asked if he could put together a very small group of entertainers to accompany me on a handshake and Merry Christmas tour. Wayne gathered up Neal McCoy, Drew Carey, and two Dallas Cowboys Cheerleaders, and the "Deliver America 2001" USO tour headed to Oman, Afghanistan, and Pakistan.

Over the next two years as commander in chief, United States Central Command (2001–2003), I saw just how committed the Cheerleaders were to giving their best for our troops, enduring exhausting days spent traveling from base to base and even going so far as to rehearse in the back of a C-17 aircraft just to perfect their routine. I watched as they performed on everything from quickly constructed plywood stages in Afghanistan's far-reaching outposts to flatbed trucks in the desert camps of Iraq and flight decks on amphibious assault ships in the Persian Gulf. No matter when the show, no matter where the event, they always brought a refreshing energy that I know those soldiers will always remember.

> **NOT ONLY DID THEY SERVE THANKSGIVING DINNER TO OUR TROOPS, BUT THEY TOOK THE TIME TO SIT DOWN WITH THEM AND SHARE A MEAL. THERE WERE NO FALSE PRETENSES TO THEIR ACTIONS. THE CHEERLEADERS' CONCERN FOR OUR SOLDIERS HAS ALWAYS BEEN GENUINE.**

Easily the highlight of these events always came during Neal's singing of his hit song "The Shake." The Cheerleaders, complete with feather boas, would invite lucky servicemen onstage for an impromptu and often hilarious dance. Truly unforgettable, particularly for those chosen to participate.

But while the shows often were the focal point for these visits, the special moments for all involved came off the stage when the Cheerleaders signed autographs, posed for photos, and just took a moment to talk about home. Not only did they serve Thanksgiving dinner to our troops, but they took the time to sit down with them and share a meal. There were no false pretenses to their actions. The Cheerleaders' concern for our soldiers has always been genuine.

And then I'm reminded of a USO tour in June of 2003, "Project Salute." As part of their visit, Wayne, Neal, and the Cheerleaders had arrived at Tallil Air Base in southern Iraq expecting only to meet the soldiers and sign autographs. However, they soon found over 1,000 men and women waiting in a stifling heat for what they hoped would be a full performance.

▲ (clockwise from top left) A well-deserved hug; taking a test-drive; an appreciative audience; with General Tommy Franks.

Without the proper equipment, one of Wayne's band members asked if anyone had a guitar. A young man ran back to his barracks, returned with one in hand, and, thanks to his help, the show took place, the Cheerleaders really stealing the spotlight and shining as brightly as ever. Two months later, that young man with the guitar paid the ultimate sacrifice for his country.

The United States can boast of the finest military personnel in the world. Thanks to them and their dedication in the face of adversity, freedom and democracy still reign.

But doing their part to support our troops and bringing a welcomed moment of joy has been and continues to be America's Sweethearts, who will always play a role in our country's global effort, an impact that really has no measure.

After all, every United States soldier knows the Dallas Cowboys Cheerleaders.

General Tommy Franks led the American and coalition troops as commander in chief, United States Central Command, during Operation Enduring Freedom in Afghanistan and Operation Iraqi Freedom in Iraq. The four-star general's awards include five Distinguished Service Medals, four Legions of Merit, four Bronze Stars, and three Purple Hearts.

SALVATION ARMY

For Jerry Jones, there are five singular highlights, accomplishments really, that stand above and beyond his 20-plus years of owning the Dallas Cowboys.

"I would put what we have done with the Salvation Army right there with any of the Super Bowls and the new stadium, without question," Jones said.

Since becoming involved with the Salvation Army in 1997, the Cowboys have helped raise more than $1.3 billion, mostly through the efforts of their Thanksgiving Day halftime show. The architect of these efforts has been Charlotte Jones Anderson, who, along with Gene Jones, oversees the team's charitable work while also serving as executive vice president/vice president brand management.

The association came about when then Frito-Lay CEO Steve Reinemund broached the idea of the Cowboys becoming involved with the charity after a meeting of the Boys and Girls Clubs of America, where both he and Anderson served on the board of directors.

"I really had an incomplete understanding of the Salvation Army before that," Anderson said. "There isn't an organization in the world that reaches more children. Their problem was that despite having been around since the Civil War, serving on the front lines of both World Wars, few people really knew what they were all about. When I met with them shortly thereafter, they wanted to know if I had any ideas to increase their visibility."

Around this same time, Jerry Jones and Gene mentioned to their daughter that the Cowboys "needed to be the Jerry Lewis of the sports world," in terms of raising money for charity. After meeting with the Salvation Army, Anderson thought of an idea that would accomplish her father's goal.

'We wanted to take our visibility and do something with it," Anderson said. "There was one game every year that we were guaranteed to be on national television and that was Thanksgiving. The next day is when the Salvation Army begins their annual Red Kettle Drive. It was perfect."

Anderson decided the Cowboys would kick-start the drive with a halftime spectacular on the level of the Super Bowl. NBC was broadcasting the Turkey Day game and Anderson sold the network's president, Dick Ebersol, on airing the halftime entertainment.

"For that first show in 1997, I asked Reba McEntire to perform," said Anderson. "She immediately said yes, that the Salvation Army was her favorite charity."

Since then, the biggest names in music have performed, from Toby Keith to Sheryl Crow to the Jonas Brothers. And while the broadcast rights have changed hands on a few occasions, there has never been an issue.

"Obviously it's all for a great cause, but the networks have always been wonderful. That's $15 million of airtime they are giving us. There's no better day than Thanksgiving to tell the story of the Salvation Army," Anderson said.

In 2008, Major George Hood, the national spokesman for the Salvation Army, told the *Dallas Morning News* that, "Jerry and Charlotte have transformed us from a band of regional community programs into a national force."

Another aspect of the charity that especially appeals to Anderson is that every dollar raised in a specific city stays in that city. And since the Cowboys have become involved, donations for the Salvation Army have more than doubled nationally, with the state of Texas leading the way.

▲ (clockwise from top left) Rookies loading up Christmas gifts; Gene and Jerry Jones, former first lady Laura Bush, Salvation Army National Commander and Commissioner Israel Gaither, and Commissioner Eva Gaither; Daughtry performing during the 2009 Thanksgiving halftime show; Charlotte Anderson, Salvation Army Major Ward Matthews, and Captain Michele Matthews; Sam Hurd serving Thanksgiving dinner at the Salvation Army's homeless shelter.

"The players, the Cheerleaders, the fans, more and more people have become involved with the Salvation Army. Whether it's adopting a child for Christmas and making sure they have presents or helping out with food for the homeless, it's such a great charity. And while we still work with many other charities, this has really become our No. 1 passion," Anderson said.

For her incredible efforts on behalf of the charity, the Salvation Army named Anderson its first female Chairman of the National Advisory Board in September 2010.

"I was flabbergasted," Anderson said on hearing the news. "When they asked me, I was overwhelmed by the trust they were instilling in me. It's really hard to fathom; it's such an honor."

And her father couldn't be prouder.

"Charlotte's efforts with [the Salvation Army] have really been inspiring. We have been a better franchise since becoming involved," Jerry Jones said. "We're helping people who can't run with the ball themselves at that given moment."

ACKNOWLEDGMENTS

My grandfather wore funny hats. Fedoras and Irish scally caps. He was always watching sports on the television in his den, so there I sat, seven, eight years old, on the rug, trying to learn these games that so fascinated him.

This was just outside of Boston, and home teams were king, no matter their degree of success or lack thereof. Opposing teams and players were scum of the earth, often worse—let's just say my vocabulary was broadened well beyond the Berenstain Bears at an early age.

Then came Thanksgiving afternoon, 1984. The New England Patriots, our Pats, were playing the Dallas Cowboys. For reasons beyond a third-grader's comprehension, this was a big deal, so we ate early and headed for the den. I'm not sure if it was the first or the 100th occasion the cameras showed Tom Landry during the game that my grandfather said, "He's a great man. We should all be more like Tom Landry."

That Sunday morning, when my grandparents picked me up for church, I was wearing a suit with a clip-on tie and a fedora. Smiling, my grandfather said, "Who are you supposed to be?"

I said proudly, "Tom Landry."

Looking back, he was right: *We all should be more like Tom Landry.*

The roll call of people who were accommodating above and beyond in this project is lengthy and blanketed with class and patience. My biggest problem in writing the narrative was deciding which stories to use, as they collectively offered enough memories for at least three books. Also, with the exception of a few players, none of those interviewed knew me in the least, yet were willing to share their recollections, many of them somewhat intimate. I shall forever be indebted to each of them (in alphabetical order):

Troy Aikman, Charlotte Anderson, Bill Bates, Dee Brock, Larry Brown, Dave Campo, Kandy Schramm Court, Tony Dorsett, Misty Duncan, Billy Joe DuPree, Kelli McGonagill Finglass, Chan Gailey, Jason Garrett, Jim Garrett, Walt Garrison, La'Roi Glover, Cornell Green, Charles Haley, Bruce Hardy, Cliff Harris, Chachis Ortiz Hecht, Thomas "Hollywood" Henderson, Calvin Hill, Hudson Houck, Chuck Howley, Michael Irvin, Jim Jeffcoat, Jimmy Johnson, Daryl "Moose" Johnston, Ed "Too Tall" Jones, Jerry Jones, Jerry Jones Jr., Stephen Jones, Lee Roy Jordan, Eddie LeBaron, Leon Lett, D. D. Lewis, Bob Lilly, Brock Marion, Don Meredith, Suzanne Mitchell, Warren Morey, Burk Murchison, Clint Murchison III, Robert Murchison, Ralph Neely, Nate Newton, Dat Nguyen, John Niland, Terrell Owens, Bill Parcells, Drew Pearson, Preston Pearson, Don Perkins, Wade Phillips, Dan Reeves, Mel Renfro, Lance Rentzel, Tony Romo, David Sherer, Emmitt Smith, Roger Staubach, Mark Stepnoski, Barry Switzer, George Teague, Duane Thomas, Pat Toomay, Judy Trammell, Jerry Tubbs, Herschel Walker, Everson Walls, Dave Wannstedt, DeMarcus Ware, Charlie Waters, Danny White, Randy White, Erik Williams, Jason Witten, Darren Woodson, and Rayfield Wright.

Remember that reccurring *Sesame Street* bit where three kids would be jumping rope and the fourth would be eating a Twinkie on the couch, with the background music singing, "*One of these things is not like the other*"? Upon first seeing the mock covers of this book, there were no goose bumps, no glow or excitement, just total and utter numbness that my name was alongside Dan

Jenkins, Pat Summerall, Verne Lundquist, Steve Sabol, Paul Tagliabue, General Tommy Franks, and Brad Sham. Their essays in these pages are worthy of the men themselves, icons one and all.

Then there's Kurt Daniels, the director of publications for the Dallas Cowboys, who ran point on this project from its infancy and nurtured it through the final caption. He is the rarest of men who values team before ego. My respect and admiration of him as an editor is beyond the realm of my capacity. Thing is, though, he's even a better friend and person.

Nothing less than the highest order of the keyboard have covered the Dallas Cowboys through the years, and one of the perks of this project was the privilege of researching their words, none more so than Blackie Sherrod, Frank Luksa, Sam Blair, Bud Shrake, Bob St. John, Randy Galloway, Rick Gosselin, Ed Werner, Mickey Spagnola, Carlton Stowers, who wrote the 25th anniversary book, and, of course, Jenkins.

My sincerest appreciation goes to friends Tim Williams, Jonathan Gallugi, P. J. Cady, Mike McDonnell, Armando Petruzziello, Kevin Atkinson, Rich McCarthy, Mike Schoener, Doug Foster, David Porter, Chuck Gutilla, Brandon Lesley, and Aik Tongtharadol.

A special word of gratitude to Dave Ivey, the older brother I never had. A gifted writer and brilliant mind, his unselfish efforts on this project were above and beyond for even him. My life has been infinitely better off because of his influence and friendship.

My professional existence has been blessed by the likes of Bob Holmes, Terry Nau, and Chris Dortch, while better men one will not find than Bill Sawtelle, Jim Dryden, Mark Warsop, and Curt Cook at Panini America, my home for the last four years.

On the family front: Lisa, Mitchell, Quinn, and Drew Daley; Bill, Heather, Liam, and Sam Millette; Matthew and Staley Sullivan; Dan and Barbara Harle; and all the Spada and O'Brien families.

There aren't enough words of gratitude for my mother, Ann Marie Sullivan. Comprehending the sacrifices she has made throughout her days on this planet is hard. They say only mothers possess the ability to love unconditionally, and I've been honored and blessed to witness that firsthand. I call her every morning and night, not because all sons and daughters should, but because I want to hear her voice and know how her day is and was.

On April 10, 2003, at Fenway Park, I was lucky enough to spill a beer on the most beautiful woman I've ever seen in my entire life and, amazingly, we ended up married. And somewhere between then and now, Danielle has also evolved into my best friend. Her support for this project was nothing short of miraculous, especially in the weeks approaching deadline when my psychological stability was a combination of Travis Bickle and a woman in labor.

Jeff Sullivan
May 31, 2010
Arlington, Texas

SELECTED BIBLIOGRAPHY AND RESOURCES

America's Game: 1971 Dallas Cowboys, DVD, narrated by Martin Sheen. (Burbank, CA: Warner Home Video, 2006)

America's Game: 1977 Dallas Cowboys, DVD, narrated by Laurence Fishburne. (Burbank, CA: Warner Home Video, 2006)

America's Game: 1992 Dallas Cowboys, DVD, narrated by Alec Baldwin. (Burbank, CA: Warner Home Video, 2006)

America's Game: 1993 Dallas Cowboys, DVD, narrated by Ed Harris. (Burbank, CA: Warner Home Video, 2007)

America's Game: 1995 Dallas Cowboys, DVD, narrated by Ed Harris. (Burbank, CA: Warner Home Video, 2007)

Bayless, Skip. *God's Coach: The Hymns, Hype, and Hypocrisy of Tom Landry's Cowboys*. New York: Fireside, 1991.

Blair, Sam. *Dallas Cowboys, Pro or Con?* New York: Doubleday, 1970.

Chipman, Donald E., Randolph Campbell, and Robert Calvert. *The Dallas Cowboys and the NFL*. Norman, OK: University of Oklahoma Press, 1970.

Dallas Cowboys. Official Site of the Dallas Cowboys. www.dallascowboys.com

Dallas Cowboys: The Complete History (2003), DVD, directed by David Plaut. (Burbank, CA: Warner Home Video, 2003)

Donovan, Jim, Ken Sims, and Frank Coffee Coffey. *The Dallas Cowboys Encyclopedia: The Ultimate Guide to America's Team*. Eugene, OR: Carol Publishing Corporation, 1996.

Eisenberg, John. *Cotton Bowl Days: Growing up with Dallas and the Cowboys in the 1960s*. New York: Simon & Schuster, 1997.

Engel, Mac. *Texas Stadium: America's Home Field; Reliving the Legends and the Legendary Moments*. Overland Park, KS: Ascend Books, 2008.

Freeman, Denne H., and Jaime Aron. *I Remember Tom Landry*. New York: Sports Pub, 2001.

Golenbock, Peter. *Cowboys Have Always Been My Heroes: The Definitive Oral History of America's Team*. New York: Warner Books, 1997.

Harris, Cliff, and Charlie Waters. *Tales from the Dallas Cowboys: A Collection of the Greatest Stories Ever Told*. Champaign, IL: Sports Publishing, 2003.

Hitt, Dick. *Classic Clint: The Laughs and Times of Clint Murchison, Jr*. Plano, TX: Wordware, 1992.

Hitzges, Norm. *The Greatest Team Ever: The Dallas Cowboys Dynasty of the 1990s*. Waco, TX: Thomas Nelson, 2007.

Jensen, Brian. *Where Have All Our Cowboys Gone?* New York: Cooper Square Press, 2001.

Magee, David. *Playing to Win: Jerry Jones and the Dallas Cowboys*. Chicago: Triumph Books, 2008.

Meyers, Jeff. *Dallas Cowboys: Great Teams' Great Years*. New York: MacMillan, 1974.

NFL Enterprises LLC. Official Site of the National Football League. www.nfl.com

Pearlman, Jeff. *Boys Will Be Boys: The Glory Days and Party Nights of the Dallas Cowboys Dynasty*. New York: HarperCollins, 2008.

Sham, Brad. *Stadium Stories: Dallas Cowboys; Colorful Tales of America's Team*. Guilford, CT: Globe Pequot, 2003.

Shropshire, Mike. *When the Tuna Went Down to Texas: How Bill Parcells Led the Cowboys Back to the Promised Land*. New York: HarperCollins, 2004.

Sports Reference LLC. Pro-Football-Reference. www.pro-football-reference.com

St. John, Bob. *Landry: The Legend and the Legacy*. Waco, TX: Thomas Nelson, 2001.

———. *We Love You Cowboys*. New York: Sport Magazine Press, 1972.

Staubach, Roger, and Frank Luska. *Time Enough to Win*. Waco, TX: Word Books, 1981.

Stowers, Carlton. *Dallas Cowboys the First Twenty-Five Years*. Dallas: Taylor Pub, 1984.

Switzer, Barry, and Bud Shrake. *Bootlegger's Boy*. London: Jove, 1991.

Taylor, Jean-Jacques. *Game of My Life: Dallas Cowboys; Memorable Stories of Cowboys Football*. Champaign, IL: Sports Publishing, 2006.

Whittingham, Richard. *The Dallas Cowboys: An Illustrated History*. New York: Harper & Row Publishers, 1984.

Austin American-Statesman
Boston Globe
Dallas Cowboys Star
Dallas Morning News
Dallas Observer
Dallas Times Herald
Fort Worth Star-Telegram
Los Angeles Times
Miami Herald
New York Times
Sport
Sports Illustrated
The Sporting News
Time
USA Today
Washington Post

COLOPHON

PUBLISHER: RAOUL GOFF

CREATIVE DIRECTOR: IAIN R. MORRIS

EXECUTIVE EDITOR: SCOTT GUMMER

MANAGING EDITOR: KEVIN TOYAMA

PRODUCTION DIRECTOR: ANNA WAN

DALLAS COWBOYS PROJECT EDITOR: KURT DANIELS

DESIGN: ALTITUDE (www.altitudesf.com)

COPYEDITOR: MIKAYLA BUTCHART

PROOFREADER: JAN HUGHES

The creators of this book would like to express their deepest gratitude to Jerry Jones and his family: Gene, Stephen, Charlotte, and Jerry Jr.

Insight Editions would like to thank Brian Singer and Kirstin Kowalsky at Altitude, Dagmar Trojanek, Lucy Kee, Martina D'Alessandro, John Reynolds, Charles Gerli, and Kevin Finley.

Also deserving of much thanks are (in alphabetical order): Scott Agulnek, Greg Aiello, Doug Aydelotte, Ann Bihari, Erin Boyd, Whitney Brandon, Jancy Briles, Jim Browder, c3 Premedia Solutions (Mitch Brazell and John Adler), Sharon Carnahan, Kay Clark, Jeff Coleman, Rich Dalrymple, Brett Daniels, Lauren Daniels, Ray Daniels, Dan Devens, John Dixon, Faye Donovan, Derek Eagleton, Josh Ellis, Dina Ferreira, Laura Fryar, Shannon Gross, Col. Michael T. Hayes (ret.), Michelle Hays, Stacie Jones, Ken Kizer, Diana Lambert, Bill Littleton, Marylyn Love, Greg McElroy, Susan Meredith, Laura Miller, Noemi Miller, Sha Moffett, Doreen Nichols, Matt Owens, Bill Priakos, Scott Purcel, Emily Robbins, Kristi Scales, Alec Scheiner, Janette Scott, Werner Scott, Ken Sins, Michael Villareal, and countless other players, coaches, and staff of the Dallas Cowboys Football Club that have made the last 50 years possible.